THE HUMANITY OF THE SAVIOUR

THE HUMANITY OF THE SAVIOUR

A Biblical and Historical Study of the Human Nature of Christ in relation to Original Sin, with special reference to its Soteriological Significance

by

HARRY JOHNSON
M.TH., PH.D.

LONDON : THE EPWORTH PRESS

FIRST PUBLISHED IN 1962

© THE EPWORTH PRESS 1962

Book Steward
FRANK H. CUMBERS

232 V

J633

147865

TO MY MOTHER AND FATHER
WITH AFFECTION AND GRATITUDE

SET IN MONOTYPE BASKERVILLE AND PRINTED IN
GREAT BRITAIN BY THE CAMELOT PRESS LTD
LONDON AND SOUTHAMPTON

Table of Contents

PART I

INTRODUCTION

PART II

THE NEW TESTAMENT EVIDENCE

PART III

THE HISTORICAL EVIDENCE

PART IV

THE COMPARATIVE NEGLECT OF THE THEORY

PART V

CONSTRUCTIVE STATEMENT

Acknowledgements

The original manuscript of 'The Humanity of the Saviour' was presented as a Thesis to London University and was approved for the Degree of Doctor of Philosophy. Before this thesis could be published, certain modifications were required. This means that the present book is shorter than the original manuscript, but nothing essential to the argument has been omitted.

I am indebted to the Rev. Professor C. Kingsley Barrett, M.A., D.D., the Rev. A. Raymond George, M.A., B.D., and the Rev. John H. Atkinson, M.A., for reading the manuscript and for their helpful comments. I also pay tribute to the excellent editing of the Rev. J. Alan Kay, M.A., Ph.D. Finally, but not least, I wish to thank my wife, without whose help and constant encouragement this book would never have been completed.

Abbreviations

AV	Authorized Version
EB	*Encyclopaedia Britannica*
ERE	*Encyclopaedia of Religion and Ethics*
ET	English Translation
Ex.T	*Expository Times*
HNT	*Handbuch zum Neuen Testament*
ICC	*International Critical Commentary*
JTS	*Journal of Theological Studies*
LXX	Septuagint
MNTC	*Moffatt New Testament Commentary*
PG	*Patrologia Graeca*, ed. J. P. Migne
PL	*Patrologia Latina*, ed. J. P. Migne
RSV	Revised Standard Version
RV	Revised Version
SJT	*Scottish Journal of Theology*
TWNT	*Theologisches Wörterbuch zum Neuen Testament*
W. Bauer	*Greek-English Lexicon* (ET by W. F. Arndt and F. W. Gingrich)

PART I

Introduction

A T THE CENTRE of the Christian Faith stands the affirmation that the Son of God became man for our salvation. The richness of the love of God was shown to men through the Incarnation of the Son of God and through the redemption that He came to bring even at the cost of His death on the Cross. Mystery has always surrounded the coming of the Son of God into human life; it is a mystery that the human mind will never completely understand. Yet our finite minds must make some attempt, however inadequate, to comprehend this central truth of our faith. The investigation that we are now to undertake is concerned with one aspect of the doctrine of the Incarnation. The eternal Son of God assumed human nature; on this all Christians will agree. But what kind of human nature did He assume? Was it the human nature that was affected by the Fall, 'fallen human nature', or was it human nature as originally created by God? On this question there would appear to be no agreed answer, and it is to the study of this aspect of the Incarnation that our present enquiry is directed. We shall investigate the theory that Christ assumed 'fallen human nature'.

To do this we must first of all decide what is meant by the Fall and 'fallen human nature'. In recent years serious doubts have been cast upon the historicity of the early stories in Genesis; many passages in Genesis 1-12 have been questioned, and, on scientific grounds, have been rejected. Biblical scholars, through a new and enlightened approach to the Bible, have come to a more accurate knowledge of the types of material that compose the biblical narratives. Without questioning the spiritual power of these early Genesis narratives, they have realized the presence of myths and legends. Much discussion has centred on the story of the Fall, and, therefore, before we can use the doctrines of the Fall and Original Sin, recent objections and criticisms must be briefly examined.

THE FALL DOCTRINE

The Fall doctrine is a serious attempt to answer the problem of the origin of evil. Generally speaking, three types of answer are

3

given to this problem. First is the answer of Monism. This virtually denies the existence of evil. Evil is either good in the making or it is an illusion; to us it seems to be evil, but if we could see the whole picture, if we could visualize the complete pattern, we should realize that it was not really so at all. It is questionable whether this is intellectually satisfying, for it attains its solution by virtually denying the existence of the data on which the problem rests. As far as practical living is concerned it certainly is not sufficient; evil is a reality, and any answer that depends upon the denial of the reality of evil is inadequate for life.

The second answer is that of Dualism. Despite variations in detail this solution has one fundamental tenet; it postulates two eternal and uncreated forces behind the universe, one good and the other evil. Between these opposing forces there is a struggle, and both the world of nature and the lives of men form part of the battleground. This is a brave answer, but it is not satisfactory, especially to the Christian. The doctrine that there is one God cannot but be affirmed, and it seems necessary to give evil a subsidiary position. The essential nature of evil appears to be parasitic; it depends on the existence of good to be perverted or preyed upon.

The third type of answer to the problem is one that has found widespread acceptance among theologians, a Fall doctrine. This answer maintains the reality of evil as against monism, yet it does not fall into the errors of dualism. The sovereignty of God is not imperilled; the forces of evil are good forces that have gone wrong. Sin and evil are the result of a good and free agent rebelling against God.

The term Fall can be used to cover three different theories: (*a*) The idea of a separate fall for each individual—each man being born free, rebelling against God and thus falling. The weakness of this theory is that it fails to give any satisfactory explanation of the universality of evil, making it a chance happening. There must be some explanation of the universality of sin and evil; it is more than a mere coincidence that all men have rebelled against God. (*b*) The theory of an 'Adamic Fall', the results of which have been passed on to succeeding generations by heredity. (*c*) The theory of a 'Pre-Adamic Fall', which takes the origin of evil back before the advent of the human race—though often an 'Adamic Fall', which was facilitated by the 'Pre-Adamic Fall', is held to come later. This last theory has a definite advantage over the second; it gives an explanation of the existence of evil in nature, a kind of evil which we know existed before the appearance of man on this planet, for painful diseases existed in the animal kingdom long before the emergence of man.

The doctrine of the origin of evil that is expounded in the Bible is a Fall doctrine. To this biblical exposition we must now turn.

(a) The Fall Doctrine
in the Old Testament and Later Judaism

In the Old Testament we find two stories that are associated with the doctrine of the fall of man. The first is centred in Adam and is found in Genesis 3. Here we have the account of the ancestors of the human race dwelling in primitive felicity in the Garden of Eden. Even though they were naked, they were unashamed. They had been created by God, and were capable of fellowship with Him, but He had commanded them to abstain from the fruit of the Tree of Knowledge which was in the centre of the garden. Tempted, Adam fell and ate of the forbidden fruit. God passed the verdict. The serpent that had deceived the woman was to become the most despised of creatures; woman, who first ate the forbidden fruit, was to bear children in pain, and be subject to her husband; as for man, God said: '. . . cursed is the ground because of you; in toil you shall eat of it all the days of your life; . . . In the sweat of your face you shall eat bread till you return to the ground, for out of it you were taken; you are dust, and to dust you shall return' (Gen 3$^{17-19}$).[1]

Many scholars are of the opinion that this story originally contained no concept of original sin in the sense of an inner taint or weakness transmitted to Adam's successors, and maintain that the punishment was purely external. A typical advocate of this position is Ludwig Koehler. He maintains that 'the statement that all men are evil, that man is depraved, that this depravity originates in the Fall of his original parents and that through the Fall the whole order of creation was distorted—all this is quite foreign to the Old Testament'.[2]

This outlook, however, is not shared by all modern scholars. Gottfried Quell, for instance, accepts the aetiological interpretation of this Genesis story, and says that the narrative 'undoubtedly

---

[1] Quotations are from the *RSV*, unless otherwise stated.
[2] *Old Testament Theology*, pp. 180-1.

justifies our basing upon it the theory of "original sin" in the sense of man's universal sinfulness'.[3] This latter interpretation seems to be nearer the mark. Even though there is in the narrative no fully developed theological doctrine, it hardly seems justifiable to go to the other extreme by denying that there is any doctrine there at all. This Adam narrative, which is most probably a compilation of primitive myths, is used in masterly fashion to show how sin enters into the situation surreptitiously, and how man's sinning brings dire results upon himself. There is no doctrine of the Fall and Original Sin in the sense in which these terms are used by later theologians, but the seeds are there, and later they germinated and bore fruit.

The other story associated with the origin of evil is found in Genesis 6. Here we have the account of the lustful angels who came to earth and had intercourse with the daughters of men, thus producing a race of giants. Later apocalyptic writers used this narrative, and found in it the origin of evil spirits. This is seen in the Book of Jubilees (4, 5, 7, 10) and 1 Enoch (6-16, 19, 86), where we have an embroidery of the Genesis narrative. The Watchers were sent to instruct men in righteousness, but as they were susceptible to human charms, there resulted a union of human and heavenly beings. The outcome of this union was a new race of beings, giants. This caused the anger of God and He decreed that the race of giants should die by mutual slaughter. After they died their spirits left their bodies and became demons. In the Book of Jubilees we read that they corrupted Noah, who prayed for their imprisonment. Mastema, the chief of the demons, protested, and the result was a compromise, one-tenth of all the demons being left at the disposal of Satan.

This story had a popular vogue in Jewish circles as an account of the origin of evil, though in the end the Adam narrative gained the ascendancy in Christianity. The Watcher story adds something to the Adam narrative; it gives a picture of a kingdom of evil, a rebel kingdom that is in opposition to God. This rebel kingdom is the cause of much of the evil in the world—physical evil, for demons are the cause of disease, and moral evil, for they tempt men to sin.

N. P. Williams is of the opinion that the idea of the Fall arose

---

[3] English translation of the article on Sin from *TWNT*, p. 30. The whole section on the Fall (pp. 23-32) is relevant.

in Jewish thought because of reflection on the universality of sin.[4] This caused search to be made through the biblical narratives for an event that might be interpreted as the origin of sin. Two stories were thought to be relevant, Genesis 3 and 6. He maintains that neither is the real basis for the doctrine: 'They are rather symbolic façades, clothing a conceptual structure which rests upon spiritual experience and introspection.'[5] This statement reveals profound insight, and we can accept the truth that reflection on the facts of experience led to the idea of the Fall. (It is also interesting that the vital elements in the Genesis 6 narrative are found only in the later embroideries of the story.) Yet it is still to be maintained that the very fact that these narratives were fastened upon to bear the weight of a Fall doctrine seems to imply that they contain the doctrine in embryo. This is particularly true of the Adam story, which seems to have in its very structure the idea of the origin of sin. This is the point of the narrative and not just an interpretation foisted on to it by later thinkers for the sake of explaining a fact of experience.

One point is quite certain. Even if the Old Testament does not give a full theoretical explanation of the universality of sin, the fact itself is well attested by such passages as the following: 'If thou, O Lord, shouldst mark iniquities, Lord, who could stand?' (Ps 130[3]); 'Enter not into judgement with thy servant; for no man living is righteous before thee' (Ps 143[2]); 'Surely there is not a righteous man on earth who does good and never sins' (Eccles 7[20]).[6] All these passages declare the universality of sin. A study of the passages, however, reveals that this view is maintained, not so much for dogmatic reasons, but because it speaks of a fact of experience. In no way could these verses be called dogmatic statements.

When we try to discover which verses in the Old Testament reveal the concept of an inborn taint or weakness, we are not on such sure ground. Job 14[4], 'Who can bring a clean thing out of an unclean? There is not one', and Genesis 8[21], 'the Lord said in his heart, "I will never again curse the ground because of man, for the imagination of man's heart is evil from his youth" ', are sometimes quoted as implying an inborn taint. This is doubtful exegesis: they merely emphasize that sin is universal. Psalm 51[5]

---

[4] *Ideas of the Fall and Original Sin*, pp. 31-4.   [5] Ibid. p. xii.
[6] Cf. 1 Kings 8[46], Job 25[4], Proverbs 20[9].

is more significant ('Behold, I was brought forth in iniquity, and in sin did my mother conceive me'), but even here the interpretation is difficult. The passage may signify no more than that sexual relationships were thought of as evil; it does not of necessity imply the idea of inborn sin, though the flavour is certainly there. Other relevant passages are: Psalms 58³, Isaiah 48⁸, and Job 25⁴. H. Wheeler Robinson writes: 'To speak of inherited sinfulness in the case of these passages . . . is not justified by historical exegesis.'⁷ Though we do not maintain that any of these passages contain a fully-developed doctrine of original sin, the writers of them appear to be saying more than merely that sin is universal. Such a passage as Psalm 51⁵ is groping after the truth that the universality of sin is not an accident; there is a connection between the fact that each individual sins and the fact that we are born of sinful parents into a sinful human race. Edmond Jacob maintains that 'the author of Psalm 51 asserts the universality of sin by depicting every man as bringing with him, when he enters the world, a propensity towards evil'.⁸ C. Ryder Smith makes a similar point: 'The concept of heredity, even if not clearly defined, begins to play a part in the Old Testament thought of the doctrine of sin and its transmission.'⁹

Before we pass on to the New Testament we must look at another theory which is of importance, and which, while not strictly speaking a fall doctrine, is relevant to our discussion. This is the doctrine of the 'yetzer hara', the theory that the origin of evil is to be found in the evil imagination within man.¹⁰ This doctrine was accepted by Rabbinic Scholasticism in New Testament times. The concept has its origin in the words of Genesis 6⁵: 'The Lord saw that the wickedness of man was great in the earth, and that every imagination of the thoughts of his heart were only evil continually.' The doctrine is found in pre-Christian times, especially in Ecclesiasticus. The Talmud, which is of a later date, yields much information about the 'yetzer hara'. From the writings of the Rabbis two points seem to emerge about this 'evil imagination'. In the first place, it is definitely stated that it is created by God, though the full implications of this do not appear to have been realized. In the second place, this 'yetzer' is put into each

⁷ *The Christian Doctrine of Man*, p. 58.   ⁸ *Theology of the Old Testament*, p. 283.
⁹ *The Bible Doctrine of Sin*, p. 39.
¹⁰ See G. F. Moore, *Judaism*, I.479-93; also W. D. Davies, *Paul and Rabbinic Judaism*, pp. 20-3.

man individually either at conception or at birth. This second fact has the effect of denying that the sinful strain is passed on by heredity. It needs to be pointed out, however, that many Rabbis tended to think of this 'yetzer' rather as a neutral force which was capable of either good or evil. 'It is the urge to self-preservation and propagation and can therefore be mastered and put to a good use.'[11]

In this connection one book needs to be mentioned in more detail. The book is 4 Ezra. The author realizes that the Law is not enough to overcome sin; rather it produces the knowledge of sin. The 'yetzer hara' was planted in the heart of Adam by God. After the Fall this evil tendency was passed on to the human race by means of physical propagation and heredity (3^{21}, 4^{30}). This is quite Pauline, except for the fact that the Apostle does not put forward the idea that there was the germ of sin in Adam before the Fall. In 4 Ezra we also have an attempt to combine the Rabbinic doctrine with the popular Adamic Fall story.

(b) The Fall Doctrine in the New Testament

When we turn to the teaching of Jesus we find that He gives no support to any of the theories of the origin of evil and sin. The concern of Jesus is not to discuss origins, but to deal with the practical situation of human need. What we can say is that Jesus accepted the universality of sin. His call to repentance is couched in general terms (Mk 1^{15}); He declares in a particularly revealing saying: '. . . unless you repent you will all likewise perish' (Lk 13^{3}); and He speaks of men generally as being evil: 'If you then, who are evil, know how to give good gifts to your children . . .' (Mt 7^{11}). We can agree with E. J. Bicknell that Jesus 'speaks and acts in a way that implies the truth of original sin'.[12] But Jesus was more concerned to deal with the grave facts of the situation than to enter into the speculative question of origins.

Yet in the New Testament we see the foundations laid for the acceptance of the Adamic Fall doctrine into the dogmatic structure of the Christian Faith. This is mainly due to the teaching of Paul, for the references to the Adam Fall narrative are confined to his writings—though references to the Watcher story are found in 2 Peter 1^{4}, 2^{4}, and in Jude 6-7. In three Pauline passages we find the Adam theory: Romans 5, 1 Corinthians 15,

---

[11] W. D. Davies, *Paul and Rabbinic Judaism*, p. 22.
[12] *The Christian Doctrine of Sin and Original Sin*, p. 37.

B

and, by implication, Philippians 2. We may content ourselves here with pointing out the facts that clearly emerge.

We see that Paul thought of physical death as the result of Adam's sin: '. . . sin came into the world through one man and death through sin' (Rom 5¹²); 'in Adam all die' (1 Cor 15²²). It is not only that the simple fact of death results from Adam's sin; there is also a sinful strain in human nature that is transmitted from generation to generation: '. . . sin came into the world through one man and death through sin, and so death spread to all men because all men sinned' (Rom 5¹²); 'by one man's disobedience many were made sinners' (5¹⁹). The most discussed passage in this connection is the phrase in Romans 5¹²: ἐφ' ᾧ πάντες ἥμαρτον. It is generally agreed by modern scholars that this cannot mean 'in whom all sinned'; rather it has the meaning of 'because all sinned', 'in that all sinned'. The phrase has, however, been translated through a long period of Church History as 'in whom all sinned'; this is found in Origen and Augustine, and in the Vulgate, where we find the Latin translation 'in quo'. This mistranslation carries the definite doctrine that men sinned in Adam through seminal identity. What, however, is the meaning of the original Pauline passage? Does Paul mean us to read 'because all men sinned in Adam', or does he just mean that as a matter of fact all men have followed Adam's bad example and have sinned? Only the former interpretation will really do justice to the passage. If Paul does not mean that all men are somehow implicated in the sin of Adam, he destroys the whole force of the parallel of the redemption in Christ. But in what sense are we involved in Adam's sin? Here Paul gives no definite answer. Much discussion has taken place as to the meaning of the phrase 'in Christ', and this should give a clue as to the meaning of 'in Adam'. To be 'in Christ' has two meanings which cannot be sharply distinguished. It means to have a fellowship with Christ of the most intimate and personal kind: 'It is no longer I who live, but Christ who lives in me' (Gal 2²⁰); it is the figure of a man living in Christ almost as he lives in the atmosphere that he breathes, and of Christ filling and pervading that man. To be 'in Christ' also has another significance; it means to be part of the fellowship of the Church which is the 'Body of Christ'. Here we have guidance to the meaning of to be 'in Adam'. It does not mean simply to have some mystical identity with the primal man;

it also means to be part of the fallen and spoiled race of humanity. It is to share the defection in the race that had its origins in the rebellion of Adam. These passages of Paul taken in their context imply that there is in man an element leading to sin, which entered human nature through the fall of Adam.

The passage from Romans 5 contains no doctrine of original guilt. In fact this is virtually denied. Sin reigned until the time of the Law, but until the Law made the nature of sin apparent, sin was not imputed. There is controversy as to the meaning of sin; is it 'anything contrary to the will of God' or 'anything contrary to the *known* will of God'? Some would prefer to keep the word sin for the latter definition—sin implies a will, and a will that is opposed to the will of God. Such a definition would result in the rejection of the term 'original sin'. This position has a certain logical attractiveness, but it seems more consistent to give sin the wider connotation of anything that breaks our fellowship with God by being contrary to His will. The term guilt can be given the more restricted meaning, being applicable only where there is an act of will involved. This attitude towards guilt can certainly appeal to this Pauline passage for support. This would mean the retention of the phrase 'original sin' but the rejection of the term 'original guilt', guilt being reserved for actions where a man is held responsible, that is, where there is an act of volition.

Paul does not confine the idea of evil to man; he talks about creation groaning and travailing until now (Rom 8[22]), and makes many clear references to the powers of evil that are more than human and that are situated in the heavenly places (e.g. Eph 6[12]). It is evident that for Paul the problem of evil is not simply the question of human sin. He sees a kingdom of evil that has rebelled against God, and a world of nature that needs the redeeming power of God. In Colossians 1[15-20] we have a picture of the cosmic redemption in Christ.

In all fairness to the complexity of Pauline thought, we must refer to the presence in his writings of the Rabbinic doctrine of the '*yetzer hara*'. Romans 7[23] ('but I see in my members another law at war with the law of my mind and making me captive to the law of sin which dwells in my members') seems to refer to this idea.

From the above investigation of Paul's thought, it is obvious that the Adamic Fall story is firmly embedded in his account of the faith. It has no vital place in any other New Testament writing, but the fact of sin and of its serious and universal nature is common to all the writers and forms the essential background to the Gospel, the good news of God's redeeming love. Before we can accept the doctrines of the Fall and Original Sin we must examine the modern scientific objections to them.

(c) Modern Objections to the Theories of the Fall and Original Sin

The first serious objection is based upon the biological theory of evolution. Here we have the virtual denial of any common ancestor of the human race. We find it difficult at first sight to find a place for a fall doctrine in a theory which depicts evolution from a lower to a higher state of being. H. T. Powell, who rejects the fall doctrine because he finds it incompatible with modern knowledge, puts it bluntly: 'Science, with its tale of continuous evolution, has no place for the Doctrine of the Fall.'[13] This argument is not as impregnable as at first it might seem. If we accept the doctrine of evolution, it is hard to see any valid reason why we cannot also accept the fact that somewhere the process of evolution has taken a wrong turn, which has upset its course.

C. S. Lewis has a suggestive chapter on this very subject.[14] He draws the picture of God perfecting the animal form that was to be the physical basis of humanity, perfecting it by means of evolution over a long period of time. At the right time this creature was given self-consciousness, could then use the personal pronoun, and could apprehend the existence of God and the realms of truth, beauty, and goodness. The power of such self-consciousness over the body and over the rest of creation is something that we cannot imagine. With this new consciousness man turned towards his creator in trust and obedience. Judged by material standards, this man was in the most primitive state, but he was truly blessed in that he possessed perfect fellowship with God. How many of these men there were we do not know, and how long they remained in this paradisal state is but conjecture, but in the end they fell. They were tempted to become as gods, to turn their consciousness, their loyalty and obedience in upon themselves, instead of towards God. Pride and self came between

---

[13] *The Fall of Man*, p. 63. Cf. F. R. Tennant, *Sources of the Doctrine of the Fall and Original Sin*, p. 78.
[14] *The Problem of Pain*, Chapter 5.

them and God their maker. Such sin is possible even for paradisal man, and it is of such a grievous nature that we can see that it would be the cause of dire results. Up to that moment man's nature had been in harmony and under man's control; now this was so no more. The balance of his nature was upset; he was a spoilt species, and no longer the species that God in His love and wisdom had perfectly created. By the natural process of biological generation this fallen species passed on its characteristics to future generations.

C. S. Lewis thus attempts to fit the Fall into a historical context, but this approach is rejected by many theologians who yet maintain a Fall doctrine. They accept the criticisms which modern science has brought against the old Adamic Fall. The story is rather a myth revealing the truth about human nature. Emil Brunner emphatically rejects the conventional picture of Adam: 'The whole historic picture of "the first man" has been finally and absolutely destroyed for us today.'[15] Thinkers like Brunner repudiate the attempt to give the Fall a historic setting. Yet Brunner affirms the doctrine of the Fall:

We cannot believe, in Christian and Biblical terms, without holding firmly to the distinction between Creation and Sin, and therefore the idea of a Fall. To give this up means to abandon the Biblical faith as a whole.[16]

Brunner thus keeps the essential Christian doctrine without making use of the rejected ideas of 'Adam in Paradise' and the primitive state. The Fall is a true statement about the reality of man's nature and his relationship with God.

Here we have two conflicting views, one which attempts to fit the Fall into a historical context without violating the findings of science, the other which repudiates any such attempt, but which firmly underlines the truth that the doctrine expounds about man, his nature, and his relationship with God. The former position, despite its speculative nature, has a certain attractiveness, but the latter position seems to be the more satisfactory approach. This is particularly so if we accept the view of Oscar Cullmann that a narrative may be a myth in the sense that Brunner means, and yet also be an event in time. He points out that in Primitive Christianity there was no distinction between historically verifiable events

[15] *Man in Revolt*, p. 85.   [16] *Dogmatics*, II.51.

and myths: 'It considers Adam to be upon the same plane as is Jesus of Nazareth.'[17] Cullmann maintains that the early Christians were right in seeing myth and history on the same redemptive time-line. In this position he is far removed from the demythologizing of Bultmann, who appears to strip away the myth and so leave a timeless truth. Cullmann recognizes the myth, but insists on keeping the truth in a time context. As an illustration, he gives the case of Adam, which is our immediate concern: 'In the New Testament point of view is not the essential thing in the figure of Adam the fact that a second Adam comes *after* him?'[18] Here we have the real distinction between Cullmann's point of view and that of Bultmann; and with this necessary corrective, the Adam story, while not being treated as 'historical', is still kept in the continuous redemptive line, and does not become timeless.[19]

Thus we can answer the first objection to the Fall doctrine in this way. Even in a process of evolution from a lower to a higher state it is possible to believe that something has gone wrong with the process, that it is not exactly as was intended in the perfection of the creative mind of God. Such facts as evil, pain, and dysteleology seem to point to the truth of this interpretation. We recognize that the story of Adam as the sole ancestor of mankind is no longer tenable, yet the story of Adam reveals a profound and lasting truth about human nature; even though the Genesis narrative is mythical in form, this myth has a vital place in the development of the redemptive acts of God that take place in time.

The second objection to a Fall doctrine can again be introduced by a quotation from H. T. Powell: 'The Citadel to be defended at all costs is the truth of God's love. It can scarcely be maintained that we are safeguarding it in any scheme that postulates a pre-cosmic Fall.'[20] It is true that in this particular passage the theory of N. P. Williams is under discussion, and we would not wish to defend that theory in all its details, but the general point still remains, that the Fall doctrine is an attempt to explain the existence of evil and yet preserve a belief in the love of God. There are facts in nature which seem to militate against the acceptance of God as a loving Creator. Nature 'red in tooth and claw' (to mention but the savage brutality of the praying mantis, or the

---

[17] *Christ and Time*, p. 94.   [18] Op. cit. p. 95.
[19] For a full account of Oscar Cullmann's position, see op. cit. pp. 94-106.
[20] *The Fall of Man*, p. xix.

absolute destructive force of driver ants, is sufficient illustration), the fact that certain species of life have been tried and have become extinct through their inability to survive in the struggle of evolution, the seemingly colossal wastage in nature—all these seem to speak against the love of God. Above all, however, is the fact that over the whole of nature there are streaked the vivid hues of pain. There is much in nature that is a positive challenge to faith, and when we come to the sphere of man, we find sin and pain in a form that cannot be ignored. To affirm the love of God, and yet maintain that this world in which there is so much sin and pain is exactly as God designed and created it, presents an almost intolerable challenge to faith. If we are to believe in the love and omnipotence of God, we are almost forced to believe in a 'Fallen World'. It is true that God is ultimately responsible, in that He created not only the realm of nature but also free agents, and it is through the rebellion of these free agents that sin and evil have made their appearance. Yet in His scheme He desired men and women who of their own free will might love and serve Him, and this necessitated the gift of freedom. Free will has, as a necessary implication, the possibility of evil and sin. The Adamic Fall doctrine is the attempt to maintain the love of God, and to admit that many things contrary to His will and purpose have entered into this world through man's wrong use of this God-given freedom. The doctrine of a Pre-adamic Fall—highly speculative though it is, and certainly beyond the sphere of rational proof—is an attempt to maintain the love of God in the face of many aspects of nature which militate against the acceptance of the divine love. Thus, against H. T. Powell, we submit that the Fall doctrine, which maintains the declension of the world from God's ideal, is not a hindrance but rather an asset to Christian apologetics when we are asserting the love of God.

H. T. Powell submits yet a third objection to a Fall doctrine. He maintains that it is only with a doctrine of God's complete transcendence that this doctrine can be held. The moment God's immanence is admitted, the Fall doctrine must be abandoned. If God's continuing work in the world is affirmed, then a Fall doctrine is seen to be inadequate. We must accept an optimistic view of the universe which makes this pessimistic concept of the Fall completely out of place.[21] Two cogent arguments can be brought

[21] *The Fall of Man*, Chapter 3.

against this position. In the first place, the world as we see it calls for a severe doctrine of sin and evil; to talk about an optimistic attitude is not adequate to the facts. When man looks into the depths of his soul, he sees the dark reality of sin that calls for a drastic explanation. Something has gone radically wrong with man. He is not the creature that God meant him to be, but fallen. Human history is the bitter and tragic embodiment of this truth. This latter point has been shown by Herbert Butterfield, whose study, *Christianity and History*, reveals the reality of fallen human nature working itself out in the pages of human history.[22] 'What history does', he says, 'is . . . to uncover man's universal sin'.[23] In the second place we cannot accept the thesis that to admit the immanence of God means the denial of the Fall. The transcendence of God is to be found in the Righteous and Holy Creator as against the sinful creature; the immanence of God is His present, continuing, redemptive activity, with its focal point in the Incarnation. This redemptive activity calls for a real doctrine of sin as its necessary background, and this background is perfectly given by the Fall doctrine. The claim that the doctrine of the Fall denies the immanence and continuing work of God is not valid.

So far the modern objections which we have considered have been against the Fall doctrine; we must now turn to those levelled against the doctrine of Original Sin. We must make it perfectly clear that this doctrine of 'original sin' is not dependent for its validity on the acceptance of the Fall doctrine. Brunner says 'the contradiction between the Creation and Sin . . . has no connection with a statement of its empirical origins'.[24] Rather the reverse is true; the truth of 'original sin', some evil bias or tendency passed on by heredity, is one of the reasons that have led to the acceptance of the explanatory hypothesis of the Fall.

Serious objection has been raised against the doctrine of 'original sin' by those who stress the importance of individuality; every human being is a separate person, and to link them together as is done by this doctrine is false. This position either denies the significance of heredity as a factor in man's constitution, or, if it does not deny it, at least reduces it to an absolute minimum. This undue stress on individuality has been widely rejected by psychologists in recent years. The concept of the 'racial unconscious' reveals the present state of opinion, and shows that any emphasis

[22] See especially Chapter 2.   [23] Ibid. p. 45.   [24] *Dogmatics*, II.74.

on individuality that is taken to extremes is to be rejected. Jung makes much of this idea and uses it extensively in his explanation of art, science, philosophy, and religion. These are all projections of elements in the racial unconscious, elements that have their origin in the dim past of man's history. This collective unconscious is universal; each individual is given a piece of the common mind of humanity, and from this he has to make his own individual life. This psychological theory is obviously of great significance in this connection, and modern theology has not overlooked its relevance. 'This idea of the "collective unconscious" helps us to explain a great many elements in the mental life of the individual . . . and we can also apply this to the sphere of sin.'[25] Considering the present climate of psychological opinion, few would accept as valid this argument against 'original sin' which emphasizes individuality almost to the denial of the corporate aspects of human personality.

A strong objection has been raised against the doctrine on the ground that a fallen nature could not be passed on from generation to generation. The study of heredity is a vast and intricate subject, but certain facts seem to have emerged clearly.[26] J. B. S. Haldane defines heredity as 'the resemblance between an organism and its ancestors, in so far as this resemblance is not due to a similarity of environment'.[27] It is clear that certain dominant abnormalities are passed on by affected individuals to about half their children regardless of sex; for instance, certain eye diseases (myopia, presenile cataract, and acute glaucoma), a number of ear and skin diseases, and some malformations such as brachydactyly and lobster claw. Certain sex-linked recessive abnormalities are also quite definite—haemophilia and colour-blindness for example. When we turn to physical characteristics, stature, weight, cranial index, we have the following table of correlation.[28] (Correlation is a term used to show the relationship between two sets of statistics. If the two sets agree in every detail, then there is a perfect correlation which is 1. If there is no agreement, then there is a correlation of 0. The grading between is done by decimal points; thus ·8 is a high correlation, and ·3 is low, though it does reveal that there is still a positive correlation.)

[25] E. Brunner, *Dogmatics*, II.98
[26] In this and in the following paragraphs I must express my indebtedness to various articles in the *EB* (1951 Edition).
[27] *EB*, XI.484.   [28] *EB*, XI.493.

Brother with brother, sister with sister	about ·52
One parent with son or daughter	about ·46
Grandparent and grandchild	about ·27
Uncle or aunt and nephew or niece	about ·25
First cousins *inter se*	about ·15

Here we can see that there is a real positive correlation with respect to physical characteristics, and that the degree of correlation becomes less as the family relationship becomes more distant.

When we come to psychological characteristics, the problem is far more complex because of the difficulty of estimating environmental influence. We must count as heredity only what is carried in the genes, and is therefore settled at the moment of conception; all else, including pre-natal influences, must be termed environment. In this sphere of 'psychological heredity', by far the greatest research has been done with reference to intelligence. Sir Francis Galton in 1869 published his *Hereditary Genius*, in which he studied the background of 997 famous men from every sphere of life, and his resultant picture of the influence of heredity is very impressive: one out of three had an eminent father; one out of two had eminent brothers and sons. As more-distant relationships were studied, the percentage fell. Is it certain, however, that all this is to be accounted for by heredity? May not environment have had some part to play in producing these figures? There is a further defect in the work of Galton in that he studied achievement rather than capacity. By means of modern 'Intelligence Tests' we are able to study capacity rather than achievement, and the results show that the more remote the relationship the lower is the degree of correlation. Here again, however, the tests are not completely decisive, for where there is a genetical similarity there is also usually a similarity of environment. It has therefore been necessary to find cases where the two factors of nature and nurture can be separated. One instance can be found in the case of foster children. In this case there is a similarity of environment but not of heredity. Here there is a definite correlation between children and their foster parents, but it is not as high as in normal families. Brothers who are brought up in different families are only half as closely correlated as brothers who are brought up together. Here heredity seems to be a definite factor in the resultant intelligence. Orphanages give us a better picture, for here the environmental influences are more extensive than in the cases just considered. Nevertheless there is a distinct variety of intelligence, showing that heredity is still a determinative factor, but the differences are not as great as in the case of foster children. The most fruitful avenue of investigation is to be found in the case of twins. Twins are of two kinds, fraternal twins who have no closer heredity than two brothers but whose environment is closer, and identical twins, who have identical heredity because they come from a single fertilized cell. In fraternal twins the correlation is ·7 as against ·5 for ordinary brothers, but in identical twins the correlation is as high as ·9. Study has been made of about twenty-five pairs of identical twins, who, because of circumstances, have been separated at a very early age. The separation means that there is a difference of environment. Even here the correlation has remained higher than in the case of fraternal twins. These investigations seem to prove beyond a shadow of a doubt that heredity is a vital factor in determining intelligence.

We have thus seen that modern investigations have shown the relevance of heredity as a factor in physical and mental characteristics. Why then should the importance of heredity be denied in the spiritual sphere? With these factors before us, there seems to be no reason to accept the criticism that a tendency to sin cannot be passed on by means of heredity. F. R. Tennant, however, still rejects the doctrine of 'original sin' on scientific grounds, saying 'the question turns entirely on the possibility of the transmission of acquired modifications as distinguished from congenital variations'.[29] An acquired characteristic is defined as 'one that has developed in the course of the life of an individual in the somatic or body cells'.[30] Such characteristics as the powerful arm muscles of the blacksmith, or the increased agility of the pianist's hands, fall under this heading. Lamarckism is the theory that such characteristics can be passed on by heredity. This theory has been rejected in most scientific circles and it is now generally accepted that acquired characteristics cannot be transmitted. Be that as it may, it is to be seriously questioned whether the Christian concept of 'original sin' can come under this category of acquired characteristics. It is something far deeper than the mere effect on

[29] *Origin and Propagation of Sin*, p. 36.   [30] *EB*, XIII.607.

the body cells of the sins of a man during his lifetime; it is something far wider in sphere and extent than chance developments in various individuals. Rather, since the Fall, it is something radical in human nature. If we are to explain the obvious and undeniable fact of human sinfulness, then we must say that 'original sin' is a congenital rather than an acquired characteristic.

It may be argued, however, that even if it is congenital now, the fact that we are tracing sin back to Adam surely means that Adam passed on a characteristic which he acquired. C. S. Lewis, who attempts to give the Fall a historical setting, replies to this point:

This condition was transmitted by heredity to all later generations, for it was not simply what biologists call an acquired variation; it was the emergence of a new kind of man—a new species, never made by God, had sinned itself into existence. The change which man had undergone was not parallel to the development of a new organ or a new habit; it was a radical alteration of his constitution, a disturbance of the relation between his component parts, and an internal perversion of one of them.[31]

If on the other hand, we think of the Fall as a myth, it is to be questioned whether biological categories apply.

If this point of view is not accepted, it does not of necessity mean that there is no transmission of a moral taint. 'Some who believe in the racial inheritance of evil are not thinking of biological inheritance at all, but of a solidarity in natural humanity, so that we are born into, and are units in, a corrupted natural order.'[32] This point of view denies the assumption of Tennant that 'the question turns entirely on the possibility of the transmission of acquired modifications'.

The final objection to this concept of 'original sin' must now be examined. It seems to have as part of its essential structure a Traducian doctrine of the origin of the soul, and in recent years this doctrine has been severely criticized. F. R. Tennant, who speaks as a scientist as well as a theologian, thinks that Traducianism is psychologically barbarous. This criticism is apt against a gross form of Traducianism, but it is to be questioned whether it disproves this particular theory. The whole question of the origin

[31] *The Problem of Pain*, p. 71.
[32] *Doctrine in the Church of England*, Footnote *, pp. 62-3.

of the soul is complex and difficult, but it seems that the most satisfactory answer is to admit that, even though our personality and soul are not continuous with those of our parents in the same way as our physical bodies are, yet the raw material out of which we build our character and spiritual nature is dependent on heredity. This position appears to be self-evident to such a careful writer as Brunner: 'The transmission of the spiritual nature, of the "character", from parents to children is such an evident and tragically powerful experience that it would be strange if it were not brought into connexion with the idea of the *peccatum originis*.'[33]

FALLEN HUMAN NATURE

(a) *Original Sin: Further investigation of its meaning*

We have examined and assessed certain modern objections to this doctrine of 'original sin'; now the doctrine must be given more careful definition. The Fall doctrine sees the origin of sin as a rebellion against God, and the results of this Fall as having been passed on to later generations. What, however, is the exact content of this fallen nature which is transmitted by heredity? The balance of man's nature has been upset, and it is this disordered nature that has been passed on, but in what way has the balance of man's nature been disturbed? In the first place the disorder consists in the weakening of the will as against the emotional side of man's nature. As made by God there was perfect balance between will and emotional force; since the Fall this has gone, and the emotional side of man's nature is no longer under the full control of his will. Free will has not been destroyed, but it has been weakened and its power seriously diminished. N. P. Williams has made much of this idea, and even goes so far as to equate the inherited weakness with the weakening of the herd complex in favour of the self-regarding instinct. It is not advisable to go so far as to equate the doctrine of 'original sin' so closely with any particular instinct; the most it is advisable to say is that the balance of man's nature has been upset and his will weakened, his emotions being now only imperfectly under the control of his will, and that there is a bias in man's nature that leads to the assertion of his will against the wills of others and, what is even more important, against the will of God. Brunner's *Man in Revolt*

[33] *Man in Revolt*, p. 144.

puts this truth under the heading of 'The Decay of Personal Unity'.[34] The substance of his thought is that

the individual functions have formed different centres, and they develop like the different centres of government which exist at the same time in a civil war, each one at the cost of others.[35]

He puts the same point vividly in another passage:

As upon a chess-board which has been shaken, all the individual chessmen are still there, unbroken, 'good', as they came out of the workshop of the turner; yet at the same time everything is confused, and misplaced and meaningless—so is the nature of man.[36]

Even when we accept the tremendous influence of social environment as a determining factor in man's development, it must be admitted that man starts with a nature that has been deeply disturbed, that is no longer perfectly balanced nor an integrated unity. From the very inception of life we have a nature that is biased towards evil.

(b) *The definition of Fallen Human Nature, and its relationship to Original Sin*

The most important term for our present discussion is 'fallen human nature', and this must now be defined.

It means human nature that is open to the possibility of sin. To possess 'fallen human nature' means to dwell in a realm where sin is a reality and has become deeply entrenched, where every aspect of life has been stained and marred by its influence. To these points most theologians would agree, but it is the next point where careful definition is required. On account of man's rebellion against God, the human race has become a spoilt species, and the results of man's rebellion are passed on from generation to generation; man is born with a proclivity to sin, with a bias towards rebellion against God, born as part of a race that has become alienated from God, born into a realm over which sin and death rule. This is the truth which lies behind the doctrine of 'original sin'.

Generally speaking there have been two main ways of looking at this doctrine of 'original sin'. One group, which includes Augustine and the Reformers, has held the view that what is

---

[34] Op. cit. pp. 228-36.   [35] Ibid. p. 235.   [36] Op. cit. p. 137.

passed on from one generation to the next is a positive corruption. Man is born with a nature corrupted from the moment of conception. The other group holds that what is transmitted is a weakness, or a proclivity to sin, rather than positive corruption. This weakness, left to its own devices, tends to lead to open rebellion against God, to actual sin, and to the corruption of man's nature, yet man is born with a weakness rather than a disease. Just as some men are born with a physical frame that makes them prone to a certain disease, so all men are born with a moral and spiritual nature that is prone to sin and rebellion without actually being born corrupt. This second position has much to commend it, especially as it is easier to believe that a new-born child is born with a nature that is weakened than to believe that it is born with one that is definitely corrupted. Yet it is to be questioned whether weakness is a completely adequate word. It tends to lead to a wrong association of ideas. Man is born with a nature weakened by the sins of previous generations, but he is also born into a race that is a spoilt species, a race that has rebelled against God and so stands alienated from God and under His wrath. This does not mean that God's wrath is personally directed against each new-born child, though Augustine and Calvin would assert even this. Rather it means that each new-born child is born into an alienated race, and, because of the fact that the whole race of sinful mankind is estranged from God, the child is born in alienation and under the wrath of God.

It becomes increasingly obvious that 'original sin' is a phrase that has a certain incongruity about it. Sin, in the fullest sense, demands the use of the will. To bring in the qualifying word 'original' leads almost to a contradiction in terms. If, however, as we have suggested earlier,[37] sin is interpreted in its broadest sense as anything that comes between us and God, then the phrase may stand. The whole question has been even more complicated by the question of the relationship between 'original sin' and 'original guilt'. Theologians who hold that 'original sin' is a positive corruption usually accept, as an important part of their system of thought, the doctrine of 'original guilt', thus maintaining that we are responsible in the sight of God for the inherited nature.[38]

---

[37] See p. 11 above.
[38] Sometimes the doctrine of 'original guilt' is understood to mean that we are guilty of Adam's actual sin in that we were present in Adam's loins at the time of the Fall.

The theologians who think of 'original sin' as a weakness tend to reject the idea of 'original guilt'. While questioning whether the word 'weakness' is adequate to define the human nature that is inherited, and while maintaining that 'original sin' involves alienation, we feel nevertheless that 'original guilt' is a doctrine that cannot be accepted. It is legitimate to ask how it is possible for a man to be guilty in the sight of God for something in which he has no real personal choice, in which his will has not been involved. To many it seems to attribute to God a harshness of judgement which in a man would be condemned. The concept of responsibility is one that should be given attention. Brunner writes:

Sin and responsibility are inseparably connected, and there is no ascription of responsibility, no verdict of guilt, without accusation and proof of responsibility, that is, no one is pronounced guilty for something which he has not done.[39]

This quotation focuses the problem clearly. To talk of guilt in respect of inherited nature is to overlook the important category of responsibility. Even though the phrase 'original sin' points to a valid truth, the phrase 'original guilt' seems unacceptable and out of harmony with the biblical message. While it is possible to say that being born into a rebellious race means, in an impersonal sense, that we are born in alienation from God, to say that there is also 'original guilt', and that God's personal condemnation lies upon us, seems to be unacceptable. Not until we have joined our own will to mankind's rebellion against God, not until we have actively entered into opposition to the will of God, does guilt enter in.

We are now able to give a definition to the term 'fallen human nature' as it is to be used in our present investigation. It is a nature that has been affected by the Fall, and by the sin and rebellion of previous generations. When we come into the world we are born into a spoilt species in the sense that the power of the will has been weakened and the balance of the instincts upset, we share in all the propensities and drives of human nature as they are now in our present post-Fall human situation, we are born into a rebellious race that by its insurrection has become alienated from God. Fallen human nature is a human nature that belongs to the age of Adam, under the tyranny of sin and death. It is a nature which tends to lead men into sin and open rebellion against God; but it is only when they have actually arrived there that men become guilty in God's sight, for not until then have they added their own will to the nature that they have inherited.

(c) The subject of this present investigation:
to discover whether Christ assumed this 'fallen human nature'

The central fact of the Christian revelation is that the Son of God became incarnate in Jesus Christ. It has always been accepted, in theory at least, that Jesus assumed full human nature, but the content of full humanity has received various interpretations. Controversy has raged over the question whether Christ was liable to error in the sense that He was limited to the knowledge and thought-forms of His day. This idea was not accepted by many early theologians, but since the rise of kenotic theories of the Incarnation this concept of 'ignorance' has become a commonplace in much theological thought. One further question remains to be asked, one that has been tacitly ignored by the majority of theologians, the question whether Christ's human nature was affected by the Fall, whether He took the 'fallen human nature' that is our common inheritance. When this question has been asked it has usually been answered in the negative; it has been held that He assumed perfect human nature, human nature as it was originally created by God.

The theory that we wish to investigate in the following pages is that Jesus, the incarnate Son of God, partook of the same 'fallen human nature' as the rest of mankind—that He fully entered into our present human predicament and shared our temptations to the full, that He came to the level of our human need by entering into the post-Fall situation. Nevertheless, because He was fully God as well as fully man, He was able from the very first, and on every occasion, to counteract the effects of this fallen nature which He had assumed. It is strongly maintained that the inheritance was always overcome and was never allowed to fructify into actual sins and rebellion against God. Finally, this 'fallen nature' was completely overcome and cleansed and renewed on Calvary. This hypothesis must be investigated, not simply as a Christological problem, but as one with a very significant bearing on soteriology.

At the beginning of our enquiry we must examine the objections

c

which might be raised against this position. This will serve a twofold purpose. It will enable us to refute a number of arguments that can be levelled against the theory that Christ shared our 'fallen human nature'. Secondly, it will help to elucidate exactly what the theory means and implies.

Perhaps the most serious objection is that this hypothesis endangers the sinlessness of Jesus. If He possessed 'fallen human nature', does not this, of necessity, tend to jeopardize His sinlessness? This is an objection which needs to be considered most carefully, for, if it can be substantiated, it means that the hypothesis we are suggesting is unacceptable. If the sinlessness of Jesus is undermined, then the efficacy of His work is destroyed. No longer can He be thought of as the perfect revelation of God; no longer can He be accepted as Saviour. Before the objection can be usefully discussed, we must be quite sure what we mean by 'sin'. To this definition we must now turn.

Sin has been understood in a variety of ways, but, if we are not to go astray in our discussion, 'it cannot be sufficiently emphasized that sin is a concept which belongs entirely to the religious realm'.[40] This is a fact of the utmost importance. Frederic Greeves says: 'Whatever else the Christian may mean when he speaks of sin, he most certainly refers to the relationship between man and God . . . he cannot complete any statement about the nature of sin without reference to God.'[41] Sin is anything which break's a man's fellowship with God and causes a separation between man and God. Norman H. Snaith describes sin as being 'theofugal'.[42] This implies that sin is a reality when the relationship between God and man has been distorted by man's rebellion, when man has asserted his own will against the will of God. The results of this egocentricity, this rebellion, are diverse, but the essential nature of sin lies in this wrong and distorted relationship to God.

The New Testament makes it clear that Jesus possessed perfect communion with God the Father; certainly there is no indication of anything entering in to destroy the relationship between them,[43] We have defined 'sin' in terms of disobedience and rebellion. In

[40] G. Aulén, *The Faith of the Christian Church*, p. 260.　　[41] *The Meaning of Sin*, p. 16.
[42] *The Distinctive Ideas of the Old Testament*, pp. 60-1.
[43] The only possible suggestion is to be found in the Cry of Dereliction, but to interpret this to mean that Jesus was actually abandoned by God is to misinterpret the saying. See pp. 59-63 below.

Jesus, however, we see, not disobedience and rebellion, but perfect obedience. This concept of Christ's obedience is rooted in the Gospel narratives. It is evident in the accounts of the Baptism and the Temptations; it appears to have been one of the mainsprings of His actions during the period of the ministry; it is clearly seen in the Garden of Gethsemane as He faces the Cross. This theme is also underlined in the other New Testament writings. In Philippians 2^8 Christ is spoken of as being 'obedient unto death, even death on a cross'. Paul speaks of 'one man's obedience' making 'many righteous' (Rom 5^{19}). The author of Hebrews also emphasizes this quality in the character of Jesus: 'Although he was a Son, he learned obedience through what he suffered' (5^8). In the New Testament Jesus is portrayed as one who was perfectly obedient to the will of His Father, and an unbroken relationship was the result. If we define 'sin' in terms of rebellion and disobedience, resulting in a distorted relationship with God, then it is evident that the New Testament so describes Jesus that in no way can 'sin' be ascribed to Him.

It is quite clear, therefore, that if the theory that Jesus shared our 'fallen human nature' in any way jeopardizes His sinlessness, then it is to be rejected as being incompatible with the New Testament evidence as to the character of Jesus. It is to be questioned, however, if the hypothesis under consideration does, in any way, imperil the sinlessness of our Lord. 'Fallen human nature', as defined in the present investigation, refers to human nature which has been affected by the sin and rebellion of previous generations, a nature which produces temptation in all its seductive power, a nature with dreadful power and potentialities for evil. The definition of sin which we have given above is concerned with a man's life, his rebellion against God, his wilful disobedience, and the distorted relationship with God which ensues. The position advocated here is that 'fallen human nature' refers to that which was assumed by the Son of God at the Incarnation, and that 'sinlessness', understood in terms of obedience and an unbroken relationship with God, refers to the incarnate life of Jesus. He assumed what was imperfect, but He wrought out of it a life that was perfect.

The matter, however, cannot be considered as settled. The question needs to be asked: What is the relationship between 'fallen human nature' and actual sin? Does 'fallen human nature' inevitably lead into sin? If it does, to assert that Jesus possessed it, and then to say that He was sinless, is to be logically inconsistent. This question must now be considered.

It is recognized by many theologians that there is a paradox concerning sin: sin is inevitable, and yet man is responsible for it.[44] This position needs to be carefully stated if serious error is to be avoided. Niebuhr says that

the Christian doctrine of original sin, with its seemingly contradictory assertions about the inevitability of sin and man's responsibility, is a dialectical truth which does justice to the fact that man's self love and self centredness are inevitable, but not in such a way as to fit into the category of natural necessity. It is within and by his freedom that man sins.[45]

It seems clear that Niebuhr is using the idea of 'inevitability' in a distinctive way. He writes: 'Sin is natural to man in the sense that it is universal but not in the sense that it is necessary.'[46] Again he writes:

Sin is to be regarded as neither a necessity of man's nature nor yet as a pure caprice of his will. It proceeds rather from a defect of will, for which reason it is not completely deliberate; but since it is the will in which the defect is found, and the will presupposes freedom, the defect cannot be attributed to a taint in man's nature.[47]

Niebuhr is describing a situation in which the word 'inevitable' can be used only in a sense different from its usual one. This same paradoxical position can be illustrated from another recent penetrating discussion of the subject. Aulén describes sin as 'inevitable and volitional'.[48] He goes on to say that 'it is evident that there lies herein a certain tension-filled relationship between different viewpoints'.[49] Again it is clear that 'inevitable' is being used in a distinctive sense. This is shown by a reference which Aulén makes to Luther. ' "Necessity", says Luther, belongs to "physics", not theology. If this concept is to be used in theology we must "bathe and wash it".'[50] He then continues: 'What Luther wants to emphasize is that sin, at the same time that it is inevitable to "natural" man, nevertheless must not be understood as a natural defect, but always be conceived of as the result of a

---

[44] For a penetrating discussion of this whole question see R. Niebuhr, *The Nature and Destiny of Man*, I. ix.
[45] Ibid. p. 279.   [46] Ibid. p. 257.   [47] Ibid. p. 259.
[48] *The Faith of the Christian Church*, p. 276.   [49] Ibid. p. 276.   [50] Ibid. p. 277.

volitional act of the individual.'[51] This quotation is very pertinent
to our present discussion. In the first place it affirms that sin is
to be thought of in terms of the volitional act of the individual,
not in terms of a natural defect. This could well be interpreted,
without injustice to Aulén, to mean that sin is concerned with
man's will and is not the inevitable result of the 'fallen human
nature' which man inherits. If this is so, it seems to imply that
Jesus could assume 'fallen human nature' without becoming a
sinner, because in all His volitional acts He was sinless.

The quotation from Aulén cited above prompts the question
whether 'inevitable' is the right word to be used in this context.
Certainly Luther was not happy with it. As we have seen both
Niebuhr and Aulén use the word, but they use it with some
hesitation, as though it is the least inadequate one to express
the truth they wish to convey. It is to be questioned whether
'inevitable' is the right word. Harold Roberts rejects it.

That we are bound up in some sense with the sin of the race cannot be
denied any more than we can deny the solidarity of goodness. It is
also beyond dispute that we have a tendency, which has deep ramifications in the history of the race, to seek our own interests and to oppose
the divine will. But although that tendency is so potent as to make sin
highly probable, it does not make it inevitable.[52]

It is significant that this passage occurs when Dr Roberts is
discussing the possibility of Jesus' sharing our 'fallen human
nature'. If responsibility for sin is to have any meaning, it cannot
also be affirmed that 'fallen human nature' makes sin inevitable.
Inevitability and responsibility are mutually exclusive concepts
in the moral sphere.

D. M. Baillie makes a similar point with reference to the
perfection of Jesus, and his comments are relevant here.

His temptations were real temptations, which it was difficult and
painful for Him to resist. . . . When we say *non potuit peccare*, we do not
mean that He was completely raised above the struggle against sin, . . .
when we say that He was incapable of sinning, we mean that He was
the supreme case of what we can say with limited and relative truth
about many a good man. 'He is incapable of doing a mean and under-
hand thing', we say about a man whom we know to be honourable;
and so we say in a more universal and absolute way about Jesus,

[51] Ibid. p. 277.   [52] *Jesus and the Kingdom of God*, p. 78.

non potuit peccare, without in any way reducing the reality of His conflict with His temptations.[53]

This quotation shows, from a different standpoint, that the concept of inevitability when used in the moral sphere is, to say the least, highly dangerous. If it is used of our inherited human nature, implying that it 'inevitably' leads into sin, then in what sense can we be said to be guilty or responsible? If it is used of the sinlessness of Jesus, under the phrase *non potuit peccare*, does it not rob the perfection and sinlessness of Jesus of any moral worth?

It might be objected that to deny that 'fallen human nature' inevitably leads into sin imperils the uniqueness of Jesus. Does it not suggest that someone else might also lead a perfect life? Several points need to be made in this connection. First, we must say that even though the word 'inevitable' is not the most satisfactory one, the truth behind its usage is real. It is a fact that sin is universal, the only exception being Jesus. Harold Roberts, who rejects the word 'inevitable', says that the tendency is 'so potent as to make sin highly probable'.[54] Many would feel that the phrase 'highly probable' does not go far enough. Certainly it seems to suggest the possibility of another man living a perfect life. This is virtually impossible. Aulén, referring to Luther, says: 'What Luther wants to emphasize is that sin, at the same time that it is inevitable to "natural" man, nevertheless must not be understood as a natural defect, but always be conceived of as the result of a volitional act of the individual.'[55] Thus, even if 'fallen human nature' does not lead inevitably into sin, for 'natural' man it does in fact lead into sin, but not in such a way as to rob man of his responsibility. When we come to Jesus, it is to be questioned whether He can be placed within the category of 'natural man'. This does not mean that His humanity was in any way less real than ours; but when we are thinking of Jesus we are thinking of a unique person. To understand Jesus purely in terms of humanity is heretical. The central line of Christian thought has always affirmed that Jesus was the incarnate Son of God. For this reason it is not possible to make statements about Jesus as though He were only a man and nothing more. He was divine as well as human, two natures within one unified personality. Jesus shared our 'fallen human nature', a nature which, while it did not make

[53] *God Was in Christ*, pp. 14-15.   [54] *Jesus and the Kingdom of God*, p. 78.
[55] *The Faith of the Christian Church*, p. 277.

sin inevitable in such a way as to undermine responsibility, yet did, nevertheless, make sin 'highly probable'—some would say with Aulén and Luther that for the natural man it made it 'inevitable'. Jesus, however, cannot be understood merely as natural man; His human nature was hypostatically united with the divine nature. Through the power of this divine nature the weaknesses of His human nature were overcome so that He did live a perfect life. When discussing the 'fallen human nature' assumed by the Son of God and the sinless life that He lived, it is essential to remember that in this particular case we are dealing with a unique person, the incarnate Son of God.

If it is suggested that this gives Jesus an unfair advantage over us, we would not disagree, except with the wording of this criticism. It is not in any way our intention to reduce Jesus to our level, or to say that Jesus was exactly as we are. Rather it is our intention to say that when the Son of God became incarnate He assumed 'fallen human nature', in this respect becoming as we are; but we should whole-heartedly affirm that He was the divine Son of God. To say that this gives Him an unfair advantage over us is to miss the essential point. The Son of God came to be our Saviour in order that His victory should be ours; any 'advantage' which He possessed He used for our benefit.

Before we leave this line of criticism, we must face the question: If someone did live a perfect life—and our stress on responsibility and criticism of 'inevitability' make it a possibility, even if of the remotest kind—would this mean that the uniqueness of Jesus had been destroyed? To put it crudely, would it mean that there would be another Son of God incarnate? This criticism is invalid. Even supposing that another man did live a perfect life, this would not destroy the uniqueness of Jesus. His uniqueness lies, not simply in the fact that He lived a perfect human life, but in the fact that He was the incarnate Son of God. In Him we see the perfect revelation of God; in Him God Himself has come to be our Saviour and Redeemer. No man, even if he lived a perfect life, could be either of these things. If he could it would mean that the distinction between Creator and creature, between God and man, was destroyed, and that the perfection of humanity was the same as divinity. This simply cannot be accepted as orthodox Christian teaching. The uniqueness of Jesus lies, not merely in His perfect human life, but far more in the revelation and redemption which He brought as Son of God. No man, even if he lived a perfect life, could challenge this uniqueness of our Lord.

The doctrine under discussion implies that the possibility of sinning was a real alternative in the life of Jesus, though the thesis is that He did, in actual fact, live a sinless and perfect life. When it is stated that there was the possibility of the incarnate Son of God sinning, certain questions arise which demand attention. Does it not seem to suggest that the success of the Incarnation was endangered?

D. M. Baillie puts the question: 'Did the Incarnation depend upon the daily human choices made by Jesus, or did He always choose aright because He was God incarnate?'[56] Baillie goes on to state that on his thesis of the 'paradox of grace' there is no dilemma. 'It must, of course, be true that His choices were genuine human choices, and that in a sense everything depended upon them.'[57] 'And yet . . . we must inevitably . . . say something apparently opposite, remembering that in the last analysis such human choice is never prevenient or even co-operative, but wholly dependent on the divine prevenience.'[58] 'We must say that in the perfect life of Him . . . this divine prevenience was nothing short of Incarnation, and He lived as He did because He was God incarnate.'[59] 'Thus the dilemma disappears when we frankly recognize that in the doctrine of the Incarnation there is a paradox which cannot be rationalized but which in some small measure can be understood in the light of the "paradox of grace".'[60] This summary of the argument of D. M. Baillie is given, not because we wish to identify ourselves entirely with his theory, but because we wish to emphasize that this problem is not confined to the Christological theory under discussion. Baillie rejects the thesis that Christ assumed 'fallen human nature', yet he still has to face the problem. If the human choices of Jesus were real, real in the sense that for Him to sin was a possible alternative, then does not this mean that the Incarnation was in constant danger of failing? Yet to deny the reality of the human choices of Jesus is an extreme form of Docetism. This problem is part of the mystery of the Incarnation, and it is not merely a problem that is confined to this theory. True it may appear in an acute form in the present context, but the basic issues are to be found in any

---

[56] *God was in Christ*, p. 130.   [57] Ibid. p. 130.   [58] Ibid. p. 131.
[59] Ibid. p. 131.   [60] Ibid. p. 131.

exposition of the Incarnation. If the human nature of Jesus is taken seriously, it means that He possessed the power of choice, and that good and evil were real alternatives. Yet in Jesus we see the Incarnation of the Son of God. This means that in Jesus we see a perfect human life, but not in such a way as to imply that the human nature of Jesus was robbed of its power of choice.

William Temple maintained that 'if any man says that he understands the relation of Deity to humanity in Christ, he only makes it clear that he does not understand at all what is meant by an Incarnation'.[61] With this statement most, if not all, theologians would agree. Is this not the place where our human finite minds cannot fully give the answer? We must affirm the reality of the choices made by Jesus, with the obvious implication that to sin was a possibility; yet we are also sure that the Incarnation was such that God's purposes were certain to be achieved. Perhaps the 'paradox of grace' gives a hint as to an answer, but it is to be questioned if any logically satisfying solution is possible. This is one of the deepest mysteries of the Incarnation, one which all theologians have to face, and which is not merely a problem that is confined to the theory under discussion.

It might be argued that to say that Jesus shared our 'fallen human nature' would immediately invalidate His sense of Sonship and would destroy the perfect fellowship that He had with His Father. It must be underlined, however, that in the definition of 'fallen human nature' that has been given the alienation involved in the assumption of this nature was in no way personal. Personal alienation only arises when personal sin and rebellion enter into the situation and guilt is incurred. Jesus, even though born into an alienated race, into the aeon of sin and death, still enjoyed unbroken the Son's fellowship with His Father. He is like a man born into a country at war who yet never accepts his country's war, but repudiates completely and emphatically its whole position, thereby keeping fellowship with a country from which he was alienated by birth. Christ, because of His perfect life, continued in perfect fellowship with His Father, even though He was in the midst of the alien territory of 'fallen human nature'.

This whole position may be challenged as too paradoxical. Jesus assumed 'fallen human nature', yet He was free from actual

[61] *Christus Veritas*, p. 139.

sin. He was born into a race alienated from God, yet had perfect fellowship with His Father and possessed a deep experience of Sonship. But paradox cannot be escaped. The Incarnation and Atonement are both full of paradox. Jesus was *vere homo*, yet at the same time, in the unity of one person, *vere Deus*. In one side of His nature He was the Incarnation of the pre-existent Christ, who was concerned in creation and possessed cosmic functions; yet on another side of His nature He was a creature. In some sense He could be called the 'Sin bearer', yet He was perfect and sinless, the Holy One of God. This sense of paradox cannot be avoided in the Incarnation and Atonement; to avoid the paradoxical is to end with an emasculated form of Christianity that is unworthy of the name. In this study there is no attempt to avoid the paradoxical, but rather to trace the paradox down to a deeper and more fundamental level, and by so doing to merge all the paradoxes of the Person and Work of Christ into one fundamental paradox—Christ when He became incarnate for man's salvation assumed 'fallen human nature'. From this point flow all the paradoxes of His Person and Work, yet there is also achieved a unified conception where Christology and soteriology are inseparably linked, where the *vere Deus, vere homo* is affirmed, where the sinlessness of Christ is maintained and yet where there is a satisfactory theory of the atonement for the salvation of men who possess 'fallen human nature'.

During the investigation of the theory we shall notice that there is a variety of phrases used by those who advocate this Christological point. 'Sinful human nature' is found on more than one occasion. This seems to be dependent on Romans 8[3], 'in the likeness of sinful flesh'. Sometimes the word 'corrupt' is applied to the nature assumed by Christ. There is a variety of expressions, but the essential point is that Christ entered into our human situation as it has become because of the Fall, that Christ's human nature was consubstantial with the nature that we inherit. The present writer prefers the phrase 'fallen human nature' despite the fact that 'sinful and human nature' might claim a certain biblical warrant from Romans 8[3]. It is not because of the 'harshness' of the expression 'sinful human nature' that we prefer the term 'fallen human nature'. Rather it is because this latter phrase seems the least liable to misunderstanding. When the phrase 'sinful human nature' is used by the thinkers we shall investigate, they are using it to express the idea that Christ entered into the human predicament as it was because of the sin of previous generations. The phrase, however, might so easily be interpreted as meaning that Jesus was a sinner. This is alien to Christian thought. The term 'fallen human nature' does not seem to be so prone to misinterpretation. It is human nature that is influenced by the Fall; it is human nature that possesses the drives and propensities, that is open to the temptations and struggles of fallen mankind. In the present investigation the phrase 'fallen human nature' will be used except where the person being considered uses another phrase, or where another phrase seems essential to the context.

What support has this theory in the New Testament? What support has it received throughout the ages of Christian thought? In what way is it necessary for a satisfactory theory of the Person and Work of Christ? These are the questions that now need to be answered.

PART II

The New Testament Evidence

AVING discussed the preliminary questions that are relevant to the enquiry, we must now pass on to the actual discussion of the theory under investigation. Our main task is to discover whether or not Jesus assumed 'fallen human nature' at the Incarnation. Of necessity the investigation must first turn to the New Testament, for, whatever the desirability of the doctrine, whatever the opinions of Christian thinkers throughout the ages, it must have its roots in the New Testament if it is to be accepted.

It must be made clear that we cannot expect to find a definite or final answer within the New Testament writings. To some extent the question under discussion is a speculative one, though that must not be thought to imply that it is of no practical significance or is irrelevant to a sound theological position; and because of its very nature it can hardly have risen in any definite form in New Testament times. The interests of the apostles were far more practical than speculative, and we are struck by the lack of any exact definition of the Person of Christ in the New Testament. On reflection, however, this is what we should expect; the early Christians were drawn by the very personality of Jesus to give Him the reverence due only to God, yet no precise doctrine of His divinity is found in these early writings. So it is with the point under discussion; the humanity of Jesus is affirmed in all the New Testament writings to a greater or less degree, but a detailed discussion of the relation between His human nature and that of other men is not found. We must not look for any precise exposition of this theory in the pages of the New Testament. What we can hope to find is (a) that no passage is opposed to the theory, and (b) that the acceptance of the theory gives a more adequate exegesis to certain passages, and gives a clearer insight into the minds of the writers.

THE GOSPELS

(a) The Virgin Birth

The New Testament evidence for the Virgin Birth is confined to the following passages: Matthew 1[16, 18-25] and Luke 1[26-38], 3[23],[1] other references are open to serious question. The silence of Mark is not of great importance, for he does not record the birth of Jesus. When we turn to Paul we find a Christology that does not contradict the idea of the Virgin Birth, but the point still remains that there is silence about the doctrine.

Much discussion has taken place as to the true reading of John 1[13], since here we might possess a reference to the Virgin Birth in the Fourth Gospel. The reading 'who was born not of blood, nor of the will of the flesh, nor of the will of man but of God' is found in Tertullian.[2] This reading is a clear reference to the Virgin Birth. It must be stated, however, that this reading has the weakest attestation, and is rejected by the vast majority of scholars. It is possible, however, that the familiar reading contains a reference to the Virgin Birth. C. K. Barrett makes the point: 'The reading which refers explicitly to the birth of Jesus is to be rejected; but it remains probable that John was alluding to Jesus' birth, and declaring that the birth of Christians, being bloodless and rooted in God's will alone, followed the pattern of the birth of Christ himself.'[3] Even if this suggestion is accepted, however, it must be admitted that generally the Virgin Birth is outside the perspective of this writer.

How to interpret the silence of much of the New Testament is a controversial question. Vincent Taylor is of the opinion that it indicates that the doctrine had no place in the early apostolic preaching, and that the tradition was not widely known in the circles in which these various books were written. It can be argued, however, that it means that the doctrine was taken for granted. When we consider the content of the doctrine, it is

[1] This assumes that the true text of Luke 2[5] is 'with Mary his wife'; see J. M. Creed, *The Gospel according to St Luke*, p. 33, and Vincent Taylor, *The Virgin Birth*, pp. 32-4.
[2] *De Carne Christi*, cap. XIX, (*PL*, II.829-30).
[3] C. K. Barrett, *The Gospel according to Saint John*, pp. 137-8. Cf. W. Temple, *Readings in St John*, p. 13, and E. Hoskyns, *The Fourth Gospel*, pp. 166-8. C. H. Dodd, however, links the verse with 3[15-16] and asserts that the verse is concerned with the *sarx-pneuma* antithesis, not the birth of Jesus; see *The Interpretation of the Fourth Gospel*, p. 224.

reasonable to infer that the tradition would first be known in a limited, private circle, and only become common knowledge at a later time; this fact tends to support Dr Taylor's position. This in no way, however, implies that the tradition is not true. When we realize that the tradition was universally accepted by the end of the second century, and that it was only attacked by heretical groups, we have a strong argument for the validity of the tradition. Certainly no contradictory tradition was current in orthodox circles.

The passages in Matthew and Luke which refer to the doctrine have been subjected to searching examination. The true text of Matthew 1^{16} is uncertain because there are a number of textual variations. But whatever the true reading, it is quite clear that Matthew accepted the doctrine of the Virgin Birth; this is made certain by the passage 1^{18-25}, which has this doctrine as its very heart. The most that can be said is that the passage comes from M, which is the least trustworthy of the Gospel sources, but it is fallacious to assume that everything from this source is unreliable or spurious. The fact must be accepted that the writer of the first Gospel knew and accepted the tradition of the Virgin Birth of Jesus. The position in Luke is more complicated. Many scholars think that 1^{34-5} and 'as was supposed' in 3^{23} are interpolations. This hypothesis, however, is not universally accepted. There is no manuscript evidence to support it, and it is to be questioned whether the arguments advanced in its favour are sufficient to prove the case.[4]

A detailed study of the passages in Matthew and Luke is not necessary to our present investigation, especially as they leave the verdict as 'not proven', though the present writer thinks there is more to be said in favour of the tradition than against it. This is emphasized by the fact that there does not appear to be a satisfactory hypothesis to explain the rise of the tradition if it is not based on fact. Such rationalizations as spring from the desire to remove all traces of the miraculous are to be rejected. Theories which make the doctrine dependent on a myth of either Jewish or Pagan origin are not convincing. No really convincing explanation of the origin of the tradition has been put forward by those who reject its historicity.[5] This is the weak link in the argument

---

[4] For a careful study of the various theories that reject these Lucan passages see J. G. Machen, *The Virgin Birth of Christ*, pp. 119-68.

[5] For an exhaustive critical evaluation of the various theories see ibid. pp. 280-379.

D

of those who reject the Virgin Birth tradition; even if they can expunge the evidence from the New Testament, they are not able to give a satisfactory hypothesis to explain the rise and acceptance of the doctrine.

Vincent Taylor, after his study of the New Testament evidence, comes to the conclusion that the ultimate decision as to the validity of the doctrine must lie with the theologian—'the last word is with theology'.[6] Most Christian thinkers have been led to accept the Virgin Birth because it fits in with their idea of the Person of Christ. He was Son of God; therefore, it is argued, it was perfectly natural to expect His entry into the world to be unique. Other scholars have rejected the doctrine on theological grounds. Emil Brunner, for instance, says that it tells against the reality of the Incarnation; if the Son of God is to be truly incarnate then He must enter into the human race in the ordinary way. 'Is a man who is born without a human father a "true man"? Does he not lack the most essential thing for a human being, the fact that he has been born in exactly the same way as we all are?'[7]

Some have accepted the doctrine on the ground that it supports the theory of the two natures in Christ; this, however, seems to be reading far more into the doctrine than is warranted. Another false argument in favour of the acceptance of the tradition is the one that makes the doctrine of the Incarnation dependent on the Virgin Birth. Douglas Edwards writes:

. . . but for the preservation in the Church of the tradition of the Virgin Birth it is extremely improbable that the doctrine of the Incarnation would have ever gained a permanent lodgement in the human mind.[8]

If this position is valid, we should expect the doctrine to be stressed throughout the New Testament; yet although in all these writings the Incarnation is continually emphasized, never once is its validity made to rest on the Virgin Birth. A further reason that is adduced for the acceptance of the doctrine is that it is demanded by the sinlessness and divinity of Christ. This cannot be sustained; Paul is sure that Christ is free from actual sin and that He is divine, yet he makes no reference to the Virgin Birth. The most that can be said is that the doctrine is compatible

---

[6] *The Virgin Birth*, p. 130. [7] *Dogmatics*, II.355.
[8] *The Virgin Birth in Faith and History*, p. 25.

with these two aspects of the Person of Christ. The tradition is rejected by some and accepted by others on purely theological grounds, and the debate still continues.

It is often tacitly assumed that if the Virgin Birth is accepted then Jesus is automatically exempt from the taint of 'original sin'. This conclusion is unwarranted. The most that can be said is that the Virgin Birth is a 'pointer' to the fact that *peccatum originale* is excluded; it is not the 'cause' of its exclusion.[9] The fact that one human parent was involved in the birth of Jesus is sufficient to mean that there would be a strand of human heredity. To affirm that He was free from 'original sin' would necessitate the view that Mary was herself free from the taint of sin. The Roman Catholic doctrine of the immaculate conception of Mary is a gesture towards this need. Niebuhr sums up the situation with perfect clarity:

The son of a human mother, even born without a human father, is still organically related to the whole human situation; and the doctrine of the immaculate conception of his mother is a mere gesture in the overwhelming dilemma; for an infinite regression of immaculate conceptions would hardly serve to remove the taint.[10]

Brunner points out that the primitive idea of procreation knew nothing of the ovum; the woman's part was purely passive. This is the only background against which the ecclesiastical doctrine can be maintained.[11] On any acceptance of the modern theory of procreation and heredity Niebuhr's criticism is devastating.

In what way is the Virgin Birth relevant to the enquiry whether Jesus at the Incarnation took 'fallen human nature'? If the Virgin Birth is false, the theory that Christ assumed 'fallen human nature' can certainly be true. But if the Virgin Birth is true, the theory can still be held. It might be assumed that the acceptance of the Virgin Birth makes the theory we are examining impossible, but this is not so. It has been seen that there are New Testament scholars and theologians who reject the Virgin Birth, but even if we do not accept their arguments, and affirm the tradition, it does not mean that Christ could not possibly have assumed 'fallen human nature'. As long as one human parent was involved, the strain would be passed on. To say that it is only passed on

[9] K. Barth, *Church Dogmatics*, I.ii.191.
[10] *The Nature and Destiny of Man*, II.76.   [11] *Man in Revolt*, p. 392.

when concupiscence is present is hardly to be accepted. If the strain was not transmitted, we must assume that in some mysterious way the chain of heredity was broken between Mary and Jesus, but we have no basis on which to found this assumption. If it is argued that Jesus was sinless, this in no way invalidates the position, because, on the definitions that we have given, this is compatible with the assumption of 'fallen nature'. Christ could assume such a nature and yet throughout His life be free from actual sin.

From the study of the Birth of Jesus we can see no evidence to discredit the hypothesis under discussion. To say that the Virgin Birth does give such discrediting evidence can be maintained only by reading back into the New Testament narratives later, and unacceptable, doctrinal ideas. Rather it is to be asserted that the New Testament supports the theory that Jesus was born into humanity and took full human nature from Mary, and the obvious deduction is that part of this heredity was 'fallen human nature'. There is no evidence to suggest that the chain of heredity was broken between Mary and Jesus. Two quotations from recent notes on the Birth of Jesus are most telling. The first is by J. K. S. Reid:

Nor does the Virgin Birth wear the aspect of a rationalization of Christ's sinlessness; for it is clear that an account that would plausibly break the entail of sin would have to be much more clever than to leave him connected on even one side of his parentage with the human race and thus so far involved in corrupt human nature.[12]

The second is by J.-J. von Allmen, who, speaking about the supposed immaculate conception of Mary, says:

Such a doctrine could not have occurred to the New Testament authors, for it contradicts the true humanity of Jesus and overthrows the good news of salvation: in fact, if Mary is found outside the 'camp' where humanity is held captive by the Evil One, then the child which she has miraculously conceived will Himself also be born outside this camp: and then neither He nor His work will have relevance for men.[13]

Both these quotations seem to imply that the birth of Jesus means that He entered fully into our human situation, and that He came into human nature as it was because of the Fall. 'Involved in

---

[12] *A Theological Word Book of the Bible*, ed. by A. Richardson, pp. 276-7.
[13] *Vocabulary of the Bible*, ed. by J.-J. von Allmen, p. 294.

corrupt human nature' and being born within the camp 'where humanity is held captive by the Evil One' both suggest that Jesus assumed 'fallen human nature'. Von Allmen makes the further point that if Jesus was born outside this 'camp', then 'neither He nor His work will have relevance for men'. This is precisely the position that we wish to maintain in this present study.

The burden of proof must lie with those who accept the doctrine of an 'inherited weakness', and yet maintain that Jesus took a real humanity from His mother without inheriting the results of the Fall. It is to be questioned whether the Virgin Birth gives any evidence for such a break in the chain of heredity. The fact that one human parent was involved certainly seems to imply that Jesus assumed the human nature that was linked, through heredity, with fallen mankind.

(b) The Baptism of Jesus

The beginning of the ministry is to be found in the Baptism. John the Baptist came to Israel with a call to repentance, with a baptism for the remission of sins, and with a message of judgement for the unrepentant.[14] Jesus answered this call of John and was baptized in the River Jordan. This story has been a difficulty to Christian thinkers. If Jesus was the sinless Son of God then why did He find the initiation to His life's work in the call of the Baptist, a call that unquestionably was one to repentance, and His Baptism for the remission of sin?

We cannot reject the story of His Baptism as an invention of the Church; 'The leaders of a new movement do not create gratuitous difficulties for themselves.'[15] The question that needs to be answered is, Why then did Jesus submit to this baptism?

One extreme answer is given by J. Middleton Murry, who simply states:

For he had come to be baptized by John as a sinner among a crowd of sinners. He had come as more than a sinner, but as a sinner he had indeed come. Whatever this man was, he was the incarnation of honesty. He would have sought no baptism for the remission of sins had he not been conscious of sin.[16]

---

[14] For a lucid exposition of the origin and significance of John's Baptism see C. K. Barrett, *The Holy Spirit and the Gospel Tradition*, pp. 26-34.

[15] A. S. Peake, *The Servant of Yahweh and other Lectures*, p. 210.

[16] *Jesus, Man of Genius*, p. 22. Cf. J. F. Bethune-Baker, *The Faith of the Apostles' Creed*, p. 117.

A less extreme position is that of James MacKinnon, who thinks that we cannot go farther than 'the consciousness of the liability to sin'.[17] He thinks of the Baptism as 'a moral tonic, a consecration to the higher life'. Neither of these views commends itself. The first does not maintain the sinlessless of Christ. The second is inadequate—to talk of Jesus accepting a baptism for the remission of sins simply because He felt the possibility of future sin seems artificial in the extreme; to speak of it as a moral tonic after reading the stern words of the Baptist is quite inadequate.

T. H. Robinson refers to a statement of Josephus to find a clue to the problem. 'There is a hint (in Josephus) that John did not so much demand confession as a consciousness of moral and spiritual purity.'[18] This is hardly to be accepted as a solution, because the evidence of Josephus is against the direct and un-equivocal testimony of the New Testament. Josephus omits any reference to the note of judgement in the Baptist's teaching and ignores the prophecy of the Mighty One who is to come; he makes the baptism deal simply with the purification of the body, not the forgiveness of sins.[19]

A saying is preserved in a fragment of the non-canonical Gospel according to the Hebrews:

Behold the mother of the Lord and his brethren said to Him: John Baptist is baptizing with a view to remission of sins: let us go and be baptized by him. But He said to them, 'What sin have I done that I should go and be baptized by him? Unless indeed this very word I have spoken is a sin of ignorance.'[20]

This has all the appearance of being an early attempt to solve the problem rather than the preservation of a genuine tradition.

The problem thus remains: Why did Jesus submit to this baptism of repentance? One of the most acceptable answers is outlined by John W. Bowman.[21] He interprets the Hebrew שׁוּב and the Greek μετάνοια to mean a turning of the mind and will in response to the prophetic call.[22] Thus Jesus, though not a

---

[17] *The Historic Jesus*, p. 62, note 5.   [18] *MNTC*, 'Matthew', p. 17.
[19] *Antiquities*, XVIII, v.2. For a recent discussion of the point see W. F. Flemington, *The New Testament Doctrine of Baptism*, pp. 23-4.
[20] Quoted by Jerome, see *Dialogus contra Pelag.*, Lib. III, 2 (*PL*, XXIII.597-8).
[21] *The Intention of Jesus*.
[22] It must be pointed out that μετάνοια is never used in the *LXX* to translate שׁוּב, ἐπιστρέφω is the verb used. Since, however, John the Baptist is in the prophetic tradition, and since the prophets used the word שׁוּב for repentance, it is legitimate to interpret μετάνοια in this context in the light of the Hebrew word שׁוּב.

sinner, had to make His choice like the rest of the Jews. He defends the difficult verses Matthew 3[14-15] and maintains that John may have known enough of Jesus, either through insight or through questions put to the candidate before baptism, to realize that Jesus was a man of outstanding moral and spiritual stature and not standing in need of such a baptism as his. 'Our Lord's saying, "Thus it is fitting for us to fulfil all righteousness", would quite naturally carry the significance, "I must take this step because it accords with the will of God for my life and ministry".'[23] T. W. Manson favours a similar interpretation of the Baptism. He says 'the question is not whether Jesus has or has not sins to confess, but whether He is to obey the call of God which comes through the last and greatest of the prophets'.[24] The divine voice from heaven was the confirmation of the inner consciousness of Jesus. He had done the will of God and had obeyed the call of His Father, and now He had received His commission to be crowned Messiah by taking the road of the Suffering Servant.[25]

True though all this may be, it is to be questioned if it is the full answer. Here in the Baptism, Jesus identifies Himself with those He came to save: 'He was numbered with the transgressors.' Though He Himself was guilty of no actual sin, He so closely connected Himself with sinful mankind that He submitted Himself to the same baptism, which, as well as being a prophetic call, is most certainly a baptism for sinners. This is a case where He had 'to be made like unto his brethren' in every respect, 'that he might be a merciful and faithful high-priest in the service of God'.[26] This element must be taken seriously if the Baptism of Jesus is to be understood fully. It was His call to Messiahship through suffering, but it was also His self-identification with those He came to save. This truth has been affirmed by many theologians. H. R. Mackintosh says:

Jesus' baptism . . . formed a crucial stage in His deepening self-identification with sinful men—'a great act of loving communion with our misery' as it has been described, in which He numbered Himself with the transgressors and took all their burdens as His own.[27]

A. E. J. Rawlinson makes a similar point:

[23] J. W. Bowman, *The Intention of Jesus*, p. 37. See the whole section (pp. 36-8).
[24] *The Sayings of Jesus*, p. 150.
[25] See O. Cullmann, *Baptism in the New Testament*, pp. 16-22, and J. Jeremias, *TWNT*, V.699.
[26] Hebrews 2[17].   [27] *The Doctrine of the Person of Christ*, pp. 36-7.

It was the whole meaning of the Incarnation that God was in Christ identified with sinners, and the self-identification of Christ with a sinful people cannot with any kind of propriety be eradicated from the story of His life.[28]

This sentence is taken from the note on the significance of our Lord's Baptism. W. F. Flemington underlines the same truth:

For Jesus this acceptance of John's baptism need imply no conscious-ness of sin save in a corporate sense, but this identification of himself with the people of God was involved in the conception of Messiahship which we know our Lord found in Deutero-Isaiah.[29]

Two more quotations will suffice to confirm the point. The first is by Vincent Taylor:

He came to be baptized as an act of self-dedication to His Mission and perhaps also a self-identification with sinful Israel in the fulfilment of righteousness.[30]

The second is from J.-J. von Allmen:

Jesus Himself underwent the baptism of John, not because He needed it for Himself, but to fulfil all righteousness, that is to say, in order to assume the ministry of the Son or the servant of God, whose task it was to accept solidarity with the people and to take their sins as His burden.[31]

What then is the content of His self-identification with humanity that is stressed by these various writers? It is usually interpreted to mean that up to the point of His Baptism Jesus was completely outside the class of sinful humanity who came to John for his baptism of repentance, but that He joined Himself to them at this point by His voluntary self-humiliation. It is possible, however, that the identification is much deeper, that Jesus, in the great act of humiliation, His Incarnation, identified Himself with the fallen humanity that He came to redeem. Thus the self-identification goes right back to the Incarnation itself, and is not simply to be dated to the Baptism, which was but the open declaration of what was there from the beginning. This is not to say with Middleton Murry that Jesus was a sinner among sinners, for Jesus came to be baptized as a spotless one who had never committed any act of

---

[28] *Commentary on St Mark*, p. 253.   [29] *The New Testament Doctrine of Baptism*, p. 27.
[30] *Commentary on St Mark*, p. 618.
[31] *Vocabulary of the Bible*, ed. by J.-J. von Allmen, p. 32.

sin; but He had stooped to man's level of need in that He had assumed 'fallen human nature'. In this way, even though He had committed no actual sin, He possessed a real solidarity with the mankind that He had come to save.

To assert that the Baptism narrative is a proof that Jesus assumed 'fallen human nature' would be to claim too much. What can be claimed is that the Baptism gains in meaning if this position is accepted. It gives real meaning to Jesus' accepting a baptism which was for sinners; for His self-identification with them was not of an artificial kind. He had stooped to man's level, to the level of man's need, and taken upon Himself the 'fallen human nature' common to all the human race. No other hypothesis gives such reality to His self-identification with those He came to save; and yet His sinlessness is not jeopardized or sacrificed, for it is agreed that He was not guilty of any actual sin. Let it be emphatically stated that this does not mean that Jesus needed baptismal regeneration, or cleansing from the taint of 'original sin'; these are concepts that have become associated with baptism in certain schools of Christian thought, but they can hardly be made to apply to the baptism of John in the gospel narratives. The Baptism of Jesus was not a personal cleansing from personal sin, but an affirmation of His real self-identification with humanity in its need, and His obedience to the call of God through the voice of the Baptist.

(c) The Temptations

Immediately after the experience in the River Jordan Jesus endured the Temptations, and the two incidents are vitally linked. The divine voice spoke to the heart of Jesus at the Baptism, confirmed His own inner consciousness of Sonship and commissioned Him to Messiahship that involved the role of the Suffering Servant. The form of the Temptation story must go back to Jesus Himself, and these temptations suggest alternative methods of achieving His purpose which did not involve the road of suffering: the satisfaction of the material needs of men (turning stones to bread), the way of the spectacular (jumping down from the Temple), the way of military conquest by becoming Satan's Messiah (the vision of the kingdoms of this world). Jesus emphatically refused these supposed short cuts to success and accepted the way of suffering which His Father had revealed to

Him. The heart of the Temptations lay in the suggestion to rebel against the will of His Father, but He chose the way of filial obedience.

These temptations were not an isolated incident confined to the beginning of the ministry; He faced temptation throughout His ministry, and before the Cross there was the agony in the garden. H. R. Mackintosh says with great insight: 'Christendom speaks of "the Temptation" as if what followed His Baptism was an isolated fact. But the pressure lasted to the end; and few things in the Gospels are more subduing than the words in which Jesus gratefully acknowledges the fidelity of those who remained with Him through His trials (Lk 22$^{28-9}$).'[32] 'Echoes of inner conflict persist throughout the story of Jesus. . . . Victory through conflict is the pathway of the Son of Man.'[33]

In what sense was Jesus liable to temptation? If Jesus assumed our full human nature, then there was always the choice between right and wrong, of using His freedom of will wrongly and of not obeying the eternal purposes of His Father. Some theologians have come perilously near to denying the reality of the power of temptation in the life of Jesus. Hilary of Poitiers makes it clear that for him Christ's body was not subject to pain, nor His soul to the fear of death. The agony in the garden was for the benefit of His disciples in their trials, not an expression of His own anguish of soul.[34] This is sheer Docetism, and reduces the inner struggle of Jesus to a mere piece of play-acting for didactic purposes; He becomes 'A God wearing a mask, and playing the part of a tempted man'.[35]

Man in his original state of perfection was open to temptation and liable to the possibility of sin. If this position is rejected only two alternatives remain. Either we must maintain that God placed the bias towards evil in man's heart so that he was liable to temptation—a most damaging concept for the idea of the goodness and love of God—or we must leave the origin of temptation and sin as an inexplicable problem. To introduce the figure of Satan does not resolve the problem; it merely pushes it a stage farther back. Man as created by God was liable to temptation

---

[32] *The Doctrine of the Person of Christ*, p. 12.
[33] Vincent Taylor, *The Life and Ministry of Jesus*, p. 54.
[34] *De Trinitate*, X.23, 24, 27 (*PL*, X.363-4, 367).
[35] A. B. Bruce, *The Humiliation of Christ*, p. 263.

because there was always the choice of his turning his consciousness in on himself rather than directing it towards God in loving trust and obedience. It is thus evident that it would be going farther than the facts warrant to say that Jesus must have possessed a 'fallen human nature' in order to be tempted. The Temptation narratives will stand as valid even if Jesus assumed perfect human nature; there was always the possibility for Him to refuse to do the will of His Father. Yet there is nothing in the Temptation narratives to preclude the theory that Christ possessed a 'fallen nature' if this is found to have the warrant of other biblical passages.

One of the facts which suggest that Jesus possessed 'fallen human nature' is the kind of temptation He endured; He was tempted in every respect as we are.[36] This, it would appear, demands that Jesus assumed at His Incarnation a nature that was weakened by heredity, for it is from this weakened nature that our temptations receive so much of their power. The full discussion of this point, however, must be reserved until we come to the detailed study of the passage in Hebrews.[37] It is clear, however, that the acceptance of the hypothesis that Jesus possessed 'fallen human nature' gives fuller weight to the Temptation narrative. Jesus felt the full power of temptation because He shared our weakened nature that was affected by the rebellions of previous generations. We can go farther. He felt the power of temptation more than any man has ever done, for all other men have given in and yielded to sin, whereas Jesus took all the full force of temptation without yielding. We can believe all this without necessarily believing that Jesus sinned, for to be tempted is not to sin. He never yielded, but conquered all His temptations.

(d) The title Son of Man

Of all the titles that are applied to Jesus in the New Testament one is distinctively His own, 'Son of Man'. Apart from a reference in Acts 7[56], the question of the crowd 'Who is this Son of man?' in John 12[34], and two echoes in Revelation 1[13] and 14[14], this title is found only on the lips of Jesus. It was the title He chose in order to reveal His Work and Person.

The title is found in the Old Testament. It occurs in Psalm 8[4], where it is obviously a synonym for man, as the force of the Hebrew

---

[36] Hebrews 4[15].   [37] See pp. 117-121 below.

parallelism makes abundantly clear. Yet even here the use is significant, for it is taken up in Hebrews with reference to Jesus; the title seems to imply the insignificance of man before God, yet also the dignity of man as against the rest of creation. Verse 17 of Psalm 80 refers to the Son of Man in a redemptive context. The phrase is found more than ninety times in Ezekiel. The title tends to be a synonym for man, but there is always the idea of the weakness and frailty of man as against God. It also has a representative aspect: 'Ezekiel is a "son of man" burdened with a message not only for Israel, but for mankind; he speaks, not for the nation, but for Man.'[38] The most significant Old Testament reference is in Daniel, a book which is to be dated about 165 B.C. The significant reference is found in 7[13]. Here the phrase has a communal connotation and is applied to 'the saints of the Most High'; it is used in contrast to the beasts that represent the oppressive powers that have risen against Israel.

Two references in the inter-testamental period are significant. The first is in the 'Similitudes of Enoch' (1 Enoch 37-71).[39] Many scholars date this book as coming from the first century B.C. This date is not unanimously accepted, but most scholars would agree that it is early enough to be significant for interpreting 'Son of Man' in the New Testament. Here we have a supernatural figure of great dignity and power. T. W. Manson has argued that the meaning of the title in Enoch is communal just as in Daniel.[40] The argument, however, is not convincing and it seems preferable to take the figure in Enoch as personal. The other inter-testamental reference is found in 4 Ezra 13, which is commonly dated, in its complete form, in the first century A.D.[41] Here we have the vision of a Man rising from the sea; the earth quakes before him, and from his mouth there issues a fiery stream that consumes his enemies.

What was the source from which Jesus drew the title? This question has raised much controversy. H. Lietzmann and J. Wellhausen were the chief among a group of scholars who denied

---

[38] M. Black, *Ex.T*, LX.11.

[39] For a critical study of these chapters with special reference to 'Son of Man', see E. Sjöberg, *Der Menschensohn im Äthiopischen Henochbuch*.

[40] *The Teaching of Jesus*, pp. 228-9. Cf. Nils Messel, *Der Menschensohn in den Bilderreden des Henoch*.

[41] 4 Ezra speaks of 'The Man'—not (in its present Latin form) of Son of Man. It is generally agreed, however, that the concept of the Son of Man lies behind the passage.

that the title could have existed in the Aramaic that Jesus used.[42] All He could have used was the word 'man'. On this ground they rejected the authenticity of the title. Dalman made a convincing reply and showed that it was possible to use a title which could be accurately translated by 'Son of Man' or 'the Man'.[43]

Having established that the title is possible, we can return to the question of its source. The usual answer, carrying the support of the majority of scholars, is that Jesus took the title from Daniel. This theory has one very strong point in its favour: Jesus actually quoted from Daniel in His reply to the High Priest (Mk 14[62]). Other theories, however, have been expounded from time to time, and the more significant of these must be mentioned briefly.

Rudolf Otto puts forward the theory that Jesus took the title from 1 Enoch.[44] This hypothesis has not gained much support; the weakness is that the two chapters (70-71) on which he places the main weight of his theory are of uncertain date, and many seriously question whether Jesus could have known them in their present form. They do not appear to be sufficient evidence to support the theory that has been based upon them.

G. S. Duncan has expounded a very different theory, maintaining that the source of the title is Ezekiel.[45] He is of the opinion that Jesus spoke of Himself as 'bar Adam' rather than 'bar Nasha'. He then draws the conclusion that the usage of Jesus was not apocalyptic, but represented the 'Ideal Man'. This hypothesis is not completely convincing, since there seems to be little in the Ezekiel picture of the 'son of man' to explain our Lord's use of the title. Moreover, in the Gospels there is a close connection between Son of Man and the Kingdom. Such a relationship is found in Daniel, but it is not even hinted at in Ezekiel. Yet the suggestion of G. S. Duncan is not without value, for it does remind us that in the thought of Jesus 'Son of Man' indicated His real affinity with mankind, an idea that is clearly found in Ezekiel.

A more radical theory is one which finds the origin of the title in a wide-spread oriental myth of the Heavenly or Primal

[42] See H. Lietzmann, *Der Menschensohn*, and J. Wellhausen, *Skizzen und Vorbereiten*, VI.196.
[43] *The Words of Jesus*, pp. 234-267. Cf. O. Cullmann, *The Christology of the New Testament*, pp. 138-9.
[44] *The Kingdom of God and the Son of Man*, pp. 159-261. Cf. R. H. Charles, *The Apocrypha and Pseudepigrapha of the Old Testament*, ii.185.
[45] *Jesus Son of Man*, pp. 135-53.

Man.[46] The myth maintains that in man there is a divine element that is imprisoned in the world of nature and darkness, and to redeem this element in man the Heavenly Man came to earth as a redeemer. To suggest that Jesus was directly influenced by this myth is too extreme a hypothesis. A more probable theory is that it entered into His thought indirectly, by means of the picture in Daniel, 1 Enoch and 4 Ezra, which depends on it. Certain facts seem to favour this, for instance the glorification of the first man Adam in certain late Jewish Midrashim,[47] and in certain heretical Jewish-Christian literature, especially the pseudo-Clementine writings of the late second and early third centuries. Here we seem to have a conflation of the biblical figure of Adam with the Heavenly Man. It is not in any way improbable that some of the ideas of this Heavenly Man myth came within the orbit of these later Jewish thinkers through Persian influence. But the conception has been modified in Daniel and 1 Enoch. The cosmological significance of the Son of Man has fallen into the background and the meaning has become apocalyptic and eschatological. Even if this influence is admitted, it is apparent that Jesus used the title with His own distinct emphasis and it is questionable whether the Iranian myth had any significant influence on His thought. Dr William Manson puts the point forcibly:

While the Son of Man conception may have come to Daniel and the writer of Enoch from an Iranian source, to Jesus its presence in Daniel made it part of Holy Writ, and, as such, to be received and understood in the light of the context of all that is made known to him in his personal history concerning the Will of God.[48]

We must now turn from the question of origins, and consider the meaning of this title as used by Jesus. The sayings containing the phrase 'Son of Man' fall into three main groups. The first group consists of sayings of a general kind; the second of sayings which deal with the betrayal, death, and resurrection; and the third of predictions which are eschatological. The problem that faces the interpreter is to find room in the same picture for the second and third of these, the Passion and Parousia sayings.

[46] For an exposition of this view see W. Bousset, *Kyrios Christos*, pp. 1-27; R. Reitzenstein, *Die hellenistischen Mysterienreligionen* (3rd edn.), pp. 417-25; R. Bultmann, *Theology of the New Testament*, I.172-3.

[47] For illustrations see W. D. Davies, *Paul and Rabbinic Judaism*, pp. 45-6.

[48] *Jesus the Messiah*, p. 185.

Some scholars have tried to resolve the difficulty by denying the authenticity of one or other group. T. F. Glasson, after a critical study of the passages concerned, eliminates the Parousia sayings.[49] On the other hand, Bultmann eliminates the Passion sayings: 'To be sure, the predictions of the passion foretell his execution as divinely fore-ordained. But can there be any doubt that they are all *vaticinia ex eventu*?'[50] Despite the scholarship of these writers, it is to be questioned if their solutions can be accepted as adequate. Both types of sayings are equally well attested, and any satisfactory solution must take into account all the evidence and must not try to find a solution by excising part of the data to be explained.

The meaning of 'Son of Man' in the thought of Jesus is often connected with the conception of the Suffering Servant in Isaiah. Many scholars have felt that the distinctive feature in our Lord's use of the term is the fusion of these two concepts. Jesus poured the content of the Suffering Servant into the mould of the Son of Man. 'The Son of Man, in whom He saw Himself, is a new figure clothed in the marred form of the Servant.'[51] This position has not passed unchallenged. Bultmann denies that this connection goes back to Jesus and makes it the product of the early Church: 'This reinterpretation of the concept was done not by Jesus himself but by the Church *ex eventu*.'[52] Even if we do not accept in its entirety this thesis of Bultmann, the importance of the Servant theme in the thought of Jesus is not so obvious as many writers seem to suggest. It cannot be denied that Jesus thought in terms of His sufferings and death, but it may be seriously questioned whether the concept of the Suffering Servant was so dominant or determinative an influence as some writers suggest.[53]

T. W. Manson has expounded the theory that 'Son of Man' has a communal significance.[54] He has to face, however, the question: 'Why is the title so often obviously a personal title for Jesus?' and he maintains that it became restricted during His ministry. The vocation of Jesus was to create the Son of Man, the community

[49] *The Second Advent*, pp. 63-150.   [50] *Theology of the New Testament*, I.29.
[51] Vincent Taylor, *Jesus and His Sacrifice*, p. 282. For an excellent exposition of the theory that the idea of the Servant is of central importance for the understanding of the self-consciousness of Jesus, see O. Cullmann, *The Christology of the New Testament*, especially pp. 51-82.
[52] *Theology of the New Testament*, I.31.   [53] See M. Hooker, *Jesus and the Servant*.
[54] *The Teaching of Jesus*, pp. 211-34.

of the Saints of the Most High. He made His appeal through His preaching and through the Mission of the Twelve, but the response was inadequate. Then He concentrated on the chosen band of disciples, but finally He came to realize that even His disciples were not ready and that He alone must be the Son of Man. Manson then speaks of 'the sufferings and death of Jesus as the birth pangs of the Son of Man'.[55] He also affirms that in Paul we have the corporate idea of the Son of Man being realized in the Church as the Body of Christ.

Much in this theory, especially in details of exposition, is to be questioned, but there is much of importance in it. It gives significance to the title 'Son of Man' as an expression of the consciousness of Jesus, in that He felt a real identity with 'man'. Even if on the Cross He was on a lonely pinnacle, it was because men could not rise to the height with Him, and He stood there for the one supreme purpose that all men, through Him, might stand on that same height. To miss the fact that 'Son of Man' in the thought of Jesus speaks of His identity with mankind is to overlook part of the significance of the title. William Manson also stresses this fact:

The Son of Man is thus revealed in his solidarity with man . . . so he becomes their Saviour. (This title) gave back to him something of his sense of oneness with . . . the sinful and the ostracized among his people whom he came to save.[56]

To have a real identity with mankind whom He came to save, to be the 'Son of Man', it was essential that He should become a part of the human race in the very fullest sense. Does this mean that He became part of the humanity that had been weakened by the sin of generation after generation? Certainly if He did assume this 'fallen human nature', then in reality He was one with mankind, He was in a deep sense 'Son of Man'. T. W. Manson says that at the crucial point He stood alone; His Cross was the birth of a new and redeemed humanity. Might we not go on to say that He stood alone because He alone among all mankind had never yielded to sin, and the 'fallen nature' that He had inherited had never been allowed to issue in rebellion against the will of God? Not only was He 'Son of Man', bound to humanity with the ties of self-identification, but He was 'Son of God', and

[55] *The Teaching of Jesus*, p. 235.   [56] *Jesus the Messiah*, p. 118.

throughout His incarnate life He lived in perfect obedience to the will of His Father.

In all this, no explanation has been given for the presence of both the Passion and Parousia sayings. The Passion sayings have a vital place in the understanding of 'Son of Man'. The Parousia sayings, at first sight, seem to present more difficulty. About some of the Parousia sayings, particularly those which come early in the ministry, the suggestion of T. W. Manson is attractive. He gives them a communal significance, making them almost another phrase for the coming Kingdom of God. This, however, will not suffice for all the passages, since many are far too personal for such an exegesis. The explanation of these is that Jesus came to realize that after suffering would come exaltation.

Dr Taylor suggests the theory that these Parousia sayings represent an earlier stage in the thought of Jesus than the Passion sayings.[57] He is of the opinion that the Coming of the Son of Man refers to the establishment of the elect community; but that Jesus came to realize that the Cross was a necessary condition of the Parousia. Here there is an echo of Schweitzer, who accepts the Passion sayings as authentic and thinks of the journey to Jerusalem as 'a pilgrimage of death'. He also affirms that the Passion of the 'Son of Man' was essential before the Parousia could occur. This is a fruitful pointer to a satisfactory solution of the problem. Both the Passion and Parousia sayings are authentic, and there seems to be no need to follow Dr Taylor in placing all the Parousia sayings at an early stage in the ministry, and then making the Passion sayings take their place during the later period. The most that needs to be said is that the Passion sayings became more prominent towards the end of the ministry, and the Parousia sayings fell more into the background. The two classes are linked in the mind of Jesus because He came to realize that only through His Passion could there be the Parousia.

In what way is the concept that Jesus assumed 'fallen human nature' relevant? It is relevant in so far as this theory would give a deep significance to the title 'Son of Man'. Jesus assumed at His Incarnation this 'fallen nature' and entered into man's alienation from God, though He Himself was never guilty of actual sin, and had perfect fellowship with His Father. Before there could be a Parousia, before the Kingdom of God could come in power, Jesus

---

[57] 'The "Son of Man" sayings relating to the Parousia', *Ex.T*, LVIII.12-15.

E

had to face the supreme struggle, enter the lists against the powers of darkness, and triumph over them through His Cross. He did this as 'Son of Man', as One having an affinity with the rest of mankind, One who through His act of self-identification was one with fallen humanity. If we are to keep the representative idea of the 'Son of Man', an important concept which cannot be ignored, and if we are to give its communal aspect any real significance, then in some essential way there must be a unity between the 'Son of Man' and the rest of mankind. This unity is maintained on the hypothesis that Christ assumed 'fallen human nature'. T. W. Manson speaks of the death of Jesus as the birth pangs of the Son of Man, the Passion of Jesus as the necessary prelude to the Parousia. Only as Jesus redeemed the 'fallen human nature' that He had assumed was He able to found a new and redeemed humanity, so paving the way for the coming of the Kingdom of God in all its fullness, and to become the One who will come with power and majesty at the consummation of the ages.

This section on the 'Son of Man' should be read in conjunction with the section on Paul's theory of Christ as the Second Adam. It is argued there that the concept of the Second Adam is connected with the title 'Son of Man' in the Gospels.[58] What needs to be said at this point, however, is that there appears to be a connection between the concept 'Son of Man' and Adam. Dr Austin Farrer has made a careful study of the material and comes to the conclusion that the picture of the 'Son of Man' in Daniel is influenced by the concept of Adam as given in Genesis.[59] He then goes on to argue that the idea of Adam lies behind 'Son of Man' in Mark, and that this dependence goes back to the mind of Jesus Himself.[60] 'Let it be granted that Christ thought in the terms which His inheritance supplied. His inheritance supplied the scripture, and the scripture contained Adam; and Daniel and Enoch had cast upon the figure of Adam a Messianic light. How could Christ fail to see His destiny in Adamic terms? How else can He have understood Himself to be the Saviour of Mankind?'[61]

Dr Farrer is not alone in linking 'Son of Man' in the Gospels with the figure of Adam. This would appear to be the opinion of Jeremias. In the article on 'Adam' in the Kittel *Wörterbuch*,

[58] See pp. 69-89 below.   [59] *A Study in Mark*, Chap. 11.
[60] Ibid. Chap. 12.   [61] Ibid. p. 289.

he gives a cross-reference to the article on 'Son of Man'.[62] This latter article is not yet published. The very fact that the cross-reference is given, however, suggests that in the judgement of Jeremias there is a real and valid connection between 'Son of Man' and Adam. A similar position is advocated by Cullmann in his study, *The Christology of the New Testament*.[63]

If this link between 'Son of Man' and Adam can be substantiated, it would tend to support the idea that the title 'Son of Man', to be given its fullest interpretation, implies a connection with the human race that had fallen in Adam. Some words of Dr Farrer certainly seem to suggest this conclusion:

The Son of Man must suffer, for is he not the Son of Man? Christ takes Man upon him where he finds him, not in immortality, but in corruption, not in paradise, but expelled and in the wilderness. Adam is tempted in paradise, and then driven forth; Christ is first driven forth, then tempted, for he begins where Adam is, not where Adam was.[64]

(e) The Cry of Dereliction

This cry of Jesus from the Cross, 'My God, my God, why hast thou forsaken me?' has always been a difficulty. It is omitted by Luke and John. In D and certain Old Latin manuscripts (c and i) the verb is softened to read 'reproached' instead of 'forsaken'. In the apocryphal Gospel of Peter the difficulty is again felt and the reading is, 'My power, my power, why has thou forsaken me?'

The authenticity of the cry has been questioned by many commentators. Loisy maintains that Jesus just died with a loud cry. But he adds:

Psalm 22 dominates all the accounts of the passion, nothing was more natural than to place its opening words in the mouth of the dying Christ.[65]

Bultmann[66] and G. Bertram[67] are of the opinion that the words and thought of this psalm provided a secondary interpretation of

---

[62] *TWNT*, I.141-3. The cross-reference is given in the heading of the section, but it is also referred to in the body of the article. Cf. the cross-reference in paragraph 4 of Jeremias's article on ἄνθρωπος (ibid. I.367).
[63] See pp. 137-52.   [64] *A Study in Mark*, p. 280.
[65] *Les Évangiles synoptiques*, II.684. Cf. H. Branscomb, *MNTC*. 'Mark', p. 298.
[66] *Die Geschichte der synoptischen Tradition*, pp. 304, 342.
[67] *Die Leidensgeschichte Jesu und der Christuskult*, p. 83.

the final cry of Jesus recorded in Mark 15[37]. This radical criticism is not accepted by all scholars. Dr Taylor says that 'this line
of interpretation is altogether too doctrinaire to carry conviction'.[68]
A. H. McNeile maintains that 'of the seven utterances from the
Cross this is the least likely to be due to Christian imagination'.[69] P. W. Schmiedel says that there are nine pillars on which
a true life of Jesus must be built; these passages, he argued, could
not be the invention of the Early Church. One of these 'founda-
tion-pillars' is the Cry of Dereliction.[70] There does not seem to be
sufficient reason for denying the authenticity of this saying.

Three main interpretations have been suggested by those who
accept the genuineness of the Cry of Dereliction. The first is
closely connected with the penal theory of the atonement. Jesus
was in reality abandoned by His Father; He was made a substitute for sinners and bore the wrath of God. This exegesis is
found in Luther and Calvin, and in more recent years has been
expressed by R. W. Dale, who says: 'Immediately before His
death, He was forsaken of God.'[71] This is also the view of Karl
Barth, whose doctrine of the atonement is almost one of simple
exchange—He takes our place and we take His; Jesus was forsaken by God for our sins. Dr Taylor's comment is terse: 'Apart
altogether from the ethical and theological objections, it is enough
to say that nothing in the saying requires such an interpretation.'[72] Much of the criticism implied in this judgement is valid,
but this theory comes near to the mark. Even if we do not accept
the traditional penal theory of the atonement, this cry of Jesus
seems to demand that Jesus at that moment endured in His heart
the alienation from God which was the direct outcome of human
sin and rebellion. The obvious implication is that what Jesus said
was a true expression of His experience at that moment. Here is
the mystery of the Cross, but it is also the power of God unto
salvation.

The second explanation is a reaction against the one just
considered, and maintains that the cry, far from being a cry of
anguish and alienation, was in fact a cry of triumph. J. McLeod
Campbell expounded a theory of the atonement that was in
direct and violent reaction to the penal theory. It was quite

[68] *Jesus and His Sacrifice*, p. 158.   [69] *The Gospel according to St Matthew*, p. 421.
[70] *Encyclopaedia Biblica*, Col. 1881.   [71] *The Atonement*, p. 360; see also pp. 60-3.
[72] *Jesus and His Sacrifice*, pp. 159-60.

natural that he should reject the traditional explanation of the Cry of Dereliction. He makes considerable use of Psalm 22 in his interpretation of the atonement.[73] Taking the psalm as a whole, he sees in this cry Jesus' trust in God. This explanation rests upon the assumption that is perfectly expressed in the words of A. Menzies: 'He who quotes the first words of a poem may be thinking not of those words only but of some later part of the poem or its general course of thought.'[74] This explanation seems too artificial to be satisfactory; it takes the heart out of the cry and virtually explains it away. To do justice to the saying we must accept the fact that the experience of Jesus at that moment was of being forsaken.

Vincent Taylor in his trilogy has argued for a representative theory of the atonement with an emphasis on the category of sacrifice.[75] He is quite certain that

the saying expresses a feeling of utter desolation, a sense of abandonment by the Father, an experience of defeat and despair. . . . The suffering is not punishment directly inflicted by God, and is penal in so far as it is sharing in the sense of desolation and loss which sin brings in its train when it is seen and felt for what it is. . . . Jesus so closely identified Himself with sinners, and experienced the horror of sin to such a degree, that for a time His communion with the Father was broken, so that His face was obscured and He seemed to be forsaken by Him.[76]

This quotation has been given at length because it maintains the true meaning of desolation and dereliction, and by linking the cry with human sin does not ignore its penal aspect, though it avoids the crudities that sometimes accompany a penal interpretation. Nevertheless there is one point in which this interpretation seems to be unsatisfying; it leaves as an unexplained mystery how Jesus, the perfect Son of God, could so identify Himself with fallen mankind as to experience this sense of alienation that is the result of sin. The value of the penal theory of substitution is that it does give an answer to this problem, even if the answer is rather artificial. It is notoriously difficult to explain

---

[73] *The Nature of the Atonement*, pp. 237-44.
[74] *The Earliest Gospel*, pp. 280-1. Cf. A. T. Cadoux, *The Sources of the Second Gospel*, p. 113.
[75] *Jesus and His Sacrifice, The Atonement in New Testament Teaching, Forgiveness and Reconciliation.*
[76] *Jesus and His Sacrifice*, pp. 161-2.

how the sins of others were transferred to Jesus, and the 'sins of the whole world'—however hallowed the phrase may be through Christian devotion—is an abstraction that has no precise and concrete significance. The representative theory avoids this difficulty, but only at the expense of leaving unexplained how Jesus could so identify Himself with sinners as to experience their alienation from God. If Jesus stands outside the company of fallen mankind we must accept either the doctrine of substitution or leave the link with sinful humanity unexplained; there seems no escape from this dilemma. All the representative ideas taken from the category of sacrifice are much too external adequately to explain the situation and account for this cry.

The situation can be understood if we assume that Jesus at the Incarnation took 'fallen human nature'. This was the supreme act of humiliation. The Cross was the final battle with the powers of sin, and the battle was decisive, once for all. In that struggle the 'fallen nature' which He had assumed was nailed to the Cross, purged and cleansed even through death; thus in Jesus, risen and victorious, there is a root of sinless humanity. The heart of this decisive struggle was this cry. As T. H. Robinson says: 'In that moment Jesus knew the experience that sin brings to us all, and he alone could know how unspeakably terrible it was.'[77] In this cry there was the tension that brought salvation. He was one with mankind, He had taken our human nature in its fallen state, yet He was never guilty of actual sin and in His life we see perfection. We can understand the meaning of the cry from the Cross; we can see how He was able to have the experience of alienation; yet we see how He was our representative and through His death brought salvation. Men have always felt that on the Cross Jesus bore the sin of mankind, that paradoxically the perfect Son of God took human sin. This paradox is in the last resort inexplicable. All that we have tried to do is to trace this paradox to its source; not simply to confine it to Calvary, but to make it a central fact in the Incarnation itself. Jesus assumed 'fallen human nature', but He never added to this nature His will, and so there was no break in fellowship between Himself and His Father. On the Cross, there took place the decisive battle between Jesus and the powers of evil, not simply powers that were external, but also the power of the 'fallen nature' that He had inherited.

[77] *MNTC*, 'Matthew', p. 232.

Here on the Cross there was the purging of human nature.

This hypothesis seems to have two advantages. In the first place it gives an adequate explanation of the Cry of Dereliction, a cry which is the heart of any doctrine of the Cross; it does so without falling into the difficulties of the theory of penal substitution, and yet does not leave as an unexplained mystery how He was the representative of mankind. The second advantage is that it makes the unity of the Incarnation and the Atonement a reality. Far too many theories make the Incarnation but a necessary preliminary to the Cross and fail to make any vital connection between the two. Some theories go so far as to make us question whether the full humanity is really necessary at all. The theory that has been suggested avoids this danger and gives an inherent and logical connection between Incarnation and Atonement, and makes the humanity of the Saviour just as necessary as His divinity if there is to be a true redemption.

(f) The Resurrection Appearances

After the Cross came the victory of the Resurrection. A. E. J. Rawlinson comments: 'Thus the verdict of man was reversed by the verdict of God.'[78] A. M. Ramsey has made an analysis of the New Testament evidence for the Resurrection:[79]

- i) A brief declaration of the news: Luke 24[34].
- ii) A vivid story of one of His appearances: Luke 24[36-43].
- iii) Stories that tell of the dejection and bewilderment of the disciples and then record the gradual dawning of the truth: Luke 24[13-35].
- iv) Accounts of the teaching given by the Risen Jesus: Luke 24[44-9], Matthew 28[16-20].
- v) The narrative of the visit to the empty tomb: Mark 16[1-8].

C. H. Dodd has made a study of the 'form' of these narratives[80] and comes to the conclusion that 'formally, there is nothing to distinguish the narratives' from those found elsewhere in the Gospels. He affirms that 'they merit the same degree of critical consideration, not only in their aspect as witness to the faith of the early Church, but also as ostensible records of things that happened'.[81]

---

[78] The New Testament Doctrine of the Christ, p. 31.   [79] The Resurrection of Christ, p. 59.
[80] In Studies in the Gospels, ed. by D. E. Nineham, pp. 9-35.   [81] Ibid. p. 35.

The task of interpreting the evidence must now be faced. Two facts emerge quite clearly from the Gospel narratives. First, the Risen Lord was the same Jesus whom the disciples had known during the ministry. Jesus was at pains to show them that it was He Himself. There had taken place a bodily resurrection. The evidence for this is:

    i) The account of the empty tomb: Mark 16$^{1-8}$, Matthew 28$^{1-8}$, Luke 24$^{1-10}$, John 20$^{1-10}$.[82]

    ii) They touched Him: Matthew 28^{9}, John 20^{27}.

    iii) He ate with them: Luke 24$^{41-2}$, John 21$^{9-13}$, Acts 10^{41}.

    iv) He had flesh and bones: Luke 24^{39}.

    v) He still bore the marks of the wounds: Luke 24^{40}.[83]

Secondly, and equally plainly, Jesus was in some way different. It was the same Jesus, but there was also a transformation. The evidence for this is:

    i) He was not immediately recognized: Luke 24$^{13-35}$, John 20^{14}.

    ii) His power to appear and disappear suddenly: Luke 24$^{31, 36}$. Doors are no barrier: John 20$^{19, 26}$.

    iii) The position of the grave clothes: John 20$^{6-7}$.

    iv) His request not to be touched: John 20^{17}.

Both these elements are present in the narratives, and are equally well-attested. For a sound interpretation of the Resurrection both these elements must be given significance.

When we consider the various theories that have been propounded, it is seen that they tend to fall into certain well-defined groups. The first of these is the theory of 'Subjective Visions'. This has been expounded by D. F. Strauss,[84] E. Rénan,[85] and the Jewish writer C. G. Montefiore.[86] The chief point in the exposition is that there was no bodily resurrection of Jesus, and no empty tomb. It was the hopeful imagination of the disciples that led them to have the subjective visions and caused them to believe

[82] Bultmann maintains that 'Paul still knows nothing' of the empty tomb (*Theology of the New Testament*, I.45). Though Paul does not mention specifically the empty tomb, it is unwarranted to conclude that he did not know of it. Rather his whole stress on the death, burial, and resurrection seems to demand an empty grave and a physical resurrection.

[83] Some manuscripts omit this, but the familiar reading is to be accepted.

[84] *The Life of Jesus*, I.396-440, II.402-17.

[85] *The Life of Jesus*, pp. 230-1.   [86] *Commentary on the Gospels*, I.397-400.

in the resurrection of their Master. The famous phrase of Rénan sums it up: 'What raised Jesus? It was love.' This theory, however, is not to be accepted. It does not do justice to the two-fold strand of evidence that has been analysed above. It arrives at its conclusion only by denying part of the evidence, the chief piece of which is the empty tomb. It is not too much to say that the theory caricatures the Gospel evidence. Coupled with this objection is the equally damaging fact that it is psychologically improbable. The disciples were plunged into despair, they were certainly not expecting a resurrection of their Master, so that the psychological requirements for subjective visions were not present.

The next group of theories are those which speak in terms of 'Objective Visions'. Such names as T. Keim,[87] B. H. Streeter,[88] and C. J. Cadoux[89] come to mind. This hypothesis is not so alien to orthodox Christian thought as the one just considered. The reality of the Resurrection is accepted in the sense that the visions were not the results of the disciples' imagination but had their origin in God; they were, in Keim's famous phrase, 'a telegram from heaven'.[90] Yet here again there is a denial of the reality of the empty tomb and the bodily resurrection of Jesus. Again part of the New Testament is disregarded and one strand of the two-fold evidence is given less than justice.

After a most searching enquiry another theory has been put forward by Kirsopp Lake.[91] He argues that all the appearances were in Galilee and not in Jerusalem,[92] but that when the disciples returned to Jerusalem they found that some of the women were talking of an empty tomb. These two factors, he says, reacted one on the other; the women's story helped to confirm the disciples in the belief that they had seen the Risen Lord, and the disciples' account of their experiences convinced the women in their belief in the empty tomb. Lake suggests that the women may have gone to the wrong tomb, where they met a young man who told them plainly that this was not the place where the body of Jesus was laid and pointed to the right tomb with the words: 'See

---

[87] *History of Jesus of Nazara*, VI.274-365.   [88] *In Foundations*, pp. 127-45.
[89] *The Life of Jesus*, pp. 164-7, 206-7.   [90] *History of Jesus of Nazara*, VI.364.
[91] *The Historical Evidence for the Resurrection of Jesus Christ.*

[92] Cf. Gardner-Smith, *The Narratives of the Resurrection*. It should be noted, however, that Lake wavers in his adherence to this theory—see *The Beginnings of Christianity*, V.14.

the place where they laid him.' He conjectures that the words
'He has risen' are a later addition to the young man's actual
words. This study of Lake is instructive, for even though he
rejects the story of the empty tomb, he admits that the historical
evidence will fit either interpretation, and goes on to say: 'Thus
the story of the empty tomb must be fought out on doctrinal, not
on historical grounds.'[93] These words of Lake give us our cue: it
can be accepted that in all the theories so far mentioned there
are present philosophical and doctrinal prejudices that have led
to the rejection of the empty tomb and the denial of the bodily
resurrection of Jesus.

If we are to do justice to the New Testament and to the experience of countless Christians, the evidence must be taken as it
stands and an interpretation sought which will fit all the facts
and both strands of evidence as outlined above. One theory which
does wrestle with all the facts has claimed the adherence of many
Christian thinkers; Chrysostom was one of its prominent early
adherents, and in more recent years it has been put forward by
B. F. Westcott.[94] Here it is suggested that the visibility and tangi-
bility of the Risen Jesus was no essential part of the Resurrection
Body, but an accommodation to help the disciples to understand.
This is not a mere variation of the visionary theory, for the empty
tomb and the physical resurrection are affirmed. A pertinent
quotation from Bishop Westcott will make this clear. 'A little
reflection will show that the special outward forms in which the
Lord was pleased to make Himself known were no more necessarily connected with His glorified person than the robes which He
wore.'[95] While there is a certain attractiveness in this theory, it is
not completely satisfying. Just as the various theories which
make the limited knowledge of Jesus during His ministry more
apparent than real—a concession for appearance' sake rather than
a reality in His incarnate humiliation—tend to jeopardize the
reality of the Incarnation, so this theory which makes the physical
appearance of the Risen Christ incidental—an accommodation
for the sake of the disciples—seems to jeopardize the reality of the
physical resurrection of Jesus. It seems that a theory that makes
the physical characteristics of the Risen Lord incidental, yet

---

[93] *The Historical Evidence for the Resurrection of Jesus Christ*, p. 253.
[94] *The Gospel of the Resurrection* and *The Revelation of the Risen Christ*.
[95] *The Gospel of the Resurrection*, p. 112.

stresses the reality of the empty tomb, is trying to have the best of both sides, and has yoked together two sets of ideas which fit only with the greatest difficulty. That the actual physical body was laid in the tomb and was raised is not given sufficient weight and emphasis in this theory.

We are thus left with the task of explaining the risen body of Jesus, with its obvious connection with the body that Jesus possessed during His ministry, yet also with significant differences. The usual explanation is that the risen body is a transformed body, one suitable for the realm of the spiritual and not the mundane. Lake is emphatic on this point:

An examination of Paul's teaching points to the fact that he believed that at the Resurrection the body of Jesus was changed from one of flesh and blood into one that was spiritual, incorruptible and immortal, in such a way that there was no trace left of the corruptible body that had been laid in the grave.[96]

This quotation contains a central core of truth. The body of Jesus after the Resurrection was obviously not the limited corruptible body that we possess; rather it was transfigured, transformed, perfected. What, however, is the reason for this? Merely to say that it was due to the fact that Jesus had died and risen does not seem to be sufficient; there must be some deeper explanation.

There is one possible answer—though it is suggested with great diffidence, for it is in the realm of speculation—which would give an adequate reason for the change in the risen body of our Lord. Jesus at the Incarnation took human nature and a physical body that had been affected by man's rebellion and sin. Through the Cross Jesus wrought redemption, triumphing over the powers of sin and evil and breaking their power. When He rose from the dead, sin and its results had no hold on Him—He had held them at bay all through His life, and now on the Cross He had won the final victory—and therefore in the Resurrection He assumed, not a 'body of sin', but a body as God intended it to be. To put it another way, in the resurrection body of Jesus we see the physical body as God intended it; in our bodies, and in the one that Jesus possessed before the victory of the Cross, we see the physical body as it became through the Fall and through the rebellion of men through the ages.

[96] *The Historical Evidence for the Resurrection of Jesus Christ*, p. 23.

Two points must be made to clarify this theory. It is not suggested that this risen body of Jesus was the one that 'Adam' had before the Fall, for this is to use categories that are not applicable in a day when evolution is an accepted hypothesis. What is meant is that this risen body of Jesus is the kind of body that God intended for man when the process of evolution was complete. Through sin and rebellion, both mundane and pre-mundane, something has gone wrong with the course of evolution, and the result is that instead of physical nature as it is in the risen Jesus we see the imperfect kind that is so familiar to us. The second point is that it is usually assumed that it was the resurrection body that entered into the heavenly places, and on this basis it might be objected that this theory is maintaining that flesh and blood have inherited eternity, a conception which Lake says is denied by Paul.[97] Yet Jesus says in Luke 24[39]: 'See my hands and my feet, that it is I myself: handle me, and see; for a spirit has not flesh and bones as you see that I have.' This verse needs explanation, and often it has been explained away. H. Balmforth writes:

It is not unlikely that, in the attempt to state quite definitely that the Risen Lord was no mere apparition, St Luke or his source has fallen into the common confusion between reality and materiality.[98]

W. Manson, in a similar way, attempts to explain away the passage:

The tendency of Luke's source and of his own mind was to materialize spiritual experience, and a comparison of the . . . narrative with Matthew 28[16-20] makes it probable that in Luke we have the overlaying of a less by a more corporeal conception of the Saviour's risen life.[99]

The difficulty with this kind of interpretation is that the strand of tradition which gives these distinctly physical features is not confined to this one verse in Luke.[100] The explanation may be that Jesus rose with a real physical body that was transformed in the

---

[97] This interpretation of 1 Corinthians 15[50] has been challenged by Jeremias (see *New Testament Studies*, II.3 (1956), 151-9). He maintains that the meaning of verse 50 is that 'neither the living nor the dead can take part in the Kingdom of God—as they are'. He affirms that the verse does not speak of the resurrection, but of the change of the living at the Parousia. He asserts that 'it is wrong to assume that the sentence "Flesh and blood cannot inherit the Kingdom of God" is speaking of the resurrection. It speaks of the change of the living at the parousia, and only by analogy is anything to be inferred from it for the Pauline conception of the Resurrection' (ibid. p. 158).

[98] 'St Luke', *The Clarendon Bible*, p. 310.

[99] *MNTC*, 'Luke', p. 269.   [100] See p. 64 above.

sense that the weaknesses that were the result of 'fallen nature' were stripped away. If the exposition of 1 Corinthians 15[50] suggested by Jeremias[101] is accepted, that is to say, if that passage does not refer to the Resurrection but to the Parousia, there is no reason why the risen body of Jesus should not possess physical features. If, however, it is maintained that this verse in 1 Corinthians refers to the resurrection body, it might be suggested that Jesus at the Ascension assumed the spiritual body which was not of flesh and blood, and that it was that body which was taken into the heavenly places.

It has long been pointed out that the Resurrection was a divine intervention, a mighty act in God's scheme of redemption. A. M. Ramsey says: 'The Resurrection is far more than an illustration or an example of human immortality. It is a victory uniquely won, and won in order that mankind may be enabled to share in Christ's resurrection.'[102] With this redemptive conception of the Resurrection of Jesus we heartily agree. What has just been attempted is to fill in the picture and show how the resurrection body of Jesus is a pointer to the fact that in the Cross Jesus triumphed over the powers of sin. Though it would be wrong to claim the support of A. M. Ramsey for the theory now tentatively suggested, another quotation of his is apposite; speaking of the Resurrection he says: 'It interrupts the hitherto normal workings of historical cause and effect and the hitherto normal workings of the order of human sinfulness, and ushers in a new stage in the cosmic process.'[103]

PAULINE THEOLOGY

(a) Adam and Christ

Here we come to one of the most important sections in our study of the New Testament evidence. We must consider the contrast between Adam and Christ, the conception that Adam is the origin of sinful humanity and that in Christ is the beginning of a new and redeemed humanity.

The origin of this idea in Paul's thought is a fascinating problem. There is no doubt that the whole force of the parallel depends on the idea of the solidarity of mankind in Adam and of

[101] See footnote 97 above. [102] *The Resurrection of Christ*, pp. 34-5.
[103] Ibid. p. 35.

the solidarity of Christians in the Body of Christ. The word אָדָם (Adam) in the Old Testament possesses a collective significance. 'Of the 510 times that the word אָדָם occurs, only a very few times does it with any certainty mean the individual man or an individual man and not men.'[104] W. D. Davies argues that the concept of solidarity is found in post-biblical Jewish writings,[105] and quotes, for instance, the strange and often grotesque stories about the body of Adam. Davies believes that the origin of the concept of Christ as the Second Adam is rooted in Rabbinic Judaism, and refers particularly to the cosmic functions ascribed to the Messiah.[106] He concludes his exposition:

In view of the interpretation of His Advent as a new creation the transition to the thought of Christ as the Second Adam was easy and ultimately almost inevitable.[107]

Paul's thought was deeply influenced by the Old Testament and Rabbinic Judaism, and these must have played some part in the formation of the parallel between Adam and Christ.

A very different theory finds the origin of the idea in a pre-Christian Gnostic conception of the Heavenly Man. An outline of this has been given earlier during the examination of the title 'Son of Man' in the Gospels.[108] R. Reitzenstein expounds this view. He says:

I am convinced that Paul has used for the development of his conception of Christ a conception already found in Hellenistic and Palestinian Judaism and derived ultimately from Iranian sources, of a divine Anthropos (Man) as a bearer of the true religion.[109]

A similar view is to be found in the writings of W. Bousset,[110] and more recently the theory has been championed by R. Bultmann.[111] There are certainly striking similarities between the thought of Paul and this myth, but there are also pronounced differences.[112] William Manson says:

[104] L. Koehler, *Old Testament Theology*, p. 129.
[105] *Paul and Rabbinic Judaism*, pp. 53-5.   [106] Ibid. pp. 36-41.
[107] Ibid. p. 41.   [108] See pp. 53-4 above.
[109] *Die Hellenistischen Mysterienreligionen*, p. 423.   [110] *Kyrios Christos*, pp. 158-64.
[111] *Theology of the New Testament*, pp. 166-7, 174.
[112] See W. Manson, *Jesus the Messiah*, pp. 174-90.

While it is possible and indeed likely that traditional or received ideas helped the apostle here, as at other points, to self-expression, the matter of his gospel must be pronounced independent of extraneous influences, based as it is on Christian historical revelation and on the Christian experience of God.[113]

It can be said that behind the Pauline idea of Christ as the Second Adam is the same community of ideas as we see in the 'Heavenly Man', and that these ideas, with which Paul is almost certain to have been familiar, reveal the background against which his doctrine was enunciated. Yet there are significant differences between Pauline thought and this gnostic myth, and it is to be questioned whether this myth can be the source from which he drew his teaching.

Another suggestion is that the background of the parallel is to be found in Philo. Taking the twofold creation story in Genesis as his basis, Philo talks of the first man who is heavenly and spiritual (Genesis 1[27]) and the second who is made of dust and is of the earth (Genesis 2[7]). The first man was the Ideal Man, the second is the historic Adam who sinned and was father of the fallen human race. Holtzmann admits that the Pauline doctrine is not exactly that of Philo, but finds in that writer the source of the idea.[114] It would seem, however, that if Paul knows this Philonic teaching, he does not draw upon it but rather 'he attacks all its essential points simultaneously'.[115] The first man, he says, is of the earth and the second from heaven (1 Corinthians 15). This is in direct opposition to the teaching of Philo. As Moffatt says, commenting on 1 Corinthians 15[45-9]: 'If this speculation ever occurred to Paul, he reverses it, not on any speculative ground, but owing to the facts of revelation in history and providence.'[116]

Whatever the exact influence of these various ideas on the thought of Paul, the concept of the Second Adam seems to have affinities with the term Son of Man in the Gospels. It is true that Paul never uses this phrase, but almost certainly he was familiar with it. This is suggested by his citation of Psalm 8[6] in 1 Corinthians 15[27]. Matthew Black writes:

[113] Ibid. p. 190.
[114] H. J. Holtzmann, *Lehrbuch der Neutestamentlichen Theologie*, p. 61.
[115] O. Cullmann, *The Christology of the New Testament*, p. 167.
[116] *MNTC*, '1 Corinthians', p. 263.

The Apostle is still thinking of Christ as the Second Adam; that is clear from verse 26, where Christ abolishes at the parousia the last enemy, Death, the legacy of the first Adam. Did he have the Synoptic Son of Man in mind, and is the Second Adam his substitute for it? Verse 25 removes any doubts on the first point: the closing words of the quotation from Psalm 8[6] speaks of 'all things' being put 'in subjection' beneath Christ's feet, including death.[117]

Matthew Black links the two concepts 'Son of Man' and 'Second Adam'. This opinion is accepted by many scholars. E. Stauffer maintains that 'the idea of the Son of Man lives on in the Pauline letters under a new christological word that gives linguistic expression to the same thing under the term "Man" and its further development and correlatives'.[118] Jeremias[119] and Cullmann[120] advocate a similar interpretation. If the concept 'Son of Man' does lie behind the thought of Paul, then it is legitimate to ask why he never uses the phrase. Much is to be said for the conjecture of Lake and Foakes-Jackson. They affirm that Paul 'was too good a Grecian to translate Bar-nāshā by so impossible a phrase as ὁ υἱὸς τοῦ ἀνθρώπου, and rendered it idiomatically by ὁ ἄνθρωπος'.[121] E. Stauffer suggests that Paul used the new terminology because, to Hellenistic ears, it would give 'a far more distinct expression to the antithesis between Christ and Adam than the name Son of Man could do'.[122] From this it may be concluded that the idea of Christ as the Second Adam has affinity with the 'Son of Man' of the Gospels. This does not mean that Rabbinic and Hellenistic ideas have not coloured Paul's thought, but it at least appears probable that our Lord's distinctive self-designation influenced it to some extent, and his terminology as well. T. W. Manson puts the position admirably: 'We have in the Pauline teaching the same conception of the Son of Man as in the teaching of Jesus, with just that difference of orientation which arises from the historic facts of the death of Jesus and the Resurrection.'[123]

We now turn to the question whether this concept of Jesus as the Second Adam is Pauline, or whether Paul took it over from the Christian tradition that he received. There is reason to believe

---

[117] 'The Pauline Doctrine of the Second Adam', *SJT*, VII.173.
[118] *New Testament Theology*, p. 111.   [119] *TWNT*, I.143.
[120] *The Christology of the New Testament*, pp. 166-81.
[121] *The Beginnings of Christianity*, I.380.
[122] *New Testament Theology*, p. 111.   [123] *The Teaching of Jesus*, p. 234.

that the picture of Adam lies behind the temptation story of Jesus as recorded in Mark, and if this is so, the parallel is to be found in the Gospel. Adam was tempted and so was Jesus; Adam was among the wild beasts and received angels' food, Christ was with the wild beasts and the angels ministered unto Him.[124] Again, we have already considered the possibility that 'Son of Man' in the Gospels is linked with the concept of Adam.[125]

There are a number of scholars who believe that Philippians 2[5-11] is pre-Pauline. E. Lohmeyer affirms that it is pre-Pauline and demonstrates its liturgical character.[126] This position is accepted by Bultmann[127] and A. M. Hunter.[128] The latter argues that, if the theory be sound, 'Paul's conception of Christ as the Second Adam goes back to pre-Pauline Christian tradition'.[129] The validity of this argument rests on the assumption that the figure of Adam lies behind Philippians 2, which is a probable, but not universally accepted, interpretation of the passage.[130] Cullman also favours a pre-Pauline authorship of this passage. He believes that it is a Christian Psalm taken over by Paul from the early Church.[131]

C. F. Burney thinks that the whole passage in 1 Corinthians 15[45] is a quotation.[132] He then draws his conclusion: 'If then this interpretation . . . be correct the implication is that some time before St Paul wrote this epistle in A.D. 55-6 the anti-thesis between the first Adam and Christ as the second Adam has been worked out in Christian Rabbinic circles and was used in argument.'

The arguments for the pre-Pauline authorship of Philippians 2[5-11] and 1 Corinthians 15[45] have not passed unchallenged. Stauffer thinks that the Philippian passage is a 'credal hymn, which Paul composed at an earlier date and quotes here'.[133] W. D. Davies argues powerfully against the theory of Burney.[134] He also rejects the argument for making Philippians 2 a pre-Pauline hymn, asserting that there is no proof that it is not a

---

[124] See V. Taylor, *Commentary on Mark*, p. 164, and J. Jeremias, *TWNT*, I.141-3, and *Jesus als Weltvollender*, p. 56.
[125] See pp. 58-9 above.
[126] '*Kyrios Jesus, Eine Untersuchung zu Phil* 2[5-11]', *Sitzungsberichte der Heidelberger Akadamie der Wissenschaften* (1928). Cf. *Die Briefe an die Philipper*, pp. 90-9.
[127] *Theology of the New Testament*, I.125.   [128] *Paul and His Predecessors*, pp. 46-51.
[129] Ibid. p. 51.   [130] See pp. 80-5 below.
[131] *The Earliest Christian Confessions*, p. 22.
[132] *The Aramaic Origin of the Fourth Gospel*, pp. 43-8.
[133] *New Testament Theology*, p. 284.   [134] *Paul and Rabbinic Judaism*, pp. 43-4.

hymn composed by Paul or by one of his disciples.[135] Davies concludes: 'Whereas the idea of the Christian Dispensation as a new creation was pre-Pauline, the concept of Christ as the Second Adam was probably introduced by Paul himself.'[136] There are no grounds for dogmatism, especially as there is no explicit reference to Adam in Philippians 2, and perhaps (as some maintain) not even an implicit reference. Nevertheless it seems probable that the idea of Jesus as the Second Adam is pre-Pauline, and may even go back to the self-designation of our Lord as 'Son of Man'.

Having dealt briefly with these preliminary questions, we must now turn to a consideration of the actual passages where the contrast between Adam and Christ is found. They are three in number: Romans 5, 1 Corinthians 15, and Philippians 2.[137] We might be tempted to think that an idea that has only three references made to it in all the Pauline corpus is not of vital significance, and is hardly to be counted as of primary importance in Paul's thought. This, however, does not follow; Paul did not write theological treatises, and ideas come to the fore only when the occasion calls them forth. Recent scholarship has tended to acknowledge that this parallel is important in Paul's thought. W. D. Davies writes:

Probably, however, this conception played a far more important part in his thought than the scanty references to the Second Adam in 1 Corinthians and Romans would lead us to suppose. In particular, in his development of the idea of the Church as the body of Christ, Paul is largely influenced by the Rabbinic ideas of Adam.[138]

Anders Nygren in his commentary on Romans has argued for the centrality of this idea in the epistle. He points out that the passage in Romans 5 is not a mere interlude, or an epilogue to what has gone before, or a prologue to what is to come; 'The truth is that this passage is actually the high point of the Epistle, in the light of which the whole is best to be understood.'[139] A similar position is advocated by Karl Barth.[140] It is thus as a key

---

[135] *Paul and Rabbinic Judaism*, pp. 41-2.   [136] Ibid. p. 44.

[137] Matthew Black argues that it is probable that the Pauline doctrine of the Second Adam lies behind a number of passages in the epistles. 'The Pauline Doctrine of the Second Adam', *SJT*, VII.170-9. The passages he mentions are: 1 Corinthians 11[7], 2 Corinthians 6[3-4], Colossians 1[15], 3[10], and Ephesians 2[15], 4[22].

[138] *Paul and Rabbinic Judaism*, p. 53.   [139] *The Epistle to the Romans*, p. 20; cf. p. 209.

[140] *Christ and Adam, Man and Humanity in Romans 5*.

feature in Paul's thought that we turn to consider the contrast between Adam and Christ which is found in these passages.

(i) Romans 5¹²⁻²¹

The interpetation of these verses is full of difficulties, and a variety of interpretations has been given. The crux of the passage lies in the interpretation of ἐφ' ᾧ πάντες ἥμαρτον, though verses 18-19 throw light on the meaning of this difficult phrase. The renderings of ἐφ' ᾧ have been varied. One of the most insistent interpretations has come through Origen, Ambrosiaster, August-ine, and the Vulgate rendering 'in quo', and has dominated later Latin theology; this rendering takes the relative as being masculine and makes the antecedent 'Adam'. The meaning thus becomes 'in whom', i.e. 'in Adam'. As W. Sanday and A. C. Headlam point out, however, ἐπί is not the right preposition to bear this significance, and ᾧ is too far from its antecedent.[141] If this is the meaning, we need to have ἐν ᾧ. Some would render the phrase as 'in like manner' or 'in so far as', but this is evading the plain meaning of the words. By far the most satisfactory solution is to take the phrase as a conjunction meaning 'for this reason', 'because'—this is taking ᾧ as neuter rather than masculine. This rendering is found in the Revised Standard Version: 'There-fore as sin came into the world through man and death through sin, so death spread to all because all men sinned', and is now accepted by the majority of scholars. ἐφ' ᾧ bears this meaning in a number of cases in Greek literature[142] and, what is more significant, in other Pauline passages.[143]

When the translation 'because' has been accepted, the problem of the meaning of the clause still remains; in what way did all men sin? Here again there is a divergence of answers. One interpretation is to maintain that the clause contains a definite and explicit doctrine of man sinning in Adam through seminal identity. It is true that the translation 'in quo' contains this theory, but as we have seen this is a doubtful rendering of the Greek.

To try to give exact expression to the means by which Adam's sin has affected all mankind is to go farther than this passage warrants. Some interpreters, however, have gone to the other extreme and have denied that there is any causal relation implied

---

[141] ICC, 'Romans', p. 133.   [142] See W. Bauer, p. 287.
[143] 2 Corinthians 5⁴, Philippians 3¹²; cf. Philippians 4¹⁰.

between the sin of Adam and the sin of all mankind. This position is put forward by H. W. Robinson[144] and F. R. Tennant.[145] H. W. Robinson makes the determining feature that of corporate personality, and Tennant uses the phrase 'mystical realism'. C. H. Dodd seems to follow H. W. Robinson on this point: 'Adam is a name which stands to him for the "corporate personality" of mankind.'[146] Dodd, however, does not explicitly deny that there is a causal relation implied in the passage.

The true rendering seems to lie between the two extremes, that of denying any causal relation, and that of making this relationship too explicit and too carefully defined. Sanday and Headlam strike the balance: 'All turns on this, that the effects of Adam's Fall were transmitted to his descendents; but St Paul nowhere says how they were transmitted; nor does he even define in precise terms what is transmitted.'[147] That there is a causal relationship implied in this passage seems to be beyond doubt. To assert that men have sinned because of Adam's example is to make nonsense of the parallelism of the passage. Anders Nygren makes the same point. He affirms that Paul's idea of man is very different from 'the present individualistic and atomistic concept'[148] and that he thought of mankind as an organic unity. 'Adam is not merely a single individual who lived long ago. Adam is significant as the head of the "old" humanity, as the head of the present age (ὁ αἰὼν οὗτος)'.[149] After examining the various types of exposition, he says: 'Paul's main idea is entirely clear and beyond doubt; it was through one man, Adam, that all men are sinners and are subject to death.'[150] To substantiate that there is a causal relationship implied in this passage Nygren puts forward an argument that is decisive. If we make this passage mean that all men die because of their own sin, then we must conclude that Paul is teaching also that all men are saved by their own righteousness. This is emphatically not Pauline doctrine. If Christ's act benefited all mankind—and this is Paul's main point in this passage—so we must also say that Adam's sin affected all men.[151] This position is enunciated by Bultmann:

As the first Adam ushered in the old mankind, so Christ, the 'last

144 *The Christian Doctrine of Man*, pp. 112-13.
145 *The Fall and Original Sin*, pp. 253-67.   146 *MNTC*, 'Romans', p. 80.
147 *ICC*, 'Romans', p. 132.   148 *The Epistle to the Romans*, p. 213.
149 Ibid. p. 213.   150 Ibid. p. 214.   151 Ibid. pp. 214-15.

Adam' ushered in the new. As the old Adamitic mankind received its stamp from the transitory, earthly first parent who brought sin and death into the world, so the new received its stamp from Christ, who, through his obedience (in becoming man and dying) and his resurrection, brought life and freedom from the annihilating powers.[152]

Even though some causal relationship is implied in this passage, its nature is not specifically defined. To deny this relationship is to miss the meaning of the parallel between Adam and Christ; whereas to talk of 'seminal identity' is to go farther than the passage warrants; in fact the concept of 'corporate personality' lies nearer the heart of this passage than 'seminal identity'. The essential point is Paul's belief that 'Sin could never be a private matter, but corrupted the whole race'.[153] In expounding the doctrine that Adam's sin affected the succeeding generations of mankind, Paul seems to be following the lead given by Jewish thought (see 4 Ezra 3^{21-2}, 4^{30-2}, 7^{118}), though W. D. Davies maintains that Paul in Romans 5 goes farther than the Rabbis.[154]

The parallel between Christ and Adam must now be examined in further detail. It is true that in Romans 5^{12-21} there is a structural irregularity, the form of the sentence being broken by the insertion of a parenthetic passage, yet the ideas of the parallelism are abundantly clear from the context. Without in any way doing violence to Paul, the sentence could be reconstructed thus: 'Therefore as sin came into the world through one man and death through sin; so through one man, Christ, redemption came into the world, and life through redemption.' The parallel can be put precisely: in Adam through 'sin' and 'disobedience' came 'death', and this spread 'to all men'; so in Christ through 'righteousness' and 'obedience'[155] came 'life', and this passed 'to all'.[156] Not that the work of Adam and Christ can be really compared; Christ more than undoes the disaster wrought by Adam, as Paul's use of the phrase πολλῷ μᾶλλον (much more) makes abundantly clear.

The general meaning of this passage is evident. Adam and Christ are 'type' and 'antitype'—in one sense they stand together,

---

[152] *Theology of the New Testament*, I.300.
[153] C. K. Barrett, *A Commentary on the Epistle to the Romans*, p. 119.
[154] *Paul and Rabbinic Judaism*, p. 34.
[155] W. D. Davies shows the centrality of the idea of 'obedience' in the Pauline conception of the Work of Christ. See ibid. pp. 260-8.
[156] This phrase must not be taken to imply of necessity the doctrine of universalism. Rather it implies that life can pass to all as they become 'in Christ', just as all have entered into death because all are in fact 'in Adam'.

yet in another sense they are diametrically opposed. They are
similar in the sense that they are both 'cosmic figures' and are
heads of aeons; they are opposed in that the aeons that they
introduced are fundamentally different. Adam is the head of the
old humanity, Jesus is the head of the new humanity; the characteristic features of the age of Adam are sin and death, but those
of the age of Christ are righteousness and life; the disobedience of
Adam was man's downfall, but the obedience of Christ was for the
creation of a humanity new and redeemed. Anders Nygren
emphasizes this concept of the two aeons[157] and gives an
admirable summary of the position:

We can say that Adam and Christ signify for Paul these two aeons, the
old age and the new. In the old aeon, which began with Adam, death
rules with unlimited power over all the children of Adam. In the new
aeon, which bursts upon man with the resurrection of Christ, life has
come to dominion still more mightily.[158]

(ii) 1 *Corinthians* 15[20-3, 45-9]

In verses 21 and 22 we have the contrast, stated in the plainest
terms, between Adam and Christ:

> 'For as by a man came death, by a man has come also the
> resurrection of the dead.
> For as in Adam all die, so also in Christ shall all be made
> alive.'

Later in the chapter, in verses 45-9, Paul returns to the parallel
and gives it further emphasis.

Even though there is a community of ideas between this
passage and Romans 5—and it is necessary to bear the Romans
passage in mind if this section is to be interpreted rightly—there
is here a different emphasis; 'The chief interest of the apostle at
this point is to maintain the final triumph over death which completes God's purpose in the first Adam, rather than to bring out
(as in Romans) the reversal of Adam's disobedience with its ill
effects on the race.'[159] But even though a difference of emphasis
is admitted, the fundamental ideas are the same: through Adam
came death and through Jesus comes life, life through resurrec-
ion. Any interpretation that tries to avoid this misses the point.

---

[157] *The Epistle to the Romans*, pp. 16-26, 218-24.   [158] Ibid. p. 23.
[159] J. Moffatt, *MNTC*, '1 Corinthians', p. 264.

The force of the passage lies in the assumption that Adam's death is in some way vitally linked with the fact of universal death, and that the Resurrection of Christ is causally linked with the resurrection of all Christians. There is no need to go on to infer, as some scholars do, that this passage requires a doctrine of universalism. All that it requires is the assertion that all the human race is 'in Adam' and therefore die, and that all men can be 'in Christ' and therefore can have the resurrection to life. To deny the cosmic significance of the acts of Adam and Christ is to ignore the obvious interpretation of the verses. A. S. Peake says:

The acts of Adam and Christ are racial acts, done in their capacity as natural and spiritual heads of the race, and affecting the whole race. Christ undoes, and more than undoes, what Adam has done, physical death is cancelled by physical resurrection.[160]

In verse 20 Paul describes Jesus as 'the first fruits of them that sleep'. On the 16th Nisan, which may in fact have been the actual date of the Resurrection, the first ripe sheaf of the harvest was offered to God (Leviticus 23[10-12]), and as a result of this the whole of the harvest was consecrated on the principle that consecration of the part consecrated the whole. In the same way the Resurrection of Jesus is a proof that all who are 'in Christ' will rise. This figure of thought again underlines the idea that the acts of Adam and Christ have a representative significance:'Christ leads the way in resurrection, as Adam did in death.'[161]

H. L. Goudge takes the parallel a step farther when he says:

Christians die, not merely 'through' but 'in' Adam. He, as it were, included all humanity in himself; we die, because we inherit his fallen nature. So also we shall rise, not merely 'through', but 'in' Christ. He includes all His members; we shall rise, because we share His life, as really as we share that of Adam.[162]

'Just as we have borne the image of the man of dust, we shall also bear the image of the man of heaven' (1 Corinthians 15[49]). Here we have the full force of the parallel brought out with explicit reference to the fact that death comes because we inherited Adam's nature, his fallen nature. It is to be questioned whether anything in 1 Corinthians 15 demands such an explanation; the

---

[160] *A Commentary on the Bible*, Ed. by A. S. Peake, p. 846.
[161] A. Robertson and A. Plummer, *ICC*, '1 Corinthians', p. 352.
[162] *Westminster Commentary*, '1 Corinthians', p. 146.

idea of corporate personality alone would be sufficient. But when we read the passage in Romans 5 and when we take account of the whole tenor of Paul's thought, we feel that this interpretation of Goudge's expresses what was in Paul's mind when he penned these words to the Corinthians. Adam's sin has caused a fallen nature to be passed on to all the race; the redemptive power of Christ was the means of creating a new and redeemed humanity: 'If any one is in Christ, he is a new creation' (2 Corinthians 5[17]).

(iii) Philippians 2[5-11]

This passage is in the form of a hymn consisting of six strophes of three lines each, the first three strophes dealing with the humiliation of Christ and the second three with His exaltation. Even if we do not accept the suggestion that it is pre-Pauline,[163] we can certainly accept the analysis of it, with its rhythm and parallelism and stately liturgical style, as a hymn.

Every word in this passage has been discussed, and as A. B. Bruce says, 'The diversity of opinion prevailing among interpreters . . . is enough to fill the student with despair, and to afflict him with intellectual paralysis'.[164] Despite its difficulty, a review of this passage must be attempted because of its importance to the present study. Even though Adam is not mentioned, it can be maintained that the idea of the parallel between Adam and Christ lies behind this hymn. A detailed study of the passage will tend to establish this opinion. Before we pass on to this study mention needs to be made of the other key-feature which needs to be recognized if the passage is to be interpreted correctly, namely the concept of the Suffering Servant. Here again the reference is implicit, but a comparison of this hymn with Isaiah 53 will make the connection clear.[165]

---

[163] See p. 73 above.   [164] *The Humiliation of Christ*, p. 8.

[165] *Paul and Rabbinic Judaism*, p. 274, gives a summary of the evidence which makes abundantly clear the relevance of the idea of the servant for a true interpretation of this passage.

As the Servant idea is so obviously behind this hymn it is rather strange that, even though Paul alludes to the Servant here, the idea is comparatively neglected in his writings. Vincent Taylor has made the following interesting suggestion: 'Is the explanation to be found in the widespread institution of slavery . . .?' Paul 'may have shrunk from using it directly of Jesus, and especially so in commending Him to the acceptance of the Gentile world' (*The Atonement in New Testament Teaching*, p. 66). The explanation of the presence of the Servant idea in this passage, however, may simply be that here Paul is quoting from an early Christian hymn.

The main points of debate in this passage may be summarized as follows:

Verse 6

ὑπάρχων (being). The question is whether this means simply 'to be' or 'to be originally'. Much is to be said in favour of the latter rendering, especially as the usual Greek word for 'to be' (εἶναι) is not used. The verb used has in classical Greek the meaning of 'to be by nature', and while it is true that the full force of the verb is not always maintained in later Greek,[166] it seems best to keep its full significance in this passage.

ἐν μορφῇ θεοῦ (in the form of God). The discussion turns on the meaning of the word μορφή (*morphē*) and its relation to σχῆμα (*schēma*). The difference has been stated simply: that '*schēma*' means outward appearance whereas '*morphē*' signifies essential being.[167] J. H. Michael accepts the distinction: 'A thing cannot be said to be in the *morphē* of another unless it possesses the essential qualities of that other.'[168] It is to be questioned whether this distinction can always be pressed,[169] but it is preferable to accept '*morphē*' in this context as meaning that Jesus was divine by nature. The verse demands such an interpretation, for the force of the context is that the Son of God who was divine, through the act of incarnation, emptied Himself in His voluntary humiliation. 'It is asserted—and on the assertion hinges the thrilling moral appeal of the passage—that before he came as man, Christ's life was Divine in quality; not merely like God, but participant in His essential attributes.'[170]

ἁρπαγμός (*harpagmos*). This word is found only here in the New Testament. It can be either active or passive. The active rendering would give the translation 'a snatching', 'robbery', and this is accepted by the Authorized Version. It is to be questioned, however, whether this rendering is to be accepted here. The passive meaning yields the translation 'booty', 'a thing to be clutched'. The Revised Version and the majority of modern scholars prefer this interpretation. This, however, does not settle the question. Even though the passive rendering is accepted, there still remains the further question, is it 'booty to be retained'

---

[166] See W. Bauer, pp. 845-6.
[167] So J. B. Lightfoot, *Epistle to the Philippians*, pp. 127-33.
[168] *MNTC*, 'Philippians', p. 86.   [169] See W. Bauer, p. 530.
[170] H. R. Mackintosh, *The Doctrine of the Person of Christ*, p. 67.

(*res rapta*) or 'booty to be snatched' (*res rapienda*). The first rendering implies that the pre-incarnate Christ already possessed equality with God and therefore did not count it something to be held on to at all costs. This interpretation is favoured by Lightfoot: '. . . yet did not regard it as a prize, a treasure to be clutched and retained at all costs.'[171] It is also favoured by Barth.[172] The other interpretation, 'booty to be snatched', implies that the pre-incarnate Christ, though possessing unity of nature with God, did not yet hold equality of status. Michael prefers this interpretation and quotes with approval Lipsius: 'The sense is: Christ regarded this equality with God (which though in divine form, He did not yet possess) not as a booty, that is to say, not as an object which He might violently and against the will of God snatch for Himself . . . but rather as attainable only through self-emptying and by the favour of God.'[173] This rendering has much to commend it. The word '*harpagmos*' can also mean 'a piece of good fortune', 'a windfall', but even if this interpretation is accepted it does not solve the problem. It is still 'an open question whether the windfall has already been seized and is waiting to be used, or whether it has not yet been appropriated'.[174] The question whether we are to think in terms of '*res rapta*' or '*res rapienda*' is not easy to decide. Linguistically either is possible; the rendering most suitable to the context is to be accepted. Dogmatism is not possible, but '*res rapienda*' seems to be the more appropriate to the general context. This is certainly true if it is accepted that the figure of Adam lies behind this passage.

τὸ εἶναι ἴσα θεῷ (equality with God). The crux of the clause lies in the question, 'Why should it be neuter rather than masculine?' It seems most likely that Paul shrank from the idea of Christ as a second God—his rigid Jewish monotheism militated against it—so 'being on an equality' refers to status and dignity rather than person. This makes the phrase adverbial. J. H. Michael thinks that Jesus received equality of status with God only after his exaltation. This means that ἐν μορφῇ θεοῦ and τὸ εἶναι ἴσα θεῷ are not synomyous expressions. 'The one expression is more naturally taken as referring to essential being,

[171] *Epistle to the Philippians*, p. 111.
[172] For Barth's interpretation of this Christological passage see *Erklärung des Philipperbriefes*, pp. 53-62.
[173] Quoted by J. H. Michael, *MNTC*, 'Philippians', p. 89.
[174] W. Bauer, p. 108.

the other as referring to state or condition.[175] There appears to be here a reference to Genesis 3[5], where the serpent says 'you will be like God'.

Verse 7

ἐκένωσεν (emptied). This verb has caused much discussion among theologians, and in recent times a distinct form of Christology has taken its name from it—Kenotic Christology. The Authorized Version translates it 'made of no reputation', but the 'emptied' of the Revised Version is much more literal. Some theologians, especially among the Lutherans, make this refer to the Incarnate Christ. The more usual view is that it refers to the humiliation of the Incarnation itself. If we have to decide between these two views the latter is preferable. It is to be questioned, however, whether this is necessary. Dr S. Cave puts the case:

He (Paul) was not concerned to divide Christ's career. For him, the Man who lived on earth was continuous with the Lord in heaven, and His self-abnegation was shown, not only in His readiness to become man, but through all His earthly life.[176]

The question now arises, 'Of what did He empty Himself?' Many highly speculative answers have been suggested which have carefully considered which attributes were laid aside. Fortunately, the meaning of the verb in this passage can be discussed without entering into these intricacies. Some say that it was of His divine nature that He emptied Himself. This, however, is not to be accepted, since nothing in the passage requires this interpretation, and there is no reason to assume that the nature of divinity was incompatible with the nature of the 'servant'; to say that it was is tantamount to denying the reality of the two natures in Christ. A second suggestion is that what was laid aside was His equality with God. But if the exposition suggested above is correct, He did not possess this before the exaltation. The most satisfactory explanation would seem to be that He laid aside the heavenly glory: 'He divested Himself, not of His divine nature, for this was impossible, but of the glories, the prerogatives of Deity.'[177] So much can be said without entering into any

[175] *MNTC*, 'Philippians', p. 87.
[176] *The Gospel of St Paul*, p. 77. Cf. J. H. Michael, op. cit. p. 84: 'The probability is that the passage embraces the pre-incarnate as well as the incarnate life of Christ.'
[177] J. B. Lightfoot, *Epistle to the Philippians*, p. 112.

elaborate division of attributes. W. Warren has put forward a
theory that attempts to cut across the whole problem.[178] He
says that the verb requires no specific object; the verse simply
means that Jesus poured out Himself. Attractive as this theory is,
especially in contrast with the elaborate structure that some
Kenoticists have built upon this verse, it does not do justice to the
rich meaning of the word.

Having discussed the specific problems of the text, we must now
try to ascertain the extent and significance of the parallel between
Adam and Christ which is implied in this passage. Some scholars
would deny that the figure of Adam lies behind this passage.
H. A. W. Meyer refers to 'the groundless opinion that our passage
alludes to Genesis 2-3'.[179] Stauffer writes:

Perhaps it is Adam (cf. Gen 3⁵, Rom 5¹²ᶠᶠ)? But Adam is a terrestrial
being, whereas the pre-existent Son is a heavenly figure. In Genesis 3⁵
equality with God consists in knowledge, while in Philippians 2⁶ it
lies in having a place of divine honour (cf. $\kappa\epsilon\nu o\delta o\xi\acute{\iota}a$, 2³). The concept that Paul has before his mind's eye must, therefore, be that of a
heavenly being who wants a place of honour equal to God's. That
suits Satan. . . .[180]

Martin Dibelius refers to 'Satan . . . or the Spirits in the Region of
the Firmament',[181] but thinks such an interpretation is questionable. He emphasizes the poetic character of the passage and says
that it should probably be interpreted 'poetisch-hymnisch' rather
than 'streng terminologisch'.[182] Lohmeyer is of the opinion that the
figure of the Devil lies behind the passage.[183] He maintains that
this hymn is 'ein Triumphlied' which proclaims that 'the dominion
of the Devil . . . is broken for ever'.[184]

Other commentators argue that it is the figure of Adam which
was in Paul's mind. This position is accepted by H. A. A.
Kennedy.[185] Similarly, A. E. J. Rawlinson writes: 'The "mind"
of the first Adam was the mind of self-deification; the "mind" of
the second Adam was the mind of humility and lowliness.'[186]
Pierre Bonnard advocates the same interpretation, saying that
Jesus, the Second Adam, is compared 'not with Satan' but with
'the First Adam' who, in Genesis 3⁵, was tempted to become 'like

---

[178] JTS, XII.461-3. [179] Commentary on the New Testament, IX.88.
[180] New Testament Theology, p. 284. [181] HNT (3rd edn.), p. 76.
[182] Ibid. pp. 76-7. [183] Der Brief an der Philipper, p. 92.
[184] Ibid. pp. 92-3. [185] The Expositor's Greek Testament, III.435-9.
[186] The New Testament Doctrine of the Christ, p. 134.

God'.[187] Cullmann, in his study of New Testament Christology, accepts the same position: 'The expression μορφή (form) firmly establishes the connection between Jesus and the creation story of Adam.'[188] 'Without the background of Paul's doctrine of the two Adams . . . these words can scarcely be understood. . . .'[189]

The parallel between Christ and Adam in this passage can be seen under two categories, the contrast between 'self-exaltation' and 'humiliation' and that between 'disobedience' and 'obedience'. Adam, according to the Genesis story, accounted equality with God a thing to be clutched at. When tempted with the bait that he would be 'like God', he grasped at it, ignoring the commandment of God, and the result was the Fall. In this passage in Philippians we have the picture of Christ 'who though He was in the form of God, did not count equality with God a thing to be grasped, but emptied himself', that is, 'he determined to become a man, to enter into the humanity which had lost the likeness of God'.[190] In the second point of comparison—disobedience and obedience—the parallel between Adam and Christ is taken a stage farther. Adam received the direct and unequivocal command of God to refrain from the fruit of the tree. His eating was thus not simply a clutching after equality with God but a definite act of rebellion and disobedience to the will of God. The picture in Philippians 2 is of the complete obedience of Christ: 'And being found in human form he humbled himself and became obedient unto death, even death on a cross' (verse 8). This stress on obedience seems to indicate that the comparison with Adam lies behind this passage. It is thus possible to argue that the contrast between the first and the last Adam is one of the key features for the interpretation of this passage. This position has recently been accepted by Alan Richardson: 'The Adam-typology plays a considerable part in Paul's thinking, and it is present to his mind when he is writing passages in which the name of Adam is not mentioned. For instance, in Philippians 2[5-11] he is thinking of the contrast between Christ and Adam, who being made in the image of God, thought that equality with God was something to snatch at. . . .'[191]

Having reviewed the three passages which expound the

[187] Commentaire du Nouveau Testament, X.43.
[188] The Christology of the New Testament, p. 176.   [189] Ibid. p. 177.
[190] Ibid. p. 178.   [191] An Introduction to the Theology of the New Testament, p. 245.

parallel between Adam and Christ, we must now face the task of trying to evaluate the true significance of this Adam-Christ contrast. It was seen that in Romans 5 there is the concept of Adam's sin having been passed on to his descendants with dire results. Paul, however, does not give any detailed exposition of how the results of Adam's Fall were passed on to his posterity, though it is obvious that there is a causal relationship between Adam's sin and the universality of sin, and that this causal relationship is rooted in heredity and not simply in example or environment. In the Corinthians passage the idea is stressed that death came through the Fall of Adam, an idea that will be discussed in more detail later.[192] In Philippians 2, though the name of Adam is not mentioned, it can be argued that the parallel is carefully worked out, the disobedience of Adam and his desire to clutch at equality with God being in the writer's mind. In contrast with Adam is Christ, the 'second man from heaven', the 'last Adam'. Paul argues in Romans that just as the disobedience of Adam worked for the destruction of mankind, so the obedience of Christ worked for man's salvation. In 1 Corinthians 15 the point is slightly different. Through Adam came death; through Jesus came the Resurrection of the dead. Philippians 2 implies the parallels: Adam clutched at equality with God but Jesus emptied Himself and took the form of a servant, and Adam was disobedient but Jesus was obedient even unto death. The result was that Christ was exalted; He was given the supreme name 'Lord', before which everything should bow.

In all these three Pauline passages there is the same fundamental pattern: through Adam mankind has suffered, but through Jesus the situation has been retrieved and more than retrieved. So much would be agreed by the vast majority of commentators. The question has now to be faced: does this give any clue to the human nature that was assumed by Christ at the Incarnation?

The force of these passages may be put tersely in the following terms. Adam fell and all mankind fell with him; there was a declension from the perfect creation of God; mankind became an alienated race that had rebelled against God. Christ stooped, emptied Himself, and through His voluntary humiliation He was the means of raising fallen man, restoring him to fellowship with

[192] See pp. 110-13 below.

God, bringing many sons to glory. All this lies in the Adam-Christ parallel. Yet if this parallel is to have any meaning, Christ must have stooped to the level of fallen man, and accepted the voluntary humiliation of descending to the level to which man had fallen through the sin of Adam and through the sins of succeeding generations. If the redemptive side of the parallel is to be preserved this must be maintained. Mankind was not in the state of Adam before the Fall, and so the usual answer that Christ assumed perfect human nature, human nature as God originally created it, has the effect of weakening the force of the parallel. Man was not in the state of Adam before the Fall, and, as this was so, something far more drastic was needed if the effects of Adam's fall were to be overcome. If there was to come 'a second Adam to the fight', then He must descend to the depths to which mankind had fallen—yet without Himself becoming involved in their actual sin and rebellion—and in His own person lift mankind from its fallen depths to a new level of life. To put it pictorially, if a man has fallen into a deep pit, his rescuer must descend into the pit, go to his level, lift him on to his shoulders and raise him up. This is what this parallel between Christ and Adam seems to imply. Adam sinned and all mankind fell to a lower level, but Christ, in His divine act of condescension, stooped to the very level where mankind was, assumed 'fallen human nature', and by His complete conquest over sin became the Head of a new and redeemed humanity. He more than cancelled what man had suffered through the rebellion of Adam. To deny this fact seems to cut at the very roots of these passages and to rob them of their power and significance. Adam caused mankind to fall; Jesus stooped from the very heights to the very depths to lift us up, to be our Saviour. As Stauffer says: 'The Son of God becomes man in order to find man. He enters upon our earthly life with its mortality, descends to the depths where we are so as to raise us to the heights where he dwells.'[193]

The suggestion that this parallel implies that Jesus shared our 'fallen nature' has been accepted by some expositors. F. B. Meyer, commenting on Philippians 2, writes: 'Jesus approached always nearer and nearer to human sin and need . . . that by identifying Himself with our sin and sorrow He might ultimately identify us with the glory which He had with the Father before

[193] *New Testament Theology*, p. 119.

the world was.'[194] J. H. A. Ebrard is more explicit. He says that the phrase 'taking the form of a servant' implies that Jesus assumed human nature as it was because of sin.[195] He interprets 'the form of a servant' as human nature 'standing under the results of sin'.[196] Cullmann, commenting on Philippians 2, writes: 'In his becoming man in the flesh, and in his humbling himself unto death . . . Jesus must assume the form of fallen man in order to take the μορφὴ δούλου.'[197]

Karl Barth in his study, *Christ and Adam, Man and Humanity in Romans 5*, gives a similar interpretation to the parallel. He writes:

As we saw in verses 9-11, those sinful and dying men, those condemned and enslaved men, are not alone, but Jesus Christ is in the midst of them, the Friend of publicans and sinners, who was crucified between two thieves, who in free obedience was willing to identify Himself with Adam and his children and heirs and has identified Himself with them once and for all.[198]

Again he writes:

Adam does not become Christ, but Christ, without ceasing to be Christ, and indeed just because He is Christ, becomes Adam as well. And because Christ thus identifies Himself with Adam's sin and Adam's death, Adam the sinner becomes a witness to Christ, the Reconciler, τύπος τοῦ μέλλοντος (verse 14).[199]

Barth accepts the theory that Christ assumed 'fallen human nature';[200] these passages show that he is of the opinion that it is implied in the parallel between Christ and Adam.

The validity and force of the present argument does not depend on any literal acceptance of the historicity of Adam. Modern science has taught us that Adam is but an abstraction, and that the early narratives in Genesis are primitive tribal stories and are in the realm of myth. This, however, must not blind us to the reality and power of these Pauline passages. As long as we accept that the sin of generation after generation of mankind has an effect on the stock of mankind, and that this effect is now passed on by means of heredity, then this parallel has significance. If we accept the idea of racial degradation and racial

[194] *The Epistle to the Philippians*, p. 61.   [195] *Christliche Dogmatik*, II.220.
[196] Ibid. p. 34.   [197] *The Christology of the New Testament*, p. 178.
[198] Op. cit. p. 22.   [199] Ibid. pp. 40-1.   [200] See pp. 167-70 below.

alienation from God, then these passages are full of meaning. Translating the fundamental idea into these terms, we see that Christ stooped at His Incarnation and became part of the human race that had been affected by the sins of previous generations, and entered into the sphere of our racial degradation. Yet He Himself defeated this inheritance, resisted and destroyed the 'fallen nature' which He assumed, and in so doing became the first of a new and restored human race. This concept gives full significance to the representative work of Jesus as Redeemer.

It would be untrue to say that Paul says explicitly that Jesus assumed 'fallen human nature'; it is doubtful indeed whether the question ever arose in precisely that form to Paul. This was the stage of proclamation; the stage of systematization of belief had not yet been reached; and in these circumstances it could not be expected that Paul would deal with the point explicitly. Yet the inference is there; and if the point is denied, the force of the Adam-Christ parallel is seriously weakened; it has been robbed of its grandeur and power, and its soteriological magnificence has been obscured. When Paul calls Jesus the 'second Adam', he implies that, in order that He might become our Saviour, He stooped and became our Brother in Adam's fallen race.

(b) The Figure of 'Dying and Rising' with Christ

In Romans 6 we have the vivid picture of a Christian being crucified, buried, and then raised with Christ.[201] This figure now calls for examination.

The origin of this pattern has been much discussed. One theory suggests that here Paul has been influenced by the Hellenistic and Oriental cults. It is affirmed that here we have the familiar pattern of death and resurrection that is found in the cults of Attis, Isis and Osiris, and Adonis. This theory has been advanced by such scholars as Brückner, Bousset, Loisy, Reitzenstein, and, more recently, by Bultmann[202] and J. Leipoldt.[203] It is not easy to assess the extent to which Paul was influenced by these cults. C. K. Barrett affirms that

there are real parallels between the language of Paul and that of some

---

[201] Compare also Galatians 2²⁰ and Colossians 2¹² where the figure is found in a less extended form.
[202] *Theology of the New Testament*, I.140.
[203] *Die Urchristliche Taufe im Lichte der Religiongeschichte* (see p. 60).

G

of the Hellenistic oriental cults. That Paul knew, and on occasion used, something of their religious terminology is probable, but this is not to say that he drew his doctrine from this source.[204]

It is to be questioned whether these cults are the source from which Paul took his ideas, though they may very probably have exerted some influence on him at this point.

A very different theory is put forward by W. L. Knox and W. D. Davies. Here the source is found in Judaism, and particularly in the idea of the Passover. Davies argues that the Pauline doctrine was based on Israel's release from the bondage of Egypt, and the fact that this deliverance was made through the waters of the Red Sea. He then draws the inference: 'It is not impossible then, that this conception of the dying and rising with Christ . . . is derived from the same world of thought as is indicated for us in the liturgy of the Passover.'[205] This is a very interesting suggestion and may well represent one of the formative elements in the thought of Paul.

Perhaps the most acceptable explanation of the origin of this figure in Paul's thought traces its source to the idea of Christians as the 'body of Christ' and the stress on the unity of Christians in Him. We have already seen that this concept of the unity of the body in the head is one of the factors that lies behind the idea of Adam and Christ as the heads of the old and new humanities in Romans 5; so again we have a similar stress on the unity in Christ. Christ is the inclusive and representative man, and through baptism we are incorporated into Him. Through being united into the body of Christ through the initiation of baptism, the believer experiences the central redemptive acts that Jesus endured in His death, burial, and Resurrection. When we take into conjunction with this the symbolism of the candidate walking into the water, being completely submerged, and then coming out of the water, we can understand how the ideas of death, burial, and resurrection came to be attached to the rite. A factor which cannot be ignored in this discussion is that Jesus spoke of His coming death as a baptism (Luke 12[50]), and when we look at Mark 10[38-9], we find Jesus speaking of His disciples sharing the experience. This last factor would be sufficient to germinate the idea, and the other factors mentioned would help to develop it.

An exposition of the meaning of the figure must now be attempted. Just as Jesus by His death and resurrection, won the victory over sin and triumphed in newness of life, so the Christian, when he enters the Christian faith through the gateway of baptism, must destroy and bury his old self and rise to a newness of life. There must be a complete change in a man's life—'Self must be mortified even to the finality of burial, that so from the tomb of the dead self, he may rise to newness of life'.[206] When we become Christians something is left behind, we pass from the realm of sin and death into that of life. Nygren says:

In the death of Christ the regnant power of sin was broken; all the dominions and powers of the old aeon were cast down. And in the resurrection of Christ the new aeon began. Since the Christian shares in the death and resurrection of Christ, all of this is also true of him; he has been delivered from the dominion of darkness and transferred to the kingdom of Christ.[207]

The 'old man' has been crucified (Rom 6[6]) and the 'new man' has been born (2 Cor 5[17]). The thought of Paul is not so much that the believer repeats the experience of Christ, but rather that he is with Christ in His experience. This concept of being with Christ in these central experiences of His life is quite distinctive of Christian thought.[208]

It now remains to discuss what relevance this idea has for the study on which we are at present engaged. The point behind the Pauline idea is that the recipient of baptism puts off the old self and becomes a new creation; he passes from the dominion of death into the body of Christ. This change from being 'in Adam' to being 'in Christ' is linked with the rite of baptism, with the descent into, and the ascent from, the water. The significant point, however, is not that the symbol of baptism suggests death, burial, and resurrection, but that the Death, Burial, and Resurrection of Jesus are linked with it. Why introduce these events in the life of Jesus? To say that they are redemptive acts and as such are appropriately in mind in an initiation rite is true, but it is to be

---

[206] G. O. Griffith, *St Paul's Life of Christ*, p. 152.
[207] *The Epistle to the Romans*, p. 234.
[208] E. Lohmeyer in his article on Σὺν Χριστῷ (in *Festgabe für Adolf Deissmann*, ed. by K. L. Schmidt) maintains that the use of σύν in this connection is unique.

questioned whether it takes the matter far enough. They are introduced here because the Cross and Resurrection of Jesus were in His own life a putting off of the old and an assuming of the new. With the Cross the old reign of sin and death was defeated, and with the Resurrection the newness of life came. With the Cross the old aeon received its death-blow, and with the Resurrection the new aeon dawned. It is generally admitted that in some way Jesus bore and defeated sin on the Cross, but how this was done is often left vague. If, however, it is argued that Jesus assumed 'fallen human nature', that He in reality entered into the race of Adam, and was part of the old aeon, and yet, through His sinless life and through the victory of His Cross, He redeemed the 'fallen nature' that He had assumed, then indeed His Cross and Resurrection would be the death-blow to the old and the inauguration of the new. If this is accepted, then immediately the force of the reference to the Cross and Resurrection in the context of baptism becomes clear and full of significance.

It might be argued that this is reading more into the concept than was ever in the mind of Paul. We must admit that Paul never definitely enunciated the point, yet it can be argued that the idea was in his mind. This is made all the more probable by the fact that this passage follows almost immediately on the parallel between Christ and Adam. As we have seen, this parallel suggests that just as Adam clutched at divinity and caused mankind to fall, so Christ stooped even to the level to which mankind had fallen and then through His divine redemptive power lifted mankind to newness of life. Thus, while there is no room for any dogmatic assertion, it seems an acceptable interpretation of this idea of 'Dying and Rising with Christ' that it fits in with the view that Christ assumed 'fallen human nature'. This position is greatly strengthened when we see this pattern as a part of the whole complex of Pauline thought on the work of Christ. It has already been seen that the parallel of Adam and Christ points to the same conclusion, that Christ took 'fallen nature'; in the next section on the Pauline pattern of salvation the same position will be found. This present section should be viewed, not in isolation, but rather in the light of the other aspects of Paul's thought on the Person and Work of Christ.

(c) The Pauline Pattern of Salvation

The central theme in the Pauline writings is that of Redemption. His exposition of the Work of God in Christ is in reality the whole weight and substance of his epistles, so much so that every other theme that he treats can be fitted, without doing it injustice, into the theme of redemption.

C. A. Anderson Scott in his study of Pauline theology divides Paul's doctrine of redemption into three main sections[209] and this threefold division will be followed here.

(i) Redemption from servitude to evil spirits

Paul and his contemporaries conceived of a whole hierarchy of evil spiritual forces, cosmic powers, which were superior to demons. Ephesians 6[12] is a revealing passage: 'For we are not contending against flesh and blood, but against the principalities, against the powers, against the world rulers of this present darkness, against the spiritual hosts of wickedness in the heavenly places.' Another significant verse is Galatians 4[3]: 'So with us; when we were children we were slaves to the elemental spirits of the universe' (cf. verse 9). The rendering of στοιχεῖα (stoicheia) in this verse has been much discussed. Originally the word signified things in a row, and from this it came to be used of the letters of the alphabet; later it had two derivative meanings, 'elements of knowledge' and 'elements of the physical universe'. From the latter arose the meaning of 'angels' or 'spirits' that are associated with the various planets and heavenly bodies. Some scholars maintain that only 'elements of knowledge' is required by this passage.[210] E. D. Burton argues that it refers to elemental forms of religion which have been superseded by Jesus Christ.[211] W. L. Knox also accepts this position.[212] Other interpreters maintain that Paul is referring to the cosmic powers.[213] This same conception is found behind such passages as Romans 8[38], Colossians 2[8], and 1 Corinthians 2[6-8]. In the last passage Paul asserts that it was these powers that crucified Christ, 'the rulers

---

[209] *Christianity According to St Paul*, pp. 27-46. Cf. the similar division in J. A. T. Robinson, *The Body*: Christ's death in relation to (a) the power of death, (b) sin, (c) the Law.

[210] This rendering is seen in the 'rudiments' of the *RV*.

[211] *ICC*, 'Galatians', pp. 510-18.

[212] *St Paul and the Church of the Gentiles*, pp. 108-9.

[213] See the translations of Moffatt and *RSV*.

of this age, who are doomed to pass away . . . none of the rulers of
this age understood this; for if they had, they would not have
crucified the Lord of glory'.[214]

These powers are thought of as having been created by God,
but they are not predominantly good; on the contrary, they are
used as an explanation of the existence of evil. They had rebelled
against God and were now in opposition to Him. It was part of
Paul's belief that these powers had gained a foothold in man, and
had taken root in the σάρξ (sarx). These forces had invaded this
part of man's nature, and had placed him under bondage.

The word 'sarx' is of such importance to this discussion that
its exact meaning must be determined. The word can carry the
ordinary meaning of flesh; 1 Corinthians 15[39] and Revelation
19[17-18] illustrate this usage. Often it carries the idea of the
weakness of man over against God, as is clearly seen in Matthew
16[17]. 'Flesh represents mere man, man in contrast with God—
hence man in his weakness and mortality.'[215] But in Paul there is
a definite relationship between 'sarx' and sin, and this is the crucial
point for the present discussion. This Pauline doctrine of the
'sarx' is one of the most important concepts in Paul's thinking,
and one that has led to a variety of interpretations.

In 1872 H. Lüdemann published a work on Pauline anthropo-
logy,[216] in which he maintained that 'sarx' has two meanings in
Paul, one the simple meaning, and the other taken from a dual-
istic system. According to the first meaning, where 'sarx' means
flesh with no evil significance, sin springs from the freedom of the
will, and salvation comes through justification and imputed
righteousness. According to the second meaning, where flesh is
considered as being corrupt, sin proceeds from the flesh as a
natural necessity, and salvation comes through the abolition of
the flesh by the spirit and through a new creation. This first
idea of redemption is judicial and has Jewish origins, the second
is ethico-physical and has Greek origins. Lüdemann expounds
the thesis that the Greek strand gradually replaced the Jewish
one in the thought of Paul. This theory is expressed, in a modified
form, in the works of Otto Pfleiderer.[217] Other writers have also
looked to Hellenism to find the origin of this antithesis between

---

[214] Some think that 'rulers' here refers to earthly rulers such as Pilate, but the
interpretation suggested above seems preferable.
[215] J. A. T. Robinson, *The Body*, p. 19.
[216] *Die Anthropologie des Apostels Paulus.*   [217] *Paulinism*, pp. 47-68.

'spirit' and 'flesh'.[218] This interpretation, in its extreme form, has not gained the support of the majority of scholars. Many scholars believe that the key to the understanding of Paul's use of 'sarx' is to be found, not in Hellenism, but in Judaism. The thesis of Schweitzer is that Paul must be interpreted exclusively in terms of Jewish thought.[219] C. A. A. Scott makes the Hellenic influence almost negligible.[220] W. D. Davies argues that the essential background of Pauline thought is Rabbinic Judaism.[221] It is never an easy matter to decide the degree of influence exerted upon Paul's mind by Hellenism and Judaism. In this particular case it seems probable that the major influence came from the latter, but his own personal experience played a significant part in the formation of his thought. W. D. Stacey in his study, *The Pauline View of Man*, sums up the point:

He was aware that his words in Romans would be read by those who thought in Hellenistic terms, and he was evidently satisfied that it should be so. But his own mind on the matter was determined first by his thorough knowledge of the Old Testament usage, and, secondly, by the anguish of his unique personal struggle with sin, finding its occasion in the flesh.[222]

We must now attempt to decide what, to Paul's mind, was the relationship between 'sarx' and sin. H. A. A. Kennedy is emphatic that the Pauline doctrine of the 'sarx' does not contain the Greek conception of matter as inherently evil, nor the idea of the body as the prison-house of the soul; he maintains that 'flesh', human nature apart from God, gives sin its material to work on.[223] C. H. Dodd says:

The Flesh is the common stuff of human nature which we inherit. . . . Paul does not think of it as necessarily evil, but as itself powerless for moral ends. . . . But this powerless substrate of human nature has fallen under the power of sin. . . . Thus by no choice of his own man, as a creature of flesh, is in the thraldom of sin.[224]

G. S. Duncan gives a similar interpretation:

[218] H. J. Holtzmann, *Lehrbuch der Neutestamentlichen Theologie*, II.13-19; R. Reitzenstein, *Die Hellenistischen Mysterienreligionen*, pp. 48ff and 159ff; W. Bousset, *Kyrios Christos*, pp. 130-4; W. Morgan, *The Religion and Theology of Paul*, pp. 16-18, 27.
[219] *Paul and his Interpreters.* [220] *Christianity According to St Paul.*
[221] *Paul and Rabbinic Judaism* (see especially p. 17).
[222] *The Pauline View of Man*, p. 173. [223] *The Theology of the Epistles*, pp. 33-8.
[224] *MNTC*, 'Romans', p. 112.

It was in the flesh that these evil powers carried out their attacks on him (man) and established their sway over him—for the flesh, though not in itself evil, is weak and easily corrupted when it is not dominated by the Spirit.[225]

J. A. T. Robinson propounds the same theory:

The σάρξ . . . is not itself evil or sinful; but it is essentially 'weak' and easily beguiled. . . . It forms therefore, in the language of a later age, the *fomes peccati*.[226]

This seems to be the most widely accepted and most satisfactory interpretation of Paul's thought. In itself '*sarx*' is not evil, but it has been invaded by the 'cosmic powers'; it has become the seat of sin and evil, and as such needs to be redeemed. The citadel of evil needs to be invaded by the powers of the Spirit that men may live according to the Spirit. This appears to be the best explanation of the contrast between flesh and Spirit which is found in the Pauline writings (see Gal 5[16-23], Rom 8[3-14]). To live in the flesh is not sinful, to rely on the flesh is.

In Jesus is the redemption from these powers of evil which have become entrenched in the '*sarx*'. This idea lies behind Colossians 1[13]: 'He has delivered us from the dominion of darkness and transferred us to the kingdom of his beloved Son.' The most instructive passage in this context is Colossians 2[15]: 'He disarmed the principalities and powers and made a public example of them, triumphing over them in it' (*RSV*m). Anderson Scott thinks of this verse as referring to a stripping off of the '*sarx*' in which these powers had gained a hold. He links the verse with the idea of the circumcision of Christ in Colossians 2[11]. He also divides Ephesians 4[21] so as to give the same idea: 'that, as was actually the case with Jesus, he put off the old man and put on the new.'[227] Vincent Taylor gives a different interpretation to Colossians 2[15]:

He thought also of the work of Christ as a fight of God Himself with these hostile powers, a death grapple from which He emerged victorious, stripping His enemies of their apparel and leading them, like a Roman conqueror, in triumph.[228]

Lohmeyer says that the illustration is not from the battleground but from the court, and alludes to the public degradation of high

[225] *MNTC*, 'Galatians', p. xl.   [226] *The Body*, pp. 36-7.
[227] *Christianity According to St Paul*, pp. 36-7.
[228] *The Atonement in New Testament Teaching*, p. 63.

officials, their mantels and insignia being taken from them.[229] The interpretation of this difficult verse turns on whether ἀπεκδυσάμενος (apekdusamenos) is rendered as 'having stripped off from himself', a reading which is favoured by the *RV*, or as 'having spoiled the principalities and powers'. The latter is the rendering of the *AV*; the same interpretation is also reflected in the *RSV* ('He disarmed the principalities and powers') and is accepted by Vincent Taylor and E. F. Scott.[230] Dogmatism is not possible in a case such as this, but we feel that the former rendering has much to commend it, especially as it agrees with the idea of Christ defeating sin in the flesh, which is found elsewhere in Paul (Rom 8³). He defeated sin in the flesh by stripping off the flesh in which the hostile powers had gained their footing. J. A. T. Robinson makes a similar point in a different setting:

It is through the σάρξ that death and its forces have control over our human nature. The dying Jesus, like a king, divests Himself of that flesh, the tool and medium of their power, and thereby exposes them to ridicule for their Pyrrhic victory. From that moment death has no more dominion over Him (Rom 6⁹).[231]

The pattern of salvation here is this: Jesus assumed flesh, thus entering the sphere in which these powers had become entrenched, and having entered the invaded territory, He became victor and brought redemption. This suggests that Jesus assumed 'fallen human nature', flesh which had been invaded by the evil powers, and there in enemy-occupied territory wrought the victory. This idea certainly seems to lie behind the interpretation of Colossians 2¹⁵ that we have accepted. The unusual phrasing of Colossians 1²¹⁻²² should also be noted: '. . . he has now reconciled in his body of flesh by his death.' E. F. Scott on Colossians 2¹⁵ makes the position clear:

If the words are so taken the meaning must be that the powers of evil had entrenched themselves in Christ's fleshly nature. 'He that knew no sin was made sin for us', and in his death he threw off this contaminated nature which he had assumed for our sakes, thus breaking free from his enemies.[232]

It is significant that even though E. F. Scott prefers the other

229 *Meyer Commentary*, '*Der Kolosserbrief*', pp. 118-21.
230 E. F. Scott, *MNTC*, 'Colossians', pp. 48-9.
231 *The Body*, p. 41.   232 *MNTC*, 'Colossians', p. 48.

interpretation of the passage, it is on grammatical and not on theological grounds—he think that the subject of the sentence appears
to be not Christ but God. The position of Anderson Scott similarly suggests that Jesus, in stripping off the '*sarx*', is stripping off
something that has been affected by the invading powers of evil;
in this he implies that He assumed 'fallen nature'. Jesus defeated
the principalities and powers by stripping off the flesh in which
they had become entrenched. He could not, therefore, have
possessed human nature as it was before the Fall; for there to be a
victory it must have been flesh which the powers had invaded.
Jesus entered the territory of these tyrannical powers, but through
His perfect life He prevented them from gaining dominion over
Him. On the Cross He stripped them off, making a public
triumph over them. This position, while still preserving the fact
of His sinlessness, asserts that He assumed fallen humanity, a
nature that in its '*sarx*' had been invaded by the powers of evil.
The two other divisions within the Pauline pattern of salvation
must now be investigated to see if they confirm this interpretation.

(ii) Redemption from the bondage of Law

Paul's attitude to the Law has always been a difficult part of his
thought to interpret in that he appears to make contradictory
statements. Sometimes he speaks of the Law in the highest terms
(Rom 7[12, 22]). In contrast, however, there are verses which speak
of the tyranny of the Law and its bondage (Rom 5[20], 7[6]). He goes
so far as to make one aspect of the work of Christ redemption from
the bondage of the Law (Gal 4[4-5], Rom 6[14], 10[4]). The explanation of this seemingly contradictory attitude is a complex question. Anderson Scott maintains that Paul uses the word law in
two senses: (*a*) as a system whereby men thought that they could
acquire merit, and (*b*) as a revelation of the divine requirements.
The first was done away by Christ, but the second continues.[233]
Bultmann says: 'It is clear that Christ is the end of the Law so far
as it is claimed to be the way of salvation, or was understood by
man as the means of establishing "his own righteousness", for so
far as it contains God's demand, it retains its validity.'[234] It is
abundantly evident that Paul thought of the Work of Christ as a
repudiation of the Law as a system of salvation. His whole
emphasis on salvation by faith in contrast to the Jewish doctrine of

[233] *Christianity according to St Paul*, p. 45.   [234] *Theology of the New Testament*, I.341.

salvation by works is a clear proof of this. Christians are no longer under law but under grace. The whole argument of the Epistle to the Galatians is a plea that they, who have been released from the power of the Law and have entered the liberty of the children of God, should not retrace their steps and again become subject to the dictates of the Law. No one can read this epistle without realizing that Paul has finished with the Law as a means of salvation, and that in Christ the Law has been repudiated.

It is in the Epistle to the Galatians that we find the most significant verses for our present discussion. First there is the statement in 4⁴ that Jesus was 'born under the law'. We have already seen that Christ had to enter the sphere over which the evil cosmic powers held sway if He were to redeem men from their tyranny. Here we find the same pattern. Jesus, to redeem men from the bondage of the Law, had to enter the sphere where the Law held sway. He was born under the Law. Yet He was born under the Law that He might redeem mankind from its bondage. This leads to the crucial verse, Galatians 3¹³: 'Christ redeemed us from the curse of the law, having become a curse for us—for it is written, "Cursed be every one who hangs on a tree".' The reference is to Deuteronomy 21²³. Originally this clause in the Law referred to the practice of hanging the dead bodies of criminals on a tree as an added humiliation. The passage says that Jesus became a 'a curse', not 'accursed'. 'Paul avoids the implication that in His own person Christ was actually "accursed". He became "a curse" in the sense that He allowed Himself to come under a curse, just as it is said in 2 Corinthians 5²¹ that He was made to be "sin" though He Himself knew nothing of sin.'²³⁵ The important question is to decide under what curse Jesus came. It might be argued that He bore God's personal curse, but this is hardly likely, since the idea is quite un-Pauline. Another possible interpretation is to say that He bore the curse of men, but this is an artificial rendering. A more satisfactory view is that He bore neither the curse of God nor the curse of men, but the curse of the Law; as E. D. Burton says, this interpretation 'though without support in any other passage of the apostle's writings, is most consonant with the context, if not actually required by it'.²³⁶ Paul believed that men had passed under the bondage of the Law and because they had not fulfilled the Law

²³⁵ G. S. Duncan, *MNTC*, 'Galatians', p. 97. ²³⁶ *ICC*, 'Galatians', p. 172.

they were under its curse. Jesus had to be born under the Law,
and by bearing its curse deliver men. Jesus permitted Himself,
through His voluntary identification with men, to come under a
curse. Here in Pauline language we find expressed a similar idea
to that which lies behind the Cry of Dereliction. To Paul it is a
real curse that has to be borne. The very fact that the Law was
given by God means that in some sense the curse is God's curse
and that Jesus bore His curse, not as His own desert, but vicar-
iously for men. By bearing the curse which the Law pronounced
against those that hang on a tree, Jesus broke the curse of the Law.
For a Jew to fail in one detail of the Law was to receive the full
condemnation for breaking the whole Law; if then Christ showed
that the Law's curse was of no avail in one particular place, the
whole curse of the Law would be broken. G. S. Duncan
aptly comments:

No doubt he (Paul) felt that when the Law, even in one particular,
brings God's own Christ under its condemnation it is, as a revelation of
the mind and will of God, so thoroughly discredited as to lose its
authority and validity.[237]

Jesus, bearing the curse, abolished it. This is Paul's doctrine in
this difficult verse. Jesus bore the curse of the Law at one point,
showed it to be false, and thus broke the whole curse of the Law.

It would be going too far to say that this idea of redemption
from the bondage of the Law requires the doctrine that Christ
assumed 'fallen human nature', but there is much to be said in
favour of this position. There is a suggestion in Paul that the
Law is a consequence of human sin;[238] if men had not sinned
there would have been no need for the Law. This point is argued
by Brunner.[239] He sums up the position in this way:

The Law is therefore, on the one hand, the wrathful answer of God to
the sin of man; on the other side, it is the means through which
God brings the sinful apostasy of man to a head. . . . Through the
radical Law man must learn what the 'curse of the Law' means, in
which the curse of his sin is seen in God's sight.[240]

If this exposition is accepted it means that to be born under the
Law means to be born into a sphere that has only come into being
because of the Fall, because of sin. This would certainly be in

---

[237] *MNTC*, 'Galatians', p. 101.   [238] Romans 5[20].
[239] *Dogmatics*, II.119-21.   [240] Ibid. p. 121.

accord with the hypothesis that Christ assumed 'fallen human nature', nature that because of the Fall was 'under the Law'.

Even if this last point is not accepted, the discussion in this section is not irrelevant, for again we see the same Pauline pattern of salvation. To redeem men from the Law Jesus must be born under its dominion. This pattern was found in the previous discussion with reference to the redemption from evil spirits, and will be found again when we come to consider redemption from sin. In both these cases the pattern is confirmed if we accept that Christ assumed 'fallen nature'. This conclusion is more convincing because the same fundamental pattern is found in all the three divisions into which Paul's thought on redemption has been divided.

(iii) Redemption from the servitude to Sin

The depth of the Pauline doctrine of sin must be emphasized. He thought of sin as rebellion against God, a state of being at enmity with Him. He goes even farther and makes sin almost a personal evil force and speaks of men as slaves of sin, in bondage to its tyranny, finally drawing the wages of death. We are its slaves (Rom 6[20]); it rules over us (Rom 3[19], Gal 3[22]); it is like a king ruling over the domain of death (Rom 5[21]); and in the end it pays its wages, death (Rom 6[23]).

It is against this background of the gravity of sin that Paul puts his doctrine of redemption. In what way was this redemption achieved? Following the pattern that we have already discerned in Paul's doctrine of redemption we should expect to find that Jesus entered the sphere where sin had entrenched itself (that is, the 'sarx') and there wrought the victory that brought redemption. This is exactly what is to be found when the epistles are studied. The whole idea is expressed in Romans 8[3]: 'For God has done what the Law, weakened by the flesh, could not do: sending his own Son in the likeness[241] of sinful flesh and for sin, he condemned sin in the flesh.' Jesus entered the sphere of the flesh, 'He took upon himself the form of sinful flesh, the burden of a life that has been afflicted hereditarily ever since the days of Adam (Rom 8[3])',[242] that He might condemn sin there where it reigned. The most important verse is to be found in 2 Corinthians 5[21]: 'For our

---

[241] For a discussion of the significance of ὁμοίωμα, see pp. 107-9 below.
[242] E. Stauffer, New Testament Theology, p. 117.

sake he made him to be sin who knew no sin, so that in him we might become the righteousness of God.' This verse is notoriously difficult to interpret, and we can sympathize with the sentiment of Plummer—'No explanation of these mysterious words satisfies us. They are a bold attempt to express what cannot be grasped in human thought, still less be expressed in human language.'[243] Yet we must try to understand something of the significance of this verse, and we can certainly ascertain in what realms of thought it moves. Attempts are made to rob these words of their full power. One such attempt is the suggestion that the word 'sin' means 'sin-offering'—an exposition followed by Augustine. This explanation, however, evades the obvious significance of the words; the contrast between sin and righteousness in the passage shows that sin and not a sin-offering is in Paul's mind. Plummer thinks that here and in Galatians 3[13] Paul was probably influenced 'by the language of LXX respecting the sin offering and the guilt offering in Leviticus 4 and the scapegoat in Leviticus 16.'[244] The force of this point in connection with Galatians 3[13] is obvious, but it is to be seriously questioned whether the same applies here. H. L. Goudge tries to evade the difficulty in another way. He maintains that 'made' really means 'treated Him as though He were' —his whole point is that we are dealing 'not with fact, but with representation'.[245] To interpret 'sin' as 'sin-offering' or to explain it as 'God treated Him as though He had sin' seems to be refusing to face the real issue. What then does this crucial verse mean?

If this verse is to be interpreted correctly it will be best to treat it independently of Galatians 3[13]. The quotation cited above from Plummer tends to link them together. This is also done by Vincent Taylor.[246] We agree that there is the same rugged paradoxical statement, and admit that both move in the same realm of ideas, but there is a disadvantage in treating them together: Galatians 3[13] refers to the Cross—this is made abundantly clear by the reference to the curse of hanging on the tree —but that this verse in 2 Corinthians refers to the Cross is not so certain. Walter Grundmann holds that it refers to the Incarnation.[247] If this suggestion is accepted, we have an important difference which divides the two verses for the purpose of exposition.

[243] ICC, '2 Corinthians', p. 187.   [244] Ibid. p. 187.
[245] Westminster Commentary on 2 Corinthians, p. 60.
[246] The Atonement in New Testament Teaching, pp. 86-8.
[247] 'Sin'—E. T. from the article in TWNT, pp. 80-1.

To take this verse as referring to the Incarnation is not the usually accepted exposition, but it can be so understood, particularly when it is severed from Galatians 3[13]. This interpretation is certainly affirmed by E. F. Scott. We have seen earlier that if Colossians 2[15] is taken to mean that Christ stripped off the flesh in which the powers of evil had taken their hold it immediately links itself with this verse; E. F. Scott's words need to be quoted again because they are so relevant:

If the words are so taken the meaning must be that the powers of evil had entrenched themselves in Christ's fleshly nature. 'He that knew no sin was made sin for us' and in his death he threw off this contaminated nature which he had assumed for our sakes, thus breaking free from his enemies.[248]

The quotation of the passage from 2 Corinthians shows that he refers it to the Incarnation, and takes it to mean that Jesus assumed 'fallen human nature'. With the quotation above we must link the same writer's comments on Colossians 1[22]:

In order to do battle with sin on its own ground Christ assumed a body of flesh; as Paul boldly expresses it in 2 Corinthians 5[21]. 'He who knew no sin was made sin for us.' Thus his physical death on the Cross had a moral value, and was universal in its effect. By the destruction of his own flesh he destroyed the principle of the flesh which involves the whole race in sin.[249]

C. A. Anderson Scott also connects this verse with the Incarnation and implies that Christ assumed 'fallen nature'. 'That is to say, though He "knew no sin" in the sense that He never consented to it, was never guilty of it, in every other relation to sin He was one with His brethren of mankind.'[250]

This interpretation fits the pattern which we have already found elsewhere in Paul. Jesus came to do battle with sin where sin had its rule. Through this victory the broken relationship between man and God was restored. This interpretation also implies that Christ assumed 'fallen human nature'; He who had no personal aquaintance with sin 'was made to be sin for us'— yet He never became a sinner; He never allowed the sin to have sway over him. J. A. T. Robinson commenting on 2 Corinthians 5[21] underlines this point:

[248] MNTC, 'Colossians', p. 48.   [249] Ibid. p. 28.
[250] Christianity According to St Paul, p. 249.

Yet even in this total identification, he (Paul) is again most careful in his choice of words. He never says that Christ was a sinner. In fact he joins this last statement with the most positive assertion that He 'knew no sin'. . . . It is by disobedience that men are 'made sinners': Christ's life was one of utter 'obedience' (Rom 5[19]).[251]

In His Cross was the redemption from the power of sin; it was defeated and its tyranny broken; man was reconciled to God.

Having examined the Pauline doctrine of redemption under these three heads we find the same essential pattern. Christ entered the sphere from which men needed to be redeemed, yet He did not allow the evil to take control of Him; finally through His Cross He won the victory and wrought the redemption. In two of these heads, redemption from evil powers and from sin, we have found a definite suggestion that Christ assumed 'fallen human nature', so much so that the meaning and force of the Pauline pattern is seriously weakened if this position is denied. This position has been put forward by J. A. T. Robinson in his study of Pauline theology under the category of 'The Body'. His words are so relevant to our present discussion that we quote him at length:

The first act in the drama of redemption is, the self-identification of the Son of God *to the limit*, yet without sin, with the body of flesh in its fallen state. It is necessary to stress these words because the Christian theology has been extraordinarily reluctant to accept at their face value, the bold, and almost barbarous phrases which Paul uses to bring home the offence of the Gospel at this point. . . . [There are, however,] pressing grounds for requiring, the ascription to Christ, of a manhood standing under all the effects and consequences of the Fall. At any rate, it is clear that this is Paul's view of Christ's person, and that it is essential to his whole understanding of His redeeming work.[252]

The whole work of Christ in redemption can be summed up for Paul in the words [of Colossians 1[21-2]]. Both the Incarnation and the Cross are necessary: first, the complete identification in the body of His flesh with the whole mass of sin and death; and, secondly, the stripping off of this body, in the power of an obedience perfect unto death, whereby the forces of evil are deprived of assault and exposed to ridicule.[253]

These words of J. A. T. Robinson are quoted with complete

[251] *The Body*, p. 39.   [252] Ibid. pp. 37-8.   [253] Ibid. p. 45.

approval. It is true, as he points out, that this conception of Christ assuming 'fallen human nature' is a theory that has been little accepted in the history of Christian thought—to which study we must turn in the next part of this investigation—but its presence in the thought of Paul seems to be certain. If this pattern of redemption is studied, it appears to indicate that Jesus stooped to enter our 'fallen nature'; He entered enemy-occupied territory to set mankind free. In some places this seems to be the obvious interpretation of his language—particularly when he speaks of condemning sin in the flesh, of stripping off the flesh, and of Christ being made sin for us. Stauffer says 'the Son of God comes to carry alien burdens (cf. Gal 6²), and enters into the position of fallen man, who is under sin (Rom 3¹⁰) and the law and the curse (Gal 4⁴, 3¹³), and he redeems that position'.²⁵⁴ The fact that this position has not been generally accepted, and that these Pauline phrases have rarely been given this interpretation, seems to lie in doctrinal prejudice rather than in sound biblical exposition. No doubt the idea that Jesus assumed 'fallen nature' is a doctrine that needs careful exposition if serious errors are to be avoided; it is also true that often it has been expounded by unfortunate advocates; and coupled with these factors is the truth that other doctrines have tended to cloud the issue. All these factors have tended to militate against the acceptance of the doctrine; yet the result is that Paul's doctrine of redemption has been robbed of some of its meaning. Something of the wonder of redemption, the grandeur of deliverance, the infinite love of the condescension of the Incarnation have been lost when Paul's pattern of redemption has not been given this interpretation. To do justice to the thought of Paul it is necessary to accept the doctrine that Christ assumed 'fallen human nature'.

There is one objection to this conclusion that must be met. It is based on the fact that several passages in Paul seem to be almost docetic in character and appear at first to mean much less than the doctrine which has just been enunciated.

Two main passages call for investigation—Romans 8³; 'For God has done what the law, weakened by the flesh, could not do: sending his own Son in the likeness of sinful flesh and for sin, he condemned sin in the flesh', and Philippians 2⁷⁻⁸: Christ 'emptied himself, taking the form of a servant, being born in the likeness of

---

²⁵⁴ *New Testament Theology*, p. 117.

men. And being found in human form he humbled himself and became obedient unto death.' Certainly both these passages appear to contain phrases which seem to suggest that Paul was hesitant to call Jesus man in the ordinary sense. J. Weiss has gone so far as to say that Paul 'grazes the later heresy of "Docetism" '.[255] This judgement is not to be accepted. A study of the Pauline epistles makes it clear that he emphasizes the full humanity of Christ (see Rom 1[3], Gal 4[4], Col 1[24], Phil 3[10]). The position of Bousset is less extreme:

These are all beginnings which could issue in docetism, but Paul glides over conceptions of this kind; he has never seriously applied his reflection to the problem how the pre-existent being in Jesus has been connected with an actual humanity.[256]

There is, however, another explanation which makes the investigation of these passages of prime importance for our present study. The suggestion is that these qualifying phrases are introduced because of Paul's idea of the flesh. Paul asserts that Jesus assumed full humanity, but wishes also to affirm that in His flesh sin had not taken root. J. Weiss says: 'He does not wish to state that Christ has borne flesh which, like our own, was ruled by sin. It would have seemed to him like blasphemy. Therefore he uses— we cannot put it differently—an expression of double meaning.'[257] Vincent Taylor expresses a similar opinion.[258] If this exposition is true, the whole of the present argument regarding Paul falls to the ground.

The crucial phrases in the Philippian passage must now be examined.

'*Taking the form* (morphē) *of a servant*'. This might in the English translation give support to the idea of Docetism, but certainly not in the Greek. It was seen earlier that '*morphē*' usually has the meaning of essential nature.[259] This is so here. Christ in reality took the nature of a servant. This meaning is confirmed when it is realized that the phrase is parallel to 'form of God' which is used to express the reality of His divinity; it was not intended to convey that He was only divine in form and appearance. J. H. Michael makes the point clearly: 'It points to the reality of the

[255] *History of Primitive Christianity*, II.490.   [256] *Kyrios Christos*, p. 183.
[257] *History of Primitive Christianity*, II.489.
[258] *The Person of Christ in New Testament Teaching*, pp. 39-40.   [259] See p. 81 above.

state now assumed by Christ. Not in appearance only did he become a servant.'[260] J. A. T. Robinson goes so far as to assert that the phrase means 'nothing in the least docetic, but the most realistic description of the condition of fallen humanity'.[261] Cullmann takes a similar position: 'Jesus must assume the form of fallen man in order to take' the form of a servant.[262]

'*being born in the likeness* (homoiōma) *of men*'. This phrase does not go as deep as *morphē*, but there is nothing in this context that warrants the description of Docetism, that Christ's humanity was unreal, a mere semblance. Neither is there support that Paul is trying to avoid the idea that Jesus assumed 'fallen human nature'. Such an interpretation reads more into the passage than is warranted. Cullmann even maintains the phrase 'shows that Jesus entered completely into fallen humanity'.[263] C. A. A. Scott says that Paul 'is far from suggesting any unreality in the human nature of Christ; He is registering the fact that in all that fell under the observation of other men Jesus was a man like themselves'.[264] There seems to be no necessity to make this passage an obstacle to the acceptance of the doctrine that Christ assumed 'fallen human nature'.

In the New Testament, the word ὁμοίωμα (homoiōma) is restricted to the Pauline epistles, where it occurs five times. The passage in Philippians 2[7] has already been referred to, and it is clear from the context that there is no suggestion that the humanity of Christ was only an 'imitation' or 'appearance'. Christ was true man. The other occurrences of the word are to be found in Romans. Before examining Romans 8[3]—the vital passage for our present investigation—it will be useful to look at the use of the word in the other three contexts. In 1[23] there is the phrase 'images resembling mortal man'; the point here is that an image corresponds to the original, and it is to be questioned whether the idea of mere 'imitation' is sufficient. In 5[14] Paul writes, 'whose sins were not like the transgression of Adam'; W. Bauer interprets this to mean 'just as Adam did, who transgressed one of God's express commands'.[265] The third instance of the use of '*homoiōma*' is in 6[5]: 'For if we have been united with him in a death like his'; Bauer renders this 'in the same death that he

[260] *MNTC*, 'Philippians', p. 91. [261] *The Body*, p. 39.
[262] *Christology of the New Testament*, p. 178. [263] Ibid. p. 178.
[264] *Christianity According to St Paul*, p. 248. [265] W. Bauer, p. 570.

died'.[266] If these interpretations are accepted, and such meanings seem to be demanded by the contexts, then it is evident that 'homoiōma' does not mean merely 'imitation'. Perhaps the word 'form' gives a better rendering than 'appearance'. What seems to be implied is a valid likeness, not a mere imitation. It is reasonable to think that a similar meaning will apply in 8³.

When we turn to Romans 8³ we come to the passage which, more than any other, suggests to commentators that Jesus assumed a humanity untouched by the Fall. Dr Taylor, speaking of Philippians 2⁷ and Romans 8³, says:

These passages are important because they clearly imply a difference between the humanity of Christ and ordinary humanity. This difference—indicated by the word 'likeness' (ὁμοίωμα)—is certainly not a difference in the mode of origin. Its character is manifest in Romans 8³; it lies in the sinlessness and moral perfection of Jesus.[267]

It is obvious that the Romans passage is the determining one in Vincent Taylor's thought. There is nothing in his statement with which we should disagree, but when we know that he means that Jesus took human nature that was not affected by the Fall,[268] then his inference must be seriously questioned. W. Sanday and A. C. Headlam make the same inference when they say, 'the flesh of Christ is "like" ours inasmuch as it is flesh; "like" and only "like" because it is not sinful'.[269] Nothing in the wording of this comment can be questioned if it means that Christ was sinless, yet the obvious implication of the sentence is that it rules out of court the theory that Christ assumed 'fallen human nature'. C. H. Dodd is explicit in rejecting this hypothesis and his comments are forceful:

Since Paul has assumed that all flesh, as such, is now under the dominion of sin, he cannot here say outright . . . that Christ became flesh. . . . But in saying that Christ came in the guise of sinful flesh, he does not mean to deny that Christ lived a truly human life. . . . Fallen humanity in Adam is not the only humanity. . . . Christ then came, in all the glory of the true humanity, in the guise of that flesh which in Adam is sinful, to deal with sin within the same sphere of physical life in which Adam had lost the glory.[270]

[266] W. Bauer, p. 570.   [267] The Virgin Birth, p. 5.
[268] This position was expounded in lectures given by Dr Taylor in Wesley College, Headingley, Leeds.
[269] ICC, 'Romans', p. 193.
[270] MNTC, 'Romans', pp. 119-20.

This passage gives an exposition which explicitly denies that Christ entered the sphere of fallen humanity. If this is accepted, all that we have said about the Pauline pattern of salvation is false. Is it to be accepted?

The evidence that was examined with reference to the Pauline concept of redemption was drawn from many aspects of his thought and based on a wide variety of passages, and the general conclusion reached was that Paul taught that Jesus, to conquer the evil powers, the Law, and sin, had to enter into the sphere in which they ruled, the sphere of 'fallen human nature'. It is hardly likely that a conclusion that is so widely based will be overthrown by one passage. Is the line of exposition found in C. H. Dodd really demanded by this verse? Paul here in Romans 8[3] and Philippians 2[7] is using language very carefully, not because his desire is to refute the idea that Jesus assumed 'fallen human nature', but because he desires to preserve the sinlessness of Jesus. He wants to avoid saying anything that might be interpreted to mean that Jesus was a sinner, which was obviously untrue. His aim was to bring Jesus into the sphere where the powers of sin and darkness held their sway, yet without asserting that He became subservient or obedient to them. He entered the territory where they ruled, but He was never subject to them. It was to maintain this point, yet without in any way giving the false impression that Jesus was a sinner, that Paul said 'in the likeness of sinful flesh'. Rudolf Bultmann in his translation of Romans 8[3] makes this point and certainly seems to say that Jesus assumed 'fallen human nature': 'having sent his own son (clad) in (our) self-same, sin-ruled flesh and (sent him) to take sin's place, God (in condemning Christ to die) condemned (our) sin (= Christ) in the flesh (he shared with us).'[271] Anders Nygren takes the same position:

Paul is firmly convinced that, in some way, Christ stood under the power of sin. But here a special difficulty arises. For it is just as clear to Paul that sin had no place in Christ. He says of Him that He 'knew no sin' (2 Cor 5[21]). Paul can therefore not use the absolute expression σὰρξ ἁμαρτίας, 'sinful flesh'; for that would mean that Christ was subject to the power of sin in the same way as we who are sinners. Paul wants to come as close to that as possible without falling into conflict with the sinlessness of Christ, of which he is utterly certain. He

271 *Theology of the New Testament*, I.296.

comes to the dividing line; but does not step over it. He says ἐν ὁμοιώματι σαρκὸς ἁμαρτίας, 'in the form of sinful flesh'; or 'in the likeness of sinful flesh'. In that expression there is no trace of docetism. . . . [Paul] here deals with two relationships which seem to be in conflict, but as to neither of which must he go too far: on the one hand, the sinlessness of Christ, and on the other hand, that Christ was placed under the same conditions and under the same powers as we.[272]

Accepting this interpretation we find that this verse in Romans is far from denying the fact that Jesus assumed 'fallen human nature'. On the contrary, it would seem to affirm it. In fact its language is carefully chosen to express the view that Jesus at the Incarnation assumed human nature that had been affected by the Fall, that He was the son of Adam before He was the head of a new and redeemed humanity, but to express it in such a way as not to jeopardize the truth that Jesus was free from actual sin. This verse thus becomes an added reason for accepting the view, already put forward, that the Pauline doctrine of redemption has, as one of its central features, the doctrine that Christ was born with the self-same 'fallen human nature' that all men inherit from Adam. J. A. T. Robinson expresses this opinion explicitly: 'God sent his own Son in the likeness of sinful flesh (ἐν ὁμοιώματι σαρκὸς ἁμαρτίας, flesh that belonged to sin: Rom 8³). Nothing apparently could be more explicit.'[273] C. K. Barrett expresses the same opinion, though more tentatively:

The word 'form' or 'likeness' (ὁμοίωμα) has already been used several times in the epistle (1²³, 5¹⁴, 6⁵) and in none of these places does it mean simply 'imitation'. . . . We are probably justified therefore in our translation [the form of flesh which had passed under sin's rule] and in deducing that Christ took precisely the same fallen nature that we ourselves have, and that he remained sinless because he constantly overcame a proclivity to sin.[274]

(d) Paul's teaching on death

In the Bible there is a close connection between sin and death. Ezekiel 18⁴ says 'The soul that sins shall die'. The whole tenor of the Old Testament is to make death something that is alien to man's true nature. It is not an original part of God's plan and purpose in creation. It is a fact that is vitally linked with human

---

[272] *Commentary on Romans*, p. 315.   [273] *The Body*, p. 39.
[274] *A Commentary on the Epistle to the Romans*, p. 165.

sin. Death is a thing of which to be afraid: 'My heart is in anguish within me, the terrors of death have fallen upon me' (Ps 55⁴).

A crucial passage for the interpretation of the Old Testament conception of death is Genesis 2-3. It is by no means clear that this story was originally intended to convey the idea that man was created immortal. Genesis 2¹⁷ reads 'for in the day that you eat of it you shall die'; at first sight this might suggest that man was created immortal, but 3¹⁹ gives a very different idea: 'You are dust, and to dust you shall return.' What is certain, however, is that later Jewish thinkers connected death with sin, and this is clearly seen in late Jewish writings: 'From a woman was the beginning of sin, and because of her we all die' (Sir 25²⁴); 'God created man for incorruption, . . . but by the envy of the devil death entered into the world' (Wis 2²³⁻⁴); 'Unto him [i.e. Adam] Thou gavest Thy commandment, which he transgressed, and immediately Thou appointedst death for him and his generations' (4 Ezra 3⁷).

When we turn to Paul we find this same idea present. Bultmann affirms that 'For Paul, in the train of Old Testament-Jewish tradition, it is axiomatic that sin draws death after it'.²⁷⁵ A study of Paul's writings reveals the truth of this estimate. He considers that death is a direct result of sin, and that it was the sin of Adam that brought the curse of death upon mankind. Certain passages leap immediately to mind: 'Therefore as sin came into the world through one man and death through sin, and so death spread to all men because all men sinned' (Rom 5¹²); 'For if many died through one man's trespass' (Rom 5¹⁵); 'If, because of one man's trespass, death reigned through that one man' (Rom 5¹⁷); 'For the wages of sin is death' (Rom 6²³); 'For as by a man came death . . . for as in Adam all die' (1 Cor 15²¹⁻²). These quotations show conclusively that in Paul's thought, following the Rabbinic ideas of his day, death came through the sin of Adam.

The Epistles leave us in no doubt as to the fact that Jesus really died and was buried. The references to this fact are so numerous that it would be superfluous to list them. This fact of the reality of His death can be seen in the way in which Paul speaks of God raising Jesus from the dead; He was really dead and it took the power of His Father God to raise Him to life:

²⁷⁵ *Theology of the New Testament*, I.246.

'Christ was raised from the dead by the glory of the Father' (Rom 6⁴; cf. Rom 8¹¹, 1 Cor 15⁴, Gal 1¹). This carefully chosen terminology only serves to strengthen the truth that Paul believed that Jesus entered the realm of death, and to such an extent that it needed the power of God to raise Him from the dead.

Here we have two facts. Paul accepts on the one hand the current Jewish belief that death entered into the human race through Adam's sin, and on the other hand that Jesus died in reality and needed the power of His Father to raise Him. The obvious conclusion seems to be that Jesus possessed human nature that had been affected by the Fall of Adam in that it was subject to death. No other explanation is really adequate. To deny the reality of His death is to cut at the heart of the Gospel and is untrue to Paul's thought. If we try to evade the issue by saying that Jesus was not subject to death on the Cross but that by an act of divine condescension He allowed Himself to die, we are introducing an explanation that is far too hypothetical to carry conviction. The inference is obvious: when the Son of God became incarnate, part of His condescension was to enter the sphere of mankind that was liable to death, and in fact He died upon a Cross. It is true that death is connected with sin in the thought of Paul, but Jesus Himself was sinless and therefore death had no real claim over Him personally, but He was subject to death in that He was one of the race of Adam—'He assumed a "mortal body"; the Son of Man, like every other fallen son of man, must die.'²⁷⁶ He was subject to death not because of any personal sin, but because of the 'fallen human nature' which He had assumed. Because death had no personal claim on Him, His death was such that it broke the power of death; He did not deserve to die and God vindicated Him in the Resurrection. The fact is perfectly clear, Jesus in becoming man became subject to death like all the sons of Adam, and to Paul death was accounted to be a result of the Fall. This leads to the conclusion that, at this point at least, Paul definitely teaches that Christ assumed 'fallen human nature', human nature that has been affected by Adam's transgression.

Niebuhr says that Paul, in expressing the idea that death came into the situation as a result of sin, is introducing an element into Christian thought which is not in harmony with the biblical

²⁷⁶ J. A. T. Robinson, *The Body*, pp. 38-9.

doctrine of the finiteness of man.[277] The suggestion that man was originally immortal, and that physical death is the result of sin, receives scant support from science, which says that the physical organism, by its very nature and composition, is mortal and subject to death. We may accept both these points; nevertheless the validity of the argument is not weakened in any way. Paul implies that Jesus assumed 'fallen human nature', and even if at this point his premises are wrong, it still does not undermine our present argument that this is part of Paul's thought on the Person of Christ.

When we take the preceding sections together and weigh their testimony, the cumulative effect is to substantiate the assertion that Pauline thought contains the belief that Christ assumed 'fallen human nature'. Paul affirms the sinlessness of our Lord, but he also maintains that this fallen nature was assumed that it might be healed. It was part of the redemptive purpose of God in Christ that this nature should be assumed in order that it might be stripped of its power, and that a new humanity might be founded in the Second Adam.

THE THEOLOGY OF THE EPISTLE TO THE HEBREWS

(a) Christ's affinity with those to be saved

There is a feature of this epistle which is of the utmost significance, namely the conception that Jesus, in order to be a Saviour, must have an affinity with those He came to save.

The first passage which calls for consideration in this connection is 2^{5-18}. Psalm 8 is quoted, which speaks of man being made a little lower than the angels, crowned with glory and honour, and set in dominion over the works of God. The writer of the epistle says that this is not revealed in the world as we see it, but we do see that the psalm has been fulfilled in Jesus, and in this fulfilment Jesus, Son of Man, becomes the Saviour. This leads the author to explain the relationship between Jesus and the human race. Before the thought of the passage can be examined in more detail there are certain exegetical points which must be considered.

The rendering of βραχύ τι in 2^7 is often given as 'Thou hast made him a little lower than the angels'—this is the rendering of both the Authorized and Revised Versions. A more satisfactory

[277] *The Nature and Destiny of Man*, I.185-9.

rendering, however, is 'Thou didst make him for a little while lower than the angels'—this is the rendering of the Revised Standard Version and is supported by many scholars. James Moffatt says:

In applying the psalm, however, our writer takes $\beta\rho\alpha\chi\acute{u}$ $\tau\iota$ in the sense of 'temporarily' rather than 'slightly', and so has to make the 'inferiority' and 'exaltation' two successive phases, in applying the description to the career of Jesus.[278]

The best interpretation of the quotation is to make it refer to man. Then in verse 9, with the mention of Jesus, we come to the contrast. As Peake says, 'We do not see all things subjected to man, but we do see Jesus crowned with glory and honour',[279] or, as Moffatt says: 'The argument of v. [8, 9] therefore is that, however inapplicable to man the rhapsody of the psalm is, at present, the words of the psalm are true, notwithstanding. For we see Jesus who was "put lower than the angels for a little while" . . . now "crowned with glory and honour".'[280] The fact that Jesus has been so crowned is a guarantee that mankind, through Him, will be established as this psalm says. This interpretation is followed by the vast majority of scholars. It seems probable that this passage has affinities with the concepts of 'Son of Man' and 'Second Adam'.[281]

There is a diversity of opinion as to the exact reference of the words 'because of the suffering of death' in 2[9]. Westcott, Peake, and *RSV* take it with $\dot{\epsilon}\sigma\tau\epsilon\phi\alpha\nu\omega\mu\acute{\epsilon}\nu\sigma\nu$ (crowned) but Moffatt takes it with $\dot{\eta}\lambda\alpha\tau\tau\omega\mu\acute{\epsilon}\nu\sigma\nu$ (was made lower), and this rendering is followed by W. Manson: 'He is "made for a little time lower than the angels" in order to suffer death.'[282] The point at issue is whether the suffering of death is connected with Jesus being made 'lower', or whether it is part of His crowning. There is nothing in the order of the Greek to decide for either rendering. Dr Taylor's suggestion has a certain attraction. He suggests that the phrase refers to both—the death which seems to make Him low was in reality His crowning.[283]

[278] *ICC*, 'Hebrews', pp. 22-3. Cf. O. Michel, *Der Brief an die Hebräer*, p. 71; J. Héring, *L'Épître aux Hébreux*, p. 31; W. Manson, *The Epistle to the Hebrews*, p. 98.
[279] 'Hebrews', *The Century Bible*, p. 98.   [280] *ICC*, 'Hebrews', p. 24.
[281] See J. Héring, *L'Épître aux Hébreux*, p. 31, and William Neil, *The Epistle to the Hebrews*, p. 39.
[282] *The Epistle to the Hebrews*, p. 98.
[283] This suggestion was made during a series of lectures given at Wesley College, Headingley, Leeds.

There is a textual problem in 2⁹. χάριτι θεοῦ (by the grace of God) is the reading of the vast majority of manuscripts and versions, and has the support of the majority of the fathers. There is, however, another reading, χωρὶς θεοῦ. Origen interpreted this reading to mean that Jesus died for all except God. It was a reading much favoured by the Nestorians who interpreted it to mean that He died apart from His divine nature. The textual problem is very complicated, but it seems best to accept the familiar reading.[284]

We must now turn from textual points to the general exposition of the passage. The whole passage turns upon the idea of the affinity of Christ with those whom He came to save, an affinity which was of vital soteriological significance. This affinity has two focal points, suffering and temptation. In 2¹¹ there is the significant phrase: 'For he who sanctifies and those who are sanctified have all one origin. That is why he is not ashamed to call them brethren.' This is sometimes interpreted to mean that Jesus and men have all one parent, God; it is claimed that it is unlikely that the reference is to Jesus and men being the sons of Adam, especially as 'many sons' in 2¹⁰ refers to sons of God. This exposition is advocated by a number of scholars.[285] It is rejected, however, by Héring. He maintains that everything in the universe has its origin in God, and therefore some more particular link between Jesus and men is in the author's mind. He argues that the reference is to the fact that the Son, by His Incarnation, becomes, like the rest of mankind, a descendant of Adam.[286] There is much to be said in favour of this exposition. Even if it is not accepted, however, the fact that Jesus became a Son of Adam along with the rest of mankind is clearly indicated in 2¹⁴⁻¹⁵:

Since therefore the children share in flesh and blood, he himself likewise partook of the same nature, that through death he might destroy him who has the power of death, that is, the devil, and deliver all those who through fear of death were subject to lifelong bondage.

[284] For a full textual note see Moffatt, *ICC*, 'Hebrews', pp. 26-7. For a critical discussion see Moffatt, ibid.; Westcott, *The Epistle to the Hebrews*, pp. 60-2; Peake 'Hebrews', *The Century Bible*, pp. 102-3; O. Michel, *Der Brief an die Hebräer*, pp. 72-3. The classical discussion of this reading is by Harnack *Studien zur Geschichte des Neuen Testaments und der Alten Kirche*, I (1931), pp. 236-45, reprinted from *Sitzungsberichte der Preussischen Akademie* (1929), pp. 63-9. Harnack favours χωρὶς θεοῦ.
[285] See A. S. Peake, 'Hebrews', *The Century Bible*, p. 106; J. Moffatt *ICC*, 'Hebrews', p. 32; O. Michel, *Der Brief an die Hebräer*, p. 80.
[286] *L'Épître aux Hébreux*, p. 34.

This is a clear statement that Jesus assumed man's nature, for flesh and blood here means 'human nature on its weak and perishable side'.[287] Jesus, if He was to be really our Saviour, if He was to deliver men from the dire situation they were in, had to enter that situation. The devil held sway over men by wielding the power of death. Therefore, to be an effective Saviour, Jesus had to enter the territory over which the devil ruled, and enter the realm of death so as to break its tyranny and power.

This soteriological significance of the identity of Jesus with man is clearly found in 2^{17-18}:

Therefore he had to be made like his brethren in every respect, so that he might become a merciful and faithful high priest in the service of God, to make expiation for the sins of the people. For because he himself has suffered and been tempted, he is able to help those who are tempted.

Here is the clear realization of the need for a community of nature between Jesus and those whom He came to save. This has been recognized by scholars. A. B. Bruce has a striking passage in his study, *The Humiliation of Christ*:

The Holy one descended into the state of the unholy, that He might raise them in turn to His own proper level in privilege and character.[288]

A. S. Peake, commenting on Hebrews 2^{17-18}, says of the relation of Jesus to men: 'As such they [i.e. men] were of corruptible nature, liable to death and in bondage to the fear of it. To become capable of death He must assume their nature.'[289] Moffatt gives a similar interpretation:

To die for everyone meant that Jesus had to enter human life and identify himself with men; suffering is the badge and lot of the race, and a Saviour must be a sufferer if he is to carry out God's saving purpose.[290]

A final quotation from a more recent study of the epistle must suffice to show how unanimous scholarship is in finding in this passage the doctrine of the real affinity between Christ and those whom He came to save. W. Manson affirms that it was necessary that Jesus 'should in His own person not only exhibit perfect

---

[287] A. S. Peake, 'Hebrews', *The Century Bible*, p. 108.
[288] Op. cit. p. 34; see the whole section, pp. 33-44.
[289] 'Hebrews', *The Century Bible*, p. 107.   [290] *ICC*, 'Hebrews', p. 28.

obedience to God, but achieve also a perfect identification of Himself with men, and thus be qualified to be our perfect Minister with God'.[291]

Yet despite this unanimity of opinion, there is no explicit exposition of the doctrine that Jesus assumed 'fallen human nature'. The only writer among those quoted who makes any discussion of the point, A. B. Bruce, rejects the hypothesis that Christ shared our 'fallen nature'. It seems, however, that the obvious exposition of this passage in Hebrews—and some of the quotations cited above come at the very least within a hair-breadth of saying it—is that Jesus assumed a human nature that was affected by the Fall. He entered the realm of suffering and death, the realm over which the devil held sway. Here was His affinity with us; yet He was not one with us in the sense that He alone remained sinless, since the powers of sin and death did not obtain control. It was in this tension between oneness and separateness that He became the Saviour.

All this is reflected in the writer's use of ἀρχηγός (archēgos). It is the picture of a pioneer, a pathbreaker who makes a path in uncharted land. Jesus is our pathbreaker, making a path out of the realm into which we have fallen and opening a way for us into the Kingdom of the sons of God. He is 'the first' and 'thus supplies the impetus' for those who follow.[292] Another meaning found in this suggestive word is that of a leader going in front of a redeemed host, beating down his enemies and winning the victory. Again the figure is apposite. Jesus comes and joins mankind in its captivity, puts Himself at the head of mankind, and as the leader wins the battle against sin and death and gains the victory for them. This passage, which teaches the affinity between Christ and those He came to save, seems to demand for its adequate exposition the concept that the Son of God took upon Himself our nature, not as it was before the Fall, but as it had become through the sin and rebellion of mankind. He Himself, despite this assumption of our 'fallen nature', preserved His freedom from actual sin, and so was our 'archēgos', and became our Saviour.

Before leaving this section in the study of the Epistle, it is necessary to examine a little more closely Christ's affinity with

[291] *The Epistle to the Hebrews*, p. 101.
[292] W. Bauer, p. 112. This is following the suggestion of C. K. Barrett, who puts Hebrews 2[10] in Bauer's third paragraph rather than in the second—*The Background of the New Testament and its Eschatology*, ed. by Davies and Daube, p. 390, note 1.

man in temptation. We find this alluded to in the passage just reviewed, but the most important verse in this context is Hebrews 4[15].
Here there is the declaration that Jesus was tempted in all
points as we are, yet without sinning. This was necessary in
order that He might have a true sympathy with those who face
the ordeal of temptation. The verse quite obviously means that
He was tempted on every side of His human nature and yet,
because He never succumbed to temptation, He felt its full force
as no sinful man ever did; as T. H. Robinson says: 'The powers of
evil have never had to exert their full strength upon us; we have
always surrendered before the limit was reached.'[293] Yet despite
the fierceness of this temptation, Jesus was without sin. This is the
usual interpretation of χωρὶς ἁμαρτίας, and is clearly reflected
in Moffatt's translation 'without sinning'. This interpretation is
also accepted by the Revised Standard Version. His sinlessness
depended, not on an absence of temptation, but in a constant
victory over it. A. S. Peake says that there is another possible
interpretation, though he himself says 'perhaps it is better' to
accept the rendering 'without sinning'. This alternative exposition mentioned by Peake is relevant to the present discussion
because, if it were accepted, it would militate against the hypothesis that is under investigation. He says that χωρὶς ἁμαρτίας
'may mean that, unlike us, Christ had no sin in himself, there was
no traitor in the camp to which temptation could appeal'.[294]
This exegesis is strained, and is certainly not required by the
passage. The obvious interpretation is the one which makes the
phrase define what was the outcome of His encounter with
temptation—He endured the full force of temptation yet without
sinning.

This verse, in fact, may be said to suggest a theory which is the
direct opposite of the one that Peake refers to. The passage says
that Jesus was tempted in all points as we are, that His temptations were of the same kind as ours. This must be taken seriously.
Cullmann writes:

The author of Hebrews really thinks of the common temptations
connected with our human weakness, the temptations to which we are
exposed simply because we are men. 'In every respect as we are' refers
not only to form but also to content.[295]

[293] MNTC, 'Hebrews', p. 51.   [294] 'Hebrews', The Century Bible, p. 131.
[295] Christology of the New Testament, p. 95.

Temptations are of two kinds, those which are purely external, and those which receive some of their power by appealing to a weakness within. Unless we admit that a purely external temptation is possible we are denying the possibility of the temptation of Adam before the Fall. As long as a person has the power of choice he can be faced with the alternative between good and evil, and he can choose evil, even though there is nothing in his nature that gives him a predisposition one way or the other. When, however, we are considering temptation as it applies to man since Adam, we face a very different situation; man has inherited a nature that has been weakened by the sins of previous generations and he is part of a spoilt species. There is therefore in his nature that to which temptation can make its appeal. It is this fact which makes the struggle against temptation far more difficult a fight than it would be if temptation had nothing within to which it could appeal, if there were no traitor in the camp. This passage says that Jesus was tempted as we are. He was our brother in the struggle against temptation and thus He could sympathize with us in our need. His temptations were of the same kind as ours, though greater in degree because He did not yield. The conclusion which suggests itself is that Jesus took our 'fallen nature' and faced temptation as we do; in His nature too there was that to which temptation could appeal. The writer of this epistle 'would have nothing to do with any suggestion that Jesus was naturally good, or that he started with an unfair advantage'.[296] If this interpretation is accepted, the phrase 'without sinning' becomes full of meaning. Despite the fact that He had assumed 'fallen human nature', He was without sin. Here we see the only kind of temptation that Jesus did not face, temptation that springs from previous acts of sin. Despite this inheritance, He never yielded, He never sinned. Thus in no way does this detract from the sinlessness of Christ; on the contrary, it enhances it, and gives it a new and richer significance. This interpretation not only fits the wording of this verse, but it would also appear to give it a deeper meaning. This exposition of the passage is tentatively accepted by J. Héring. Commenting on the passage he affirms that 'without sin' refers to 'actual sin'. The author of Hebrews did not ask himself the question whether Jesus shared the 'human weaknesses' which we place under the heading of 'original

[296] William Neil, *The Epistle to the Hebrews*, p. 54.

sin'. If he had, 'perhaps he would have replied in the affirmative' to show in what a radical way Jesus resisted and vanquished evil.[297]

This position has not gone unchallenged, and A. B. Bruce is emphatic that there is no need to postulate that Christ assumed 'fallen human nature' to account for the statement that 'He was tempted in all points as we are'. He makes the phrase 'without sin' refer not simply to the outcome of the issue with temptation, but also to its origin. As we have pointed out above, this seems to be a strained and artificial exegesis, and certainly not one that would carry the weight of scholarship with it. Bruce maintains that the same temptation can arise from a different cause, even from morally opposite causes, and adds that 'the temptation which proceeds from a holy source may be in a degree fiercer than that which has its origin in sinful lust'.[298] He gives the illustration of two men in business, both tempted to sharp practice. One man thinks of his family and the benefits that would accrue from the added wealth, the other possesses a character which is merely avaricious. The former faces the fiercer temptation. This hardly seems to meet the point. It is true that temptation can arise from different sources, some of which may be better than others, but the fact still remains unshaken that there is a difference of kind between temptations that arise and have no fallen nature to appeal to, and those which, when they arise, have an ally within the nature of man himself. It is artificial in the extreme to say that a perfectly good nature could be the cause of temptation arising from within.

A. B. Bruce then goes on to say: 'It thus appears that sinful dispositions, though certainly making men more liable to fall before the temptation do not increase the painful sense of being tempted but rather diminish it.'[299] It is hard to see any justification for such a statement. It seems perfectly clear that temptation that has an ally within will be all the more fierce and all the more difficult to defeat than temptation which is meeting a nature which has nothing within to which it can appeal. The truth that this statement of Bruce contains is that a fallen nature tends to yield before the full force of temptation is felt. Jesus did not so yield, and therefore He experienced the full power of temptation as no other man has ever done. If this passage in Hebrews is

[297] *L'Épître aux Hébreux*, p. 48, note 5.
[298] *The Humiliation of Christ*, p. 265.   [299] Ibid. p. 266.

interpreted to mean that Christ possessed 'fallen human nature' and that His temptations were not different from ours in kind, then we can accept that they were different in degree in so far as He never yielded, and so He felt the force of temptation as no other man has ever done. Only so far, and no farther, can we agree that it is the good man rather than the bad who is tempted.

Thus, to sum up, this epistle is concerned to stress that Jesus had to possess a real affinity with those whom He came to save. It was necessary that He should share the same humanity, and to be tempted in all points as the rest of mankind. This affirmation of the nature of Christ seems to demand the hypothesis that the Son of God assumed 'fallen human nature'. In so doing He shared in the same humanity as those He came to redeem. Yet because He was without sin, He led the way for the rest of mankind to a new life. No better summary can be found than the words of E. K. A. Riehm commenting on Hebrews 2:

It would be quite contrary to the sense of the writer to say that Christ took human nature as it was before the fall, in its original power and completeness. [Men] are such as need to be sanctified, and their flesh and blood, in which Christ took part likewise, is the human corporeal nature weakened through the curse of sin, receptive of all outward impressions tending to tempt or to cause pain, and liable to death.[300]

(b) The High-priesthood of Christ

This is the central theme of the epistle. In Jesus there is the completion and fulfilment of the priesthood and sacrifice of the Old Testament. Emphasis is laid on the person of the High Priest, on the sacrifice he makes, and on his entrance into the sanctuary on behalf of Israel. The obvious background to all this is the Jewish day of Atonement.

The doctrine of Christ as priest is not confined to this one letter—we have the picture of Christ interceding for us in Paul, we have the Great High-priestly Prayer in John, there is the concept of the priestly task behind Revelation 1[13] and 1 Peter 2[9], and Dr Taylor has shown how important is the sacrificial terminology in the thought of Jesus.[301] But in this epistle the concept occupies a central place, and is a key to the thought of the author.

[300] Der Lehrbegriff des Hebräerbriefes, pp. 314-15. It is worthy of note that at this point Riehm, in a footnote, refers to Gottfried Menken, see pp. 148-51 below.
[301] Jesus and His Sacrifice.

I

Many passages in Hebrews contain this idea, and, taken together, they form an impressive picture of the writer's conception
of the High Priest. To be a High Priest Jesus must have an
affinity with those He represents before God (2^{17-18})—this part
of the writer's thought has been investigated in the last section,
but the conclusions are relevant here—and this affinity is seen in
two specific aspects, suffering and temptation. Because of this
unity with men, He is able to sympathize with them and offer
them succour. He is able to range Himself beside humanity, and,
representing them before God, to make the perfect sacrifice of
Himself. Likeness to His brethren is part of His necessary quali-
fication for being an effectual High Priest. A. S. Peake makes the
point that 'we need more than human nature in our divine high
priest. We need human experience. He must have felt the extreme pressure of our difficulties that he may sympathize with
us.'[302] The Jewish High Priest could sympathize because he
himself was a sinner, but this has the effect of making his ministry
of no abiding value. Jesus could help in a permanent way because
He was 'without sin', yet He shared our nature, experienced
human life, was tempted as we are (4^{14-16}).

The High Priest is called to represent men before God, and
to offer sacrifices that will bring the cleansing from sin (5^1).
It is true that Jesus was not a High Priest of the levitical order,
but was appointed by God a High Priest for ever after the
order of Melchizedek (5^{5-6}); nevertheless He is indeed man's
representative. The passage continues:

In the days of his flesh, Jesus offered up prayers and supplications,
with loud cries and tears, to him who was able to save him from death,
and he was heard for his godly fear. Although he was a Son, he learned
obedience through what he suffered; and being made perfect he became
the source of eternal salvation to all who obey him (5^{7-9}).

'The purpose of these moving words . . . is to show how intensely
Jesus entered into the human lot.'[303] Nowhere in the New Testament is the humanity of Christ set forward in such realistic colours
and with such power as in this epistle.

It is not sufficient, however, for a High Priest to have a close
affinity with men; he must also have contact with God; he must
be able to enter the Holy of Holies, and so to mediate between

302 'Hebrews', *The Century Bible*, pp. 129-30.
303 W. Manson, *The Epistle to the Hebrews*, p. 109.

men and God. This Jesus can do to perfection, for He is not only man; He is also divine. The writer of Hebrews has a profound grasp of the two natures in Christ, because it is demanded by his soteriological teaching. Christ has entered the heavenly places; He has passed beyond the veil into the heavenly sanctuary where He performs an eternal ministry for man (6^{19-20}). His high-priesthood is not one that passes to another, like the levitical priesthood:

"He holds his priesthood permanently. . . . Consequently he is able for all time to save those who draw near to God through him, since he always lives to make intercession for them" (7^{24-5})

The ministration of Christ is eternal in the heavenly sanctuary. Jesus Christ is divine, and so His high-priestly ministry has an eternal quality that the Jewish high-priesthood never possessed.

There is yet another aspect which differentiates Jesus as High Priest from the Jewish levitical High Priests: they needed to offer sacrifices for their own sins, and this meant that their mediation was imperfect; Jesus, who was free from sin, had not to sacrifice for Himself, and this meant that His sacrifice was complete and perfect, and was offered once for all.

For it was fitting that we should have such a high priest, holy, blame-less, unstained, separated from sinners, exalted above the heavens. He has no need, like those high priests, to offer sacrifices daily, first for his own sins and then for those of the people; he did this once for all when he offered up himself (7^{26-7}).

He is a High Priest 'who is seated at the right hand of the throne of the Majesty in heaven' (8^{1}). He 'entered once for all into the Holy Place, taking not the blood of goats and calves but his own blood, thus securing an eternal redemption' (9^{12}).

We thus see Christ as a High Priest who perfects the imperfect system of the levitical sacrifices. He is a true representative of mankind; yet He is Son of God, and therefore the limitations of the merely human High Priests no longer apply. This brings to the fore the two natures in Christ. Jesus is man and as such can represent man before God; He is also divine, and therefore His ministry is perfect, and the old defects of the sacrificial system are no longer there. The sacrifice He makes is once for all, and the Holy of Holies He enters is the heavenly one, of which the earthly is but a copy.

The matter cannot be left at this point of development, for further exposition is needed if the full significance of this thought is to be grasped. Jesus, as High Priest, is to represent, and to mediate on behalf of, sinful humanity, humanity as it is because of the Fall. If Jesus assumed perfect human nature untouched by the Fall, then it would mean that He did not stand side by side with man in his need. It is not sufficient to say that Jesus stood by us in that He was tempted and endured suffering. If Jesus had assumed 'unfallen human nature' there would have been a gulf between Jesus and those whom He represented before God, the gulf created by sin. It is to deal with precisely this situation that He came. It was fallen humanity that He was to represent before God. It would be foolish to say that Jesus stood beside man as a fellow sinner—that would invalidate all His work—but it is true to say that He stood at the side of sinners in that He had assumed a human nature affected by the Fall. By this hypothesis there can be an effective mediation between man in his sinful state and God in His holiness. It seems apparent that, if Jesus assumed perfect human nature, then He could not really represent fallen mankind. To say that sin is not an essential part of humanity, and to assert that Jesus needed to assume only that which was originally in the constitution of man, is to beg the question. Since the Fall, human nature has been so radically affected that it is very different from the original creation of God. A new element has entered in—sin. It was to deal with this new element that the Son of God became incarnate, and to take no account of the one factor in human nature that needed redemption seems to be avoiding the point at issue. If the hypothesis is accepted that Jesus shared 'fallen human nature' with the rest of mankind, then we see how He is able to represent sinful mankind before God, and is fitted to be the High Priest who represents fallen humanity. Yet being Himself free from actual sin, despite His inheritance of 'fallen nature', He is able to approach the throne of God on man's behalf.

Side by side with this fact that Jesus shared 'fallen human nature', must be placed the equally important truth that He was different from the rest of mankind in that He was not a sinner. This cannot be too emphatically stated, and Hebrews is concerned to make the point: 'For it was fitting that we should have such a high priest, holy, blameless, unstained, separated from sinners, exalted above the heavens' (7^{26}). This element is necessary for Jesus to be the perfect High Priest. He is identified with men, in that He has inherited the same human nature as the rest of mankind, yet He is separate from them, in that He has never allowed that inheritance to lead Him into sin. In this He is unique. It is only for this reason that He is able to approach the throne of God without having first to sacrifice for Himself.

In the doctrine of the High-priesthood of Christ there is a paradox, yet a paradox that holds within it the glory of redeeming love and power. Jesus, the High Priest, is one with men whom He represents before God; yet, at the precise point of sin, He is not with them, for He is sinless. The power of the atonement is to be found in this paradox. The paradox is admitted by all orthodox interpreters of the High-priesthood of Christ; it is agreed that Jesus was both human and divine. To affirm that the Son of God took 'fallen human nature' is simply to make the content of the essential paradox more explicit, showing how great was His affinity with man in his need, while still maintaining His sinlessness. This theory, however, is not put forward to make the paradox more startling, but to obviate a difficulty in exposition. It eliminates the gulf between the human nature that Christ came to save and that which He assumed. On the usual exposition this gulf not only exists, but is so deep and wide that it turns the work of Christ as High Priest into a spectacle that men can only watch from a distance; for between Christ their representative and themselves there yawns the great chasm created by the Fall. This hypothesis turns the High-priestly work of Christ into a vital act of mediation which men can accept in faith. To put the matter in other terms: if Jesus assumed perfect human nature, He spanned the gulf between God and man, but that between fallen and unfallen man still needed to be bridged. If, however, Christ shared our 'fallen human nature', then His mediatorial work as High Priest bridges the whole gulf from fallen man in his dire need to God. It is for reasons of soteriology that this hypothesis about the Person of Christ is needed. Behind the emphasis laid by the writer of this epistle on the affinity of Christ with those whom He came to save, behind the doctrine of Christ's High-priesthood, seems to be the doctrine that Christ assumed 'fallen human nature', and in some phrases the doctrine is all but explicit.

SUMMARY OF THE NEW TESTAMENT EVIDENCE

Nothing in the Gospels absolutely demands the hypothesis that Jesus possessed 'fallen human nature', though several parts of the narrative suggest it, and other parts are given a more adequate interpretation if it is accepted. In Paul, the position is very different; here the theory is to be found. It is not defined explicitly, for no quotation puts the matter beyond doubt, but that is what we should expect at this early stage in the development of Christian thought. A study of Paul's thought, however, shows that this idea has its place in his conception of the person of Christ, and is an integral part of his estimate of His saving work. The Epistle to the Hebrews is not quite so definite as Paul, but the obvious interpretation of the thought of this epistle leads to the conclusion that this theory of Christ's possessing 'fallen human nature' is a part of the writer's thought. The other parts of the New Testament have not been examined in this section, because they have nothing relevant to say on the particular point under discussion.

Thus we have found that the New Testament evidence supports the doctrine, though this conclusion is, to some extent, based upon legitimate inference rather than on explicit references.

PART III

The Historical Evidence

HAVING DISCUSSED the New Testament evidence for the theory that Christ assumed 'fallen human nature', we must now turn to an examination of the later historical evidence. This will be considered in two ways. First the various exponents of the doctrine will be reviewed, and an attempt will be made to indicate what principle of unity holds them together. The advocates of the theory are not many; the doctrine has been a neglected one during the centuries of Christian thought, often indeed not merely neglected but rejected. This being so, after the various defenders of the theory have been reviewed, we shall attempt in Part IV to explain why this doctrine, which is rooted in the New Testament, has been given such scant treatment during nineteen centuries of Christian thinking.

GREGORY OF NYSSA

The Cappadocian Fathers—Basil of Caesarea, Gregory of Nazianzus, and Gregory of Nyssa—were firmly Nicene in their theology, and brought about the final defeat of Arianism in the East. The struggle with Arianism, however, is not sufficient background against which to understand their Christological position, especially that of the two Gregorys, because they also faced, in its earliest stages, the doctrine of Apollinarianism. In this connection they were led to emphasize the full humanity of Christ, and their main point was soteriological. The position is put clearly by Nazianzen: 'For that which He has not assumed He has not healed; but that which is united to His Godhead is also saved.'[1] Our main concern, however, is with Gregory of Nyssa, and we now turn to his exposition of the human nature assumed at the Incarnation.

The passages with which we are immediately concerned are to be found in the *Antirrheticus adversus Apollinarem*,[2] at which we

---

[1] *First Epistle to Cledonius*, PG, XXXVII.181. This is sometimes quoted as meaning that Christ assumed 'fallen human nature'. Gregory enunciates a principle which, carried to its logical conclusion, would lead to the doctrine under discussion; nevertheless the phrase is used to show that Christ assumed, not simply a body as Apollinarius said, but also a rational soul.

[2] *PG*, XLV.1123-1269.

129

must look in some detail. The *Apodeixis* of Apollinarius was a vindication of the writer's whole position, the *Antirrheticus* of Nyssen was designed to answer this major work of Apollinarius paragraph by paragraph. C. E. Raven comments: 'When he attempts to pour scorn upon every passage he quotes, the result is a pathetic display of incompetence.'[3] We admit that Apollinarius was a far deeper thinker than his adversaries ever realized, and that the *Antirrheticus* is not one of the greatest of Gregory's writings, yet there is much of value in this work which must not be overlooked; in fact many of the weaknesses are the direct result of Gregory's plan of attempting to reply to Apollinarius section by section.

In this work Gregory emphasizes the human figure of Jesus that is portrayed in the Gospels. Jesus possessed a human will, was subject to human ignorance, grew in knowledge, faced temptations, shrank from death in the Garden, endured pain and sorrow, and on the Cross endured dereliction.[4] Gregory insists that Jesus possessed a full and complete rational soul.[5] All this is in contrast to the teaching of Apollinarius, who denied the rational soul in Christ, and whom Gregory accused of teaching that the body of Jesus came from heaven.[6]

Gregory is so emphatic about the fullness of the humanity of Christ, that in several passages he appears to state that Christ assumed human nature as it was after the Fall. The relevant passages must be quoted in full. He discusses the Pauline text that Jesus was made sin for us, and explains it as meaning 'that He united to Himself the sinful soul of man'[7] (cf. 'But the word of the Apostle testifies that He became sin for us, who clothed Himself in our sinful nature').[8] The second passage is much longer:

For we say that God who is essentially free from matter . . . when the time of the consummation of all things was drawing near . . . with a view to the destruction of sin was blended with human nature, like a Sun as it were dwelling in a murky cave and by his presence dissipating the darkness by means of his light. For though he took our filth upon himself, yet he was not defiled by the pollution; but in his own self he purifies the filth. For, it says, the light shone in the darkness, but the darkness did not overcome it. It is just what happens in the case of

---

[3] *Apollinarianism*, p. 263.   [4] *Antirrheticus*, 11, 14, 24, 32.
[5] Ibid. 11, 17.   [6] In this accusation Gregory seems to have been wrong.
[7] *Antirrheticus*, 23.   [8] *De Vita Moysis*, PG, XLIV.336.

medicine. When curative medicine is brought to bear upon disease, the ailment yields and vanishes, but it is not changed into the art of medicine.[9]

The final passage says:

In His great longsuffering He endured not to repel from communion with Himself our nature fallen though it was as a result of sin, but to receive it to Himself again.[10]

These passages seem to show that Gregory of Nyssa taught that the human nature assumed by the Son of God was 'fallen human nature' which was polluted by the sins of previous generations, and, to use his own term, was 'filth'. J. F. Bethune-Baker accepts this interpretation: 'Gregory of Nyssa, however, does seem to regard the human nature assumed by Christ as fallen (sinful) human nature.'[11]

The matter, however, cannot be decided simply on these passages, for there is another strand in the thought of Gregory which must be examined. There is a strong suggestion in his writings that in Christ the human is transmuted into the divine. Passages are found in the *Antirrheticus* which tend to suggest this transmutation.[12] He speaks of the humanity of Christ as a drop of vinegar in the ocean of the divinity;[13] he regarded the union of the two natures as only becoming complete at the Ascension, when the human nature ceased to retain its own characteristics. He speaks of the human nature as 'transformed into the sea of incorruptibility', 'changed into the divine and immortal nature', no longer possessing 'weight, shape, colour, resistance, softness, limitation of quantity, in a word anything of what could have been seen then, since the mixture with the divine had raised to the divine properties the lowliness of the bodily nature'.[14] In *Antirrheticus* 53, where Nyssen has spoken of Christ taking our sinful nature, he also speaks of the human nature being transmuted in Christ. He emphatically states that the divine nature was in both body and soul, and rendered each sinless.[15] In the 5th and 6th Books against Eunomius his position is virtually Apollinarian; let one significant quotation suffice:

---

[9] *Antirrheticus*, 26.   [10] Ibid. 53.
[11] *An Introduction to the Early History of Christian Doctrine*, p. 251. It is interesting to note that he himself is sympathetic to the position: 'That is to say, the human will, though fallen, is able by union with the divine will to realize its true power. In this conception the solution to the problem may be found' (p. 252).
[12] Op. cit. 25, 42, 53, 55.   [13] Ibid. 42.   [14] Ibid. 42.   [15] Ibid. 54.

We assert that even the body in which He underwent His passion, by being mingled with the divine nature, was made by that commixture to be that which the assuming nature is . . . if anything belonging to our lowly nature was assumed in His dispensation of love for man, we believe that even this was transformed to what is divine and incorruptible.[16]

What is the explanation of this apparent inconsistency in Gregory? J. H. Srawley replies to Bethune-Baker, and, after reviewing the evidence, comes to the conclusion that Gregory does not teach that Christ assumed 'fallen human nature'.[17] He interprets the passages which, at first, suggest this position to mean that human nature, before Christ assumed it, was filth and polluted by sin. Jesus, however, assumed perfect human nature, and thereby redeemed the fallen nature of men. This seems artificial, and looks like an attempt to save Gregory from a doctrine which his own words obviously imply. Yet the other strain in his thought must be accounted for, and the solution is not as difficult as it might at first appear. The teaching of Gregory of Nyssa was that the human nature assumed at the Incarnation was the 'fallen human nature' that was the result of Adam's sin; but, he maintains, it was cleansed at the moment of conception by the Virgin Mary.[18] Thus, as far as the incarnate life was concerned, he stands in agreement with the rest of the Greek theologians, giving inadequate emphasis to the humanity, and having a decidedly Monophysite tendency. Thus in Nyssen we have a very interesting position. He grasps the soteriological significance of the idea of Christ assuming 'fallen human nature', he realizes the significance of such Pauline passages as 'he was made to be sin', and in certain passages he quite unequivocally expresses the doctrine, but he undermines this strong position because he is firmly in the Greek tradition, which laid all the stress on the divine to the detriment of the human. The only way in which he could reconcile these two aspects of his thought was to say that the 'fallen nature' was purified at the moment of conception. This left him free to have the usual emphases of Greek Christology. The fact still remains, however, that this early Greek Father held that the Son of God assumed 'fallen human nature'.

---

[16] *Contra Eunomium*, V.3 (*PG*, XLV.693).
[17] *JTS*, VII.434-41.   [18] *Antirrheticus*, 54.

SPANISH ADOPTIONISM

In the eighth century in Spain there arose a dispute on the Person of Christ known as Spanish Adoptionism. The origins of this heresy are somewhat obscure, but it is generally recognized that, to some extent, it arose through Nestorian influences, and certainly it resembles that earlier heresy in many ways.[19] Adolf Harnack, while admitting Nestorian influence, nevertheless finds the origin of the movement elsewhere. He makes it the legitimate successor to the Augustinian doctrine and to the Calcedonian formulae.[20] R. L. Ottley makes the controversy yet another chapter in the struggle between Antioch and Alexandria.[21]

The controversy eventually involved the majority of the Spanish Church, but it first came to the fore in Elipandus, Archbishop of Toledo, a 'haughty, stubborn, and exceptionally hot-tempered old man'.[22] To put the position succinctly, Elipandus emphatically desired to maintain the unity of the Person of Christ, yet he also vehemently defended the phrase '*Christus Filius Dei adoptivus*'. He maintained that adoption was a convenient and accurate term to express the elevation of the human nature to the dignity of the divine. The result of this, however, was that he tended to teach two sons as well as two natures—one '*genere et natura*', the other '*adoptione et gratia*'. Herein lies the close affinity with Nestorianism.

The controversy broke out about the year A.D. 780 when Elipandus expounded his theory in various letters.[23] Abbot Beatus of Liebana and Bishop Etherius of Osma took up the challenge.[24] Elipandus appealed to Felix of Urgel, who was an acute, able and gifted thinker, and we must look to him as the theologian of the movement. The controversy spread beyond the borders of Spain, and the issue became so widespread that Pope Adrian I was forced to enter the controversy. In 792 a synod met at Ratisbon (Regensburg), where Felix defended Elipandus before Charles the Great, but he was worsted in the debate. Felix went to Rome and signed a recantation of his errors. On his return to Spain, however, he repudiated it and reaffirmed his earlier beliefs. In 794 a Council was held at Frankfurt and again

---

[19] See *ERE*, I.104; J. Tixeront, *History of Dogmas*, III.509-15.
[20] *History of Dogma*, V.278-92.   [21] *The Doctrine of the Incarnation*, p. 472.
[22] J. Tixeront, *History of Dogmas*, III.510.
[23] *PL*, XCVI.859-82.   [24] Ibid. 893-1030.

the Spanish doctrine was condemned. It was from this period that the figure of Alquin of York came to the centre of the controversy, and one is struck with the reasonableness and Christian charity that he showed towards his opponents. In 799 Felix met Alquin at the Synod of Aix-la-Chapelle and after much debate Felix re-entered the fellowship of the Church. Elipandus refused all efforts of reconciliation. Felix, however, does not seem to have recanted completely, for a posthumous treatise revealed that he had not entirely changed his views. The movement soon died out and its influence was not great.

The main thinker of the movement was Felix. He confesses the divinity and eternity of the Logos; the reality of the Incarnation and the hypostatic union with the human nature are also clearly affirmed. The union took place at the moment of conception. There is no idea of a man being exalted on account of his virtue, and Felix has no wish to divide the unity of the Person. What he does maintain, however, is that it is impossible to apply, in any accurate way, the term Son of God to Jesus as a man. In His divine nature He was Son by nature; in His human nature He was Son only by adoption. Thus, even though in one sense Felix denied the Nestorian error of splitting the Person of Christ, in another way he was guilty of the same error. Despite his wish not to divide the person, this is what in fact is done.

We must try to do justice to Felix and see the basic reasons for his position. This was due to a sincere desire to avoid two errors. The first was that of Docetism, for there was a danger of reducing the humanity to the level of a necessary garment to clothe the theophany of the coming of the Son of God. The second was that of Eutychianism and kindred heresies. One of the primary reasons for his position was to prevent any confusion of the natures.[25]

To maintain their position, the Spanish Adoptionists quoted from the Bible[26] and also from the Fathers.[27] There is no doubt that some of the Fathers used 'adopted' as a synonym for 'assumed'.

[25] See Alcuin *Contra Felix*, iii.17. (*PL*, CI.171-2).

[26] The main texts quoted are: Deuteronomy 18[15], Psalm 2[8], 21[23], 44[8], Isaiah 11[2-3]. Mark 13[32], Luke 1[80], 18[19], Matthew 17[5], John 1[14], 10[35-6], 14[28], Philippians 2[7], Hebrews 2[17], 5[5], Romans 8[29], 1 Corinthians 11[3], 1 John 3[2].

[27] Fathers quoted include Ambrose, Hilary, Augustine, Isodore of Seville, and the Mozarabic Liturgy. Hilary, for instance, in *De Trinitate* writes: '*Ita potestatis dignitas non amittitur dum carnis humilitas adoptatur.*' In the Mozarabic Liturgy '*adoptivus homo*' and '*adoptio carnis*' are used.

We now come to the part of the doctrine of Felix that is our immediate concern: what kind of human nature was 'adopted' or 'assumed' by Christ at the Incarnation? Starting from the Pauline phrase in Romans 8[29] which speaks of Christ as the first-born among many brethren, Felix argued that even though Christ had a place of pre-eminence among His brethren, yet in certain aspects He was in the same condition as they were—for instance with reference to election, adoption, and grace. Only in so far as Christ took a human nature such as ours was there the possibility of a real redemption. It is plain that Felix believed that, if the atonement was to be real and valid and not a sham, Christ must have assumed the same human nature that was the common possession of mankind. This now leads to the further question: In what terms did Felix define this humanity? Through his tendency to separate the two natures in Christ and to treat them with a distinctness which almost amounts to isolation, it is natural for him to ascribe to the human nature the full attributes of humanity. He affirms that Jesus was ignorant on certain points, for instance about the date of the last judgement.[28] In His human nature He was not impeccable or good by nature, only 'ex dono gratiae'.[29] His adoption by grace was different from ours only in that it was more perfect.[30] It is true that He was born of a virgin, but He also had to be born again through baptism.[31] The important question has now to be asked: Did Felix believe that the human nature 'adopted' by Christ was human nature as it was because of the Fall? His answer is clear. Christ assumed the body which Zechariah describes as a filthy garment:

and thus was filthy by reason of the transgression arising out of the sinful flesh which He deigned to put on; from which point, wrapped in both the cloth and rags of the human race, men looked on him until such time as a garment of innocence be woven on the shuttle of the Cross.[32]

Felix emphatically rejects the idea that Christ was a sinner: 'He was made throughout like us, the law of sin excepted.'[33]

---

[28] Agobard, *Contra Felix*, V (*PL*, CIV.37-8); Paulinus of Aquileia, *Contra Felix*, III.12 (*PL*, XCIX.444-5).
[29] Paulinus, *Contra Felix*, III.11 (*PL*, XCIX.443-4); Alcuin, *Contra Felix*, II.18, V.10, VII.8 (*PL*, CI.159-60, 198-9, 219ff).
[30] Alcuin, *Lib. adv. haeresin Felix*, xxxvi (*PL*, CI.101).
[31] Alcuin, *Contra Felix*, II.16 (*PL*, CI.157-8).
[32] Ibid. VII.8 (*PL*, CI.219).   [33] Ibid. I.15 (*PL*, CI.139).

R. L. Ottley is of the opinion that in Felix 'these strong expressions relate to the external condition of mortal humanity—its weakness, frailty, and mortality—and are not intended to impute inherited sinfulness to our Lord'.[34] In a footnote Ottley reveals the source of his estimate of Felix, namely J. A. Dorner. It is true that Dorner says that Felix is referring to 'external impurity, mortality and so forth', but he also goes on to say: 'His opinion, however, undoubtedly was not that Christ assumed the nature which Adam had prior to the fall, but in that state to which the fall had reduced it.'[35] This is a logical and accurate estimate of his position. Christ assumed human nature in all its weaknesses, but it was also human nature which had been affected by the Fall.

The great opponent of Felix was Alcuin of York. It must be admitted that on many points Alcuin was right and that Felix was often wrong. Alcuin's accusation that Felix split the person of Christ by his stress on the two natures is fully justified. In reality, however, Alcuin himself does not give any satisfactory answer to the Christological problem, but falls back on the position that it is all essentially mystery.[36] The most serious fault in the position of Alcuin is his tendency to weaken the reality of the human nature of Christ, to make it 'a mere predicate of the higher nature'.[37] It is against this background that we see the strength of Felix. He gives adequate emphasis to the reality of the humanity of Christ. This was vitally needed at this particular time, as can clearly be seen if the decisions of the Council of Frankfurt (794), a council held during the time of the controversy, are examined. Here the humanity is little more than a mere shell; Christ assumed impersonal human nature, and through the union it possessed the attributes of deity. The human limitations seen in the Gospels are placed in the categories of 'economic', 'pedagogic', or 'illusory'.

In Felix we see many theological affirmations that are inadequate, and no modern theologian would wish to defend them, but two points which he makes are of lasting worth: first his stress on the full humanity of Christ, and secondly his affirmation that Christ had to assume the human nature that needed to be redeemed if redemption was to be effective. It was in this latter

---

[34] *The Doctrine of the Incarnation*, pp. 476-7.
[35] *Doctrine of the Person of Christ*, II.1.258.   [36] *Contra Felix*, III.2-3 (*PL*, CI.163-4).
[37] R. L. Ottley, *The Doctrine of the Incarnation*, p. 480. Cf. G. C. Berkouwer, *The Person of Christ*, p. 323.

soteriological context that he propounded the concept that Christ had to assume human nature as it was as a result of the Fall. This link between the assumption of 'fallen nature' and the saving work of Christ is one that was noticed in Gregory of Nyssa, and it will be seen time and time again in this historical study.

For nearly a thousand years the theory that Christ assumed 'fallen human nature' was ignored, and the next advocate of the theory seems to have been Antoinette Bourignon in the seventeenth century. An explanation of this serious neglect is attempted in Part IV.

ANTOINETTE BOURIGNON

Antoinette Bourignon was born at Lille in 1616. Because of a facial deformity she grew up with a liking for solitude, and it was in solitude that she found communion with God. She desired to enter a Carmelite Convent, but was rejected because she did not bring any money with her. This incident helped to fashion her dislike of Churchmen and her suspicion of monastic institutions.

In 1636 her father attempted to force a marriage upon her. She fled, but after a time she was brought back home. She then went to Mons, where she unsuccessfully tried to form an ascetic community. She professed to have received certain revelations: she was to revive the teaching of the Gospel and to gather her spiritual children around her. For the remainder of her very eventful life she was concerned to establish this community, the most important attempt being on the Island of Nordstrand. She was bitterly opposed by the authorities, and during this period she published a number of controversial writings. By 1676 matters came to a crisis; she had to admit the failure of the settlement on Nordstrand. In 1679 she went to Hamburg, and there she was charged with sorcery by a former adherent. To escape arrest she fled and was forced to remain in hiding until her death in 1680 at Franeker in Friesland.[38]

Antoinette Bourignon was opposed to all the organized religious groups of her time, both Roman and Protestant. Her own theological position can be summed up in her Confession of Faith. This was published in 1675 to oppose the 'malicious

---

[38] For a balanced and sympathetic study, see A. R. MacEwen, *Antoinette Bourignon, Quietist.*

reports which some had industriously raised to make the purity of her doctrines and sentiments be suspected'.[39] This statement is vague, and tends to be evasive on the vital issues. Point four in her Confession is concerned with the Person of Christ: 'I believe that Jesus Christ is truly God, and that He is also truly man; and that He is the Saviour and Redeemer of the world.'

Our immediate concern is to show that Antoinette Bourignon accepted the doctrine that Jesus Christ shared our 'fallen human nature'. Her position is most clearly expounded in the Sixth Letter in the Second Part of *Solid Vertue*.[40] The letter is dated 1676. She is replying to a letter in which her position has been questioned. Antoinette Bourignon does not accept its interpretation of her teaching. She asserts the sinlessness of Jesus: 'Jesus Christ never contracted sin',[41] but she also affirms that He assumed 'fallen human nature', but never allowed it to issue in actual sin: 'Jesus Christ *was made sin* itself for Men. By which, nevertheless it is not meant that Jesus Christ did ever Sin, or actually follow the Rebellious Will of his Human Nature, because he never did that, neither in his Glorious Estate nor during his Mortal Life.'[42] She affirms the divinity of Christ, but says of His manhood that He 'made himself Truely Man, of the Corrupted Race of *Adam*, of the same Nature with all Men, come out of his Loyns'.[43]

It was only by entering into our predicament that Jesus Christ could face the full power of temptation; if Jesus had not had in His human nature 'a Will rebelling against the Superior part of his Soul . . . he would have had Nothing to fight against, and by Consequence could not carry the Victory'.[44] It was only because He had assumed this fallen nature that He was able to suffer: 'If Jesus Christ had not been pleased to take on him our Corrupt Will he could not have suffered, because in that Case all his Sufferings would have been insensible to him.'[45] It was only because He has shared our fallen nature that He could in any real sense say to us: 'Be ye followers of me.'[46]

For Antoinette Bourignon this doctrine had a redemptive significance: 'Jesus Christ, according to his Human Nature, is truly our Brother, sprung from our Common Father *Adam*, and he

---

[39] After her death, this Confession was included as a prefix to most of her writings.
[40] Antoinette Bourignon, *An Admirable Treatise of Solid Vertue*, pp. 72-83.
[41] Ibid. p. 77.   [42] Ibid. p. 80.   [43] Ibid. pp. 77-8.
[44] Ibid. p. 80.   [45] Ibid. p. 80.   [46] Ibid. p. 81.

saw in the Bosom of his Father that we were all perishing in the Mire of our Self-will; for which Cause he threw himself into it, that he might draw us out of it, and deliver us from these Dangers.'[47] He was like a faithful brother 'who throws himself into a Sink of Impurities, to deliver his Brother from Thence, whom he seeth perishing without his Help and Assistance'.[48] Antoinette Bourignon asserts that this is no dishonour to Christ; rather it redounds to His credit.

Few would wish to defend the teaching of Antoinette Bourignon in its entirety. Yet is it necessary to go to the opposite extreme of repudiating it all? To charge her, as many of her contemporaries did, with dishonouring Christ, is to misunderstand her true teaching and to pass a rash verdict on her writings. It is true that her Christology tended to be Socinian, but there can be no doubt of her deep reverence for Jesus and her firm adherence to His sinlessness, despite the fact that she also accepts the doctrine that He shared our 'fallen human nature'.

PETER POIRET

This prominent French mystic was born at Metz in 1646. He studied theology in Basel, Hanau, and Heidelberg. In 1672 he was appointed pastor of the French Church at Annweiler; it was here that he became acquainted with the writings of Antoinette Bourignon, and this was the most important influence on his thinking. In 1676 he went to Holland, settled in Amsterdam and there began his literary career. He went to Hamburg, and there had his first meeting with Antoinette Bourignon. From that time he became her loyal disciple. He accompanied her on her wanderings, and when her complete works were published in Amsterdam he prefaced them with a strong defence of her character and mission.

His writing was quite extensive and he made a valuable contribution to the religious and philosophical thought and discussions of his time. He was attached to the mystics and the Quietists, but he was not a Quietist in the full sense of that word. He taught that man's relation to God is not purely passive, but receptive. He refuted Predestination, and attacked Pelagianism because it did not do justice to the inherent sinfulness in man. Socinianism he rejected because it did not ascribe salvation

47 Ibid. p. 79.   48 Ibid. p. 79.

completely to the working of God's grace. Unlike many mystics he insisted on certain dogmatic definitions and constantly appealed to the authority of the Scriptures. He was a man honoured and respected, and he won for mysticism respect and consideration. He died at Rijnsburg in 1719.[49]

Peter Poiret expounds his theory in Volume IV of *The Divine Economy*, which bears as its title, *The Economy of the Restoration of Man after the Incarnation of Christ*. When the exposition of Poiret is carefully examined, we are forcibly struck by the fact that for him this theory that Christ assumed 'fallen human nature' is not a Christological speculation which stands in isolation, but a theory that is propounded because it is an essential part of his soteriological position. Jesus descended into the 'Pit and Torment of Pollution, in which we were plunged' in order that He might draw us out of that pit, if only we would hold fast to Him and faithfully follow Him.[50] Jesus was 'resolved to put Himself into the number and condition of Sinners, to become like one of them', so that He might present to them His saving remedy.[51] Poiret is convinced that if salvation was to be a reality, this was the only way; the plight of man was such that herein lay the only remedy. When Jesus decided to become our deliverer He saw men 'in so wretched a Condition that they could not be relieved but by his cloathing himself in sinful Flesh like theirs, and taking upon him their Weaknesses, Diseases and Curse'.[52] Here was a revelation of divine condescending love in all its fullness. Poiret, however, teaches that ultimately this condescending into 'fallen human nature' is no dishonour to Christ.

It is perfectly evident that any writer who holds that the Son of God, for us men and for our salvation, became man to the extent of assuming 'fallen human nature' must take the humanity of Christ seriously. This is certainly true of Poiret. He takes every opportunity to underline the reality of the Incarnation. There is no trace of Docetism in his Christology; all the full implications of the Incarnation are realized, and the language he uses is strong and forceful: 'He also loaded himself with the Passions of the Soul, and with the strong Bias with which they carry us towards their Objects, and to Excess. . . .'[53] As always when he is making a

<hr/>

[49] I am indebted to the article in the new *Schaff-Herzog Encyclopedia of Religious Knowledge* for the biographical note on Peter Poiret.
[50] *Divine Economy*, IV.15.   [51] Ibid. p. 14.
[52] Ibid. p. 27.   [53] Ibid. p. 34; cf. p. 28.

strong statement of this kind, there is explicitly and definitely made the important proviso 'with this Exception, that he never consented to any of them in a Sinful manner, against Justice and the Love of God'.[54]

When Peter Poiret is examining the conditions into which the Son of God entered by the Incarnation, particularly in connection with His assumption of 'fallen human nature', there is one truth that he underlines: the reality of the temptations. This point was of paramount importance, for without the full reality of His temptations His kinship with us would be destroyed, and without this kinship His saving power would be undermined. It was necessary that He should endure temptations, 'to experience the violence and exuberancy, the bias and tendency of our Corrupt Nature, that he might resist and conquer all these'.[55] He flatly denies that it tells against the honour of Christ to make Him face all temptations, even those that spring from a 'fallen human nature'; rather it is to give Him honour, 'for what Glory would it have been to obtain a Victory without either Engagement or Conquest?'[56] If the perfection of Christ is to have any meaning, it must be a perfection that has been tested and yet has emerged victorious. Poiret is anxious to show that Jesus had to face the full force of temptation, even if it meant His assuming 'fallen human nature'. He is equally anxious to show that for Christ there was a complete conquest and victory; that Christ was personally sinless was axiomatic to Poiret. 'Jesus Christ never sin'd, though he felt the efforts and assaults of Sin, without consenting to them, and therefore without sinning; for it is not the Sensation but the Consent that makes Sin'.[57] Jesus was always victorious; He never sinned.

Poiret tries to support his position regarding the Person and Work of Christ with the backing of Scripture. He is firmly of the opinion that he is not expounding a new and novel doctrine, but that of the Bible. 'The Gospel, the Apostles and the Prophets tell us, That he took our Diseases and Weaknesses: That he took upon him the likeness of sinful Flesh: That he was made Sin and a Curse for us: That he bore our sins in His Body.'[58] Hebrews 2[14, 17, 18] is a key passage in his exposition of the theory now

---

[54] Ibid. pp. 34-5.   [55] Ibid. pp. 14-15.   [56] Ibid. p. 27.   [57] Ibid. p. 18.
[58] p. 16. The passages referred to are: Matthew 8[17], Romans 8[3], 2 Corinthians 5[21], Galatians 3[13], 1 Peter 2[24].

under investigation; so also is the reference in Hebrews to Christ as High Priest. Poiret inserts his own interpretation into the text, which has the effect of making his point crystal clear:

Who, says the same Apostle, in the Days of his flesh, (whilst he liv'd in Flesh, laden with the Inclinations of Corrupt Nature) having with strong cries and tears (because of the mighty assaults which the Corruption or Curse of Nature made upon him) . . .[59]

It is only through this affinity with us combined with His sinlessness, that Christ becomes High Priest in a full and effective way.

The position of Poiret then is quite evident. He expounds the theory that the Son of God became incarnate by assuming 'fallen human nature'; but for him this is not so much a Christological speculation as a foundation stone for the doctrine of the work of Christ. He takes the humanity of Christ seriously: He had to face the same trials and temptations that we have to face. On one point, however, he is absolutely certain and quite explicit: he insists upon the perfect sinlessness of Christ. He fully realized that this position had not been accepted by all, but he is persuaded that his exposition leaves Jesus Christ without spot and blemish, and that it also reveals Him as One full of holiness and love, One who is a Saviour in the fullest and deepest sense of that word.

CHRISTIAN FENDE [60]

The Christological theory that we are investigating is expounded by Fende when he is commenting on Ephesians 2[11-18].[61] Christ has broken down the middle-wall of partition between Jew and Greek, and has made them one through the destruction of the enmity in His flesh, and has reconciled them both in one body through the Cross, so bringing the hostility to an end. This was done when God sent His Son 'in the likeness of sinful flesh and condemned sin in the same flesh'.[62]

Fende then refers to the concept of sacrifice, and affirms that the Old Testament sacrifices were but a foreshadowing of the true sacrifice that was to come. Jesus was that true sacrifice, and He

---

[59] *Divine Economy*, IV.18.

[60] No biographical note on Christian Fende is given, because the author has been unable to discover any details either in England or in Göttingen.

[61] *Des hocherbeichteten Apostels Pauli vortrefflicher Brieff an die Ephesier* (1727). The relevant section bears the title: '*Von desselben Sendung von Gott in der Gleichheit des Fleisches der Sünde.*'

[62] Ibid. p. 32.

entered into the sphere of fallen humanity that stood at enmity with God. Hebrews 2[14] speaks of the children being sharers in flesh and blood; Fende maintains that Jesus became 'sharer in the same way of sinful flesh and blood . . . the very same as that of the children'.[63] The only difference was the mode by which He partook of this human nature; Christ was not born because of the will of sinful man, but by the process of the Virgin Birth. Yet, Fende is emphatic that Christ did enter in reality the sphere of sin, and that in this fact lies the power of redemption. 'The holy, self-emptied Son of God was conceived in her virgin body, and therefore clothed in our poor sinful flesh and blood, and was born of her, so that in all respects He might be tempted after our likeness. . . .'[64] Fende emphasizes the idea of Christ's facing temptation; He had to face temptation in the same sphere as men. His temptations had to be the same as ours, not simply coming from without but also from within, if He were to be one with us, and so to be able to deliver us in the time of temptation. 'If Christ had been tempted merely outwardly, and not inwardly by the fleshly desire, then He would not have been able to oppose and overcome such enmity against God for us.'[65] Unless Christ has Himself overcome these temptations and offered them up on the Cross, we are not truly loosed from them.

Fende then makes the point that if Christ had not assumed this 'fallen human nature', He would not have been able to die; 'he otherwise could not have died without sinful flesh'.[66]

There are two Christological errors against which Fende is most vehement. The first is Docetism, the other Adoptionism. It is while he is discussing the latter that his own position comes to the fore, and again with a strong soteriological emphasis. If Christ had come in a different 'flesh', then our redemption would not have been wrought. We only understand the full meaning of redemption when we understand how God sent His Son 'not only in the outward form, but also in the likeness of sinful flesh'. Christ came as a sin-offering, and sin has been judged and condemned in His flesh. Through obedience, Christ has rescued us from the sting of death, from the devil, and from the power and dominion of darkness. In this passage, Fende expounds the theory under consideration with the utmost clarity, emphasizing its soteriological significance. He also traces the theory back into

[63] Ibid. p. 35.   [64] Ibid. p. 36.   [65] Ibid. p. 44.   [66] Ibid. p. 37.

the New Testament, back to the testimony of the Apostles; it is
to be found in the teaching of Peter, Paul, and John. It is, therefore, not a new theory, but an old one that has been neglected.[67]

Fende is sure that this theory does not in any way detract from
the dignity of Christ. Rather, he asserts, it redounds to His
honour, and makes Him even more worthy of adoration and
praise in that He so emptied Himself. He overcame and cleansed
that which He had assumed and bore it to the Cross, and in His
own body made an offering for sin. Because He was personally
without blemish—and Fende emphasizes the sinlessness of
Christ—He is able to purify our consciences from dead works so
that we can serve the living God (Heb 9[12-14]).

Fende reiterates that without this coming into 'fallen human
nature' there would be no redemption. He puts the matter
pointedly in the form of a question: 'How could God have condemned sin in the flesh of Christ, and how could Christ have
destroyed and taken away the same in His flesh and once for all
died for the same, if He had not had such sin in His flesh?'[68] He
continues that if Christ had not had the enemies before Him
there would not have been a true conquest, rather it would have
been a 'sham-fight'.[69] It was, however, no sham; Christ had to
fight the greatest of all battles, in which He remained obedient
even unto the Cross, and in so doing He died once for all to sin.

Those who expound the view that Christ possessed perfect
human nature believe that they are honouring Christ, because
they are affirming that He could not be tempted by 'such sinful
flesh and blood' as we possess. Fende says the truth is actually the
opposite; unless He had 'overcome such flesh in Himself' He
could not 'truly loose us therefrom'.[70] Without this doctrine
that Christ assumed our sinful nature the whole of man's salvation ceases to be; at the very best it becomes only a 'theoretical
and outward circumcision of sinful humanity'. The victory of
Christ over sin is nothing outward or theoretical, but a fact which
is rooted in the very being of Christ.[71]

Fende ends the section about the Incarnation with a reference
to Jesus as our High Priest, who was holy, guiltless, spotless
(despite the fact that He suffered temptations of sinful flesh) and
in His perfection separate from sinners. He completes the work of

---

[67] *Des hocherbeichteten Apostels Pauli vortrefflicher Brieff an die Ephesier* (1727), pp. 41-2.
[68] Ibid. p. 43.   [69] Ibid. p. 43.   [70] Ibid. p. 45.   [71] Ibid. p. 48.

redemption, an eternal redemption through His blood, and takes His place and sits on the right hand of God, there to make intercession for us. Christ assumes the highest place of honour, but He has reached it through the way of absolute victory, even to the point of having overcome human nature as it is because of the Fall.

Christian Fende is not a theologian whose entire position can be accepted. J. A. Dorner, in a brief but revealing comment, says that he 'denied the Trinity, the deity and satisfaction of Christ, and asserted a sinfulness of His human nature, though he at the same time allowed that it fought therewith, and overcame it'.[72] From the one work of Fende that the present writer has seen, this criticism appears a little sweeping, but even if it is accepted it does not imply that there is not some truth in his position. The truth of his teaching on Christ's assumption of 'fallen human nature' can only be decided in the light of the whole discussion on the subject.

JOHANN KONRAD DIPPEL

Dippel was born at Frankenstein in 1673. At the age of sixteen he went to the University of Giessen, and there showed himself as a champion of orthodoxy and an opponent of Pietism, though there does not seem to have been any great sincerity in his adherence to orthodoxy. His great ambition was to gain a professorship at Giessen. Having no success there he went to Wittenberg, again without gaining his ambition; from there he went to Strasburg. It is from this time that we see the growing influence of Pietism on Dippel. He returned home, and in Giessen he met Gottfried Arnold and became a sincere convert to Pietism.

He now began to champion the Pietist cause and attacked the orthodox position. He entered into the combat with vigour and in a brief space of time published a considerable number of polemical writings. His views brought him into severe trouble; he was persecuted by the clergy, and his life was threatened by the mob. In 1702 the Consistory decreed that he should not publish any more theological writings.

In 1704 he went to Berlin, but he was driven from Berlin because of his Pietist faith, and he fled to Köstritz, which had become a refuge for Pietists. From there he went to Holland and practised medicine at Leyden. He still continued to express

---

[72] *Doctrine of the Person of Christ*, II.II.376.

his theological opinions. In 1714 he removed to Schleswig-Holstein, but in 1719 he made an unfortunate intrusion into politics and was condemned to perpetual imprisonment. He was nevertheless kept only in partial confinement. In 1726 he went to Sweden where he again plunged into politics. Finally he became physician to King Frederick I. It was while in this position that he published his religious views in their final and most complete form in *Vera Demonstratio Evangelica* (Frankfurt, 1729). This was published under his pseudonym of Democritus Christianus. In Sweden his views brought about the hostility of the clergy and he had to leave. He returned to Germany to live near Goslar, but even though he refrained from religious controversy the clergy forced him to flee. The final years of his life were spent in controversy with Zinzendorf on the nature of the Atonement. He died in 1734.[73]

In *Vera Demonstratio Evangelica*, Dippel expounds the theory that Christ assumed human nature as it was after the fall of Adam. He maintains that Jesus took upon Himself our flesh and blood 'out of the weakened mass of fallen men',[74] and therefore was not as the first Adam before the Fall. He claims that this position is neither absurd nor irreligious; he adopts it because he is trying to show in what way Jesus came to bear and take away sin, and so to free human nature and to make it holy. In order to do these things, Jesus had to assume 'fallen human nature', that He might become like His brethren: 'All that is common to all men . . . is to be found also in Christ; yea, even more frailty than in Adam himself, for this humanity was taken from the weakened mass of the human race. . . .'[75] In one aspect He was different from His brethren: He did not sin. In Dippel there are again held together the two factors that Jesus assumed 'fallen human nature' and that He was without sin. For this writer both truths were necessary if Jesus was to be a Saviour. They were not incompatible—one statement refers to the nature He assumed, while the other is a judgement on the life He actually lived, a life lived to perfection despite the inheritance of 'fallen nature'.

Dippel says that, in the act of the Incarnation, the Son of God was born of the Virgin through the power of the Holy Spirit, but

---

[73] In this biographical note the author is greatly indebted to the article in the new *Schaff-Herzog Encyclopedia of Religious Knowledge*.

[74] Op. cit. p. 22; cf. p. 162.   [75] Ibid. pp. 275-6.

this does not in any way weaken the true humanity of Jesus. He points out that, if He is to possess a true humanity, Jesus 'must experience and overcome all temptations'.[76] If He is to be the Second Adam, the one who redeems mankind who have fallen through the first Adam, if He is to be the firstborn among many brethren, 'He must, therefore, also suffer and experience more than anyone before or after Him'.[77] It is through this that He shows His brethren that it is possible to overcome all the temptations of the devil, to overcome the world, and to overcome the 'fallen nature', and therefore to emerge out of the Fall, to come through death to life, and to be firmly planted in holiness. The reality of Christ's temptations is a vital part of Dippel's Christology.[78]

Being charged with denying the sinlessness of Christ, Dippel complains that he has been misunderstood, and that his opponents are attributing to him an idea which has never entered his mind, and a doctrine which he himself detests. He is absolutely definite about the sinlessness of Christ: 'I recognize and admit that Christ, the Holy One, set apart from sinners, had no sin nor did He commit any sin.'[79] But he is equally emphatic that the temptations of Jesus had to be real if His saving work was not to be reduced to a mere appearance. He attacks the orthodoxy of his time in that it tended to make the humanity of Christ, because of its union with the divine, far less than truly human, and thus deny the power of the incarnate Son of God to suffer temptation. Dippel asserts that this is a plain denial of Scripture. If Christ's life has been a mere 'Shadow-Fight' against temptation, then the invitation for men to follow Him as their example is sheer mockery. Unless Christ has faced what all men have to face, then His oneness with mankind, His becoming our brother, is false. It is foolish to draw the picture of a Saviour who fought evil and sin without having experienced its attractiveness and seductive power, and who chose and loved the highest good simply because it was not possible for him to do otherwise.[80] Yet, despite the fact that the possibility of sinning and falling was a real possibility, Jesus was in fact sinless: 'All the time He remained true to Himself. . . . He was never overcome or beaten by any temptations.'[81]

The point that Dippel continually makes is that this is no mere

---

[76] Ibid. p. 260. [77] Ibid. p. 260 [78] See ibid. pp. 162, 275.
[79] Ibid. p. 255. [80] See ibid. p. 257. [81] Ibid. pp. 162-3.

Christological speculation, but essential to an understanding of the saving work of Christ. It is because Christ took upon Himself 'fallen human nature' that there is an effective salvation for sinful men.[82] He is concerned to affirm this idea of Jesus as the one through whom men are led from the realms of sin to a newness of life. The Son of God became man, lived as a man among men, teaching them the living way so that they might rise again out of their fallen state. Not only did He teach, but even more He opened for them a way, and walked the way before them; He was the 'Pioneer' of the new redeemed humanity.

This redemption was wrought by Christ, and it was through His death that His saving power was really made manifest. It was on the Cross that Jesus redeemed 'fallen human nature' and opened up for men a way to newness of life. The method by which this was accomplished was that Jesus had 'offered up our sin in His body, and this death of the body of sin is pleasing to God and alone a sacrifice which is well pleasing to Him'.[83] Jesus thus died for us, that we might die with Him and be raised with Him to newness of life. Dippel states emphatically that the redemption of human nature took place first in the person of Jesus; it is not a question of imputation. This point cannot be made too forcibly: 'He bore and purged in His own flesh the sin of the world. . . . He did not bear and purge them by imputation, but threw them out, and actually fought with them. . . .'[84] The Son of God assumed human nature as it was through the Fall of Adam, and yet He lived a perfect life, and through His Cross wrought the redemption of mankind. To Dippel this does not detract from the holiness and righteousness of Christ; 'rather it increases these and makes them more glorious'.[85]

GOTTFRIED MENKEN[86]

Gottfried Menken was born in Bremen in 1768. He was a youth of rich gifts, and his home environment was such as would develop his Christian faith. In 1788 he went to the university of Jena to study, and his natural choice was theology. He was averse to the flat rationalism that was current in the university, and showed his firm adherence to the Bible as the Word of God. He believed in the

---

[82] See ibid. pp. 35-6.   [83] Ibid. pp. 273-4.   [84] Ibid. p. 261.   [85] Ibid. p. 296.
[86] For a recent study of the significance of Menken, see K. Barth, *Die protestantische Theologie im 19 Jahrhundert*, pp. 469-83.

revelation of God in history, and the middle point of this revelation was Jesus Christ. Menken moved to Duisburg in 1790, where he came into close contact with several Pietist families. The most formative influence upon him, however, was not Pietism, but a kind of evangelical Christianity which came mainly through his friendship with F. A. Hasenkamp and Dr Collenbusch; this evangelicalism was always strongly biblical.

Menken had a distinguished ministry and his influence as a preacher was great. Many of his writings are published sermons. Menken's strength lies in his ability as a biblical expositor. His ability and knowledge was rewarded when in 1828 he was awarded the degree of D. Theol. He died in 1831.

Menken expresses his belief about the Person and Work of Christ in a book of sermons based on certain chapters in the Epistle to the Hebrews.[87] These sermons make it crystal clear, even to the most casual reader, that Menken holds Christ in the very highest esteem. He has no doubt about His full divinity, and he underlines, not simply the dignity of His character, but also the finality of His work.[88] Menken ascribes to Jesus the central place in all his thinking, and he finds in Him the fullness of salvation.

In the sermon which is based on the text Hebrews 9[13-14] he expounds the theory that Christ assumed 'fallen human nature'.[89] He speaks of the full humanity of Jesus, and of His kinship with those He came to save. Menken is most concerned to expound the meaning of this consubstantiality of Christ's human nature with ours, because he is convinced that the focus of the Christian faith has been so concentrated on the stressing of the full divinity of Christ that the understanding of His humanity has thereby suffered.[90]

Menken maintains that the idea of sacrifice 'is the heart and life' of religion.[91] He asserts that this age-old idea of sacrifice—sacrifice through which man is reconciled to God—is fulfilled in Jesus. For this reconciliation to take place Jesus had to be identified with the sinners who needed to be redeemed through His sacrifice. He quotes Philippians 2[5-7] and Galatians 4[4] and

[87] *Homilien über das neunte und zehnte Capitel des Briefes an die Hebräer* (1831).
[88] See ibid. pp. 15-16, 85, 91-2.
[89] The theory is not confined to this one sermon (see also ibid. pp. 111, 145, 166-7, 177, 188, 192, 207-8), but this is the one which contains the fullest and most detailed exposition of his thinking upon the subject.
[90] Ibid. p. 94.   [91] Ibid.

emphasizes that these passages mean that Christ possessed a full human nature; the strong expressions they contain are used to show that the Son of Mary, even though He was not born in the usual physical way but through the working of the power of God, 'nevertheless from this His mother . . . received a true and full human nature, as all those born of women . . .'.[92] This, however, does not express the whole truth of the situation, since it still does not express the full identity of Jesus with those He came to save, and it is his next point which is vital for our present investigation.

God has sent His Son in the form of sinful flesh. The Son of God took, therefore, when He came into the world, not a human nature as this nature was when it came out of the hand of God before the Fall, before it had become in Adam sinful and mortal . . . on the contrary, [He took] such a human nature as it was after the Fall in Adam, and is in all his descendents.[93]

Menken's one desire is to show that it is precisely this kind of human nature that needed to be assumed at the Incarnation if the salvation of men was to be accomplished, and that it was a part of the true Incarnation of the Son of God into the human race that He came to redeem. He makes the point that the possibility of sin and death belongs to natural earthly humanity, and goes on to say that one who does not possess these features is not a true Son of Adam or a true Son of Man.[94]

At this point in the sermon, he appeals to 1 Peter 2[24]: 'He himself bore our sins in his body on the tree.' He asks what this means, and states that it implies that Christ possessed 'fallen human nature'—'He, as all the children of Adam, was in the form of sinful flesh'.[95] It is evident that as far as Menken is concerned this is not a theological hair-splitting, but a real point that involves in it the all-important question of our salvation. It is an attempt to explain the saving power of the Cross. The Son of God who took 'fallen human nature'—yet, despite its assumption, was Himself sinless—has, through His Cross, made full atonement for sin.

He kept Himself aloof from all real sin. . . . what is more, He so overcame, so denied and crucified the sinfulness of human nature . . . that at

---

[92] *Homilien über das neunte und zehnte Capitel des Briefes an die Hebräer* (1831), p. 102.
[93] Ibid.   [94] Ibid. p. 103.   [95] Ibid. p. 104.

last, by the Cry of the Cross, 'It is finished', it was completely, entirely, and for ever, destroyed.[96]

The full soteriological significance of this Christological position now becomes evident. 'His Cross could become the death sign of sin, the victory sign of life for men. He offered up the form of sinful flesh in His own person. . . . He sacrificed and destroyed in His own person the sinfulness of human nature, made this nature sinless in His own person. . . .'[97] Christ is the Second Adam who came into the situation created by the first Adam and, through His power, 'made human nature sinless'.[98]

There is one final stage that Menken needs to take to complete his exposition, and this is to explain how the victory that has been won in the person of Jesus Christ is made available for men and women. How does this work of Christ become available for us? Menken's answer is, 'through faith'.

Here in this sermon we have the complete position of Gottfried Menken with reference to this Christological point. It can be summarized briefly thus: he accepts without reservation the full divinity of Christ, and is most careful to underline the sinlessness of our Lord. Side by side with this affirmation he emphasizes the full humanity of Christ, and it is at this point that he maintains that Jesus Christ possessed the kind of human nature that was the result of Adam's Fall. He affirms that in His own life Jesus purified and presented this fallen nature to God. This position is held in such a way that the sinlessness of Jesus is not impaired; despite the fallen nature that He assumed, Christ was sinless and perfect. Through our birth into the race of Adam we are possessors of this fallen inheritance, and unlike Christ, we do become sinners; but through faith in, and union with Christ, we who are part of fallen humanity, we who have added our own personal sin to the nature that we have inherited, are cleansed and made new.

EDWARD IRVING

Edward Irving was born in Annan, Dumfriesshire, in 1792. He was brought up 'in the religious atmosphere and habits of Scotland; family religion, church-going, sabbath observance'.[99] He entered Edinburgh University and graduated M.A. in 1809.

---

[96] Ibid. p. 105.   [97] Ibid.   [98] Ibid. p. 106.
[99] P. E. Shaw, *The Catholic Apostolic Church Sometime Called Irvingite*, p. 8.

In 1815 he was licensed to preach by the presbytery of Kirkcaldy, and four years later became assistant to Dr Chalmers in Glasgow. Here he worked with great devotion as a parish minister, especially among the poor, to whom he showed a deep sympathy.

The turning point in his life came when he was called to the Caledonian Church, London, in 1822. Here his preaching gained him a great reputation and soon he attracted a vast congregation of fashionable people. His popularity, however, was comparatively shortlived. He became more and more interested in the subjects of prophecy and apocalyptic, and it was this excessive pre-occupation with apocalyptic that was his greatest weakness and led to his decline.

In the year 1828 there appeared the charge of heresy. This was first brought by a certain Rev. H. Cole, 'a skulking spy of orthodoxy',[100] and 'an obscure clerical busybody'.[101] The charge was brought against Irving because of the views that he was expounding on the Person of Christ.[102] These views can be seen in a series of sermons published in 1828 (they appear in Volume V of his collected works).[103] In 1830 he published *The Orthodox and Catholic Doctrine of Our Lord's Human Nature*[104] to state plainly his opinions, and in 1831 *Christ's Holiness in Flesh*[105] to refute the charge that he was denying the sinlessness of Christ.

The charges continued, and in 1833 he was deposed by the Presbytery of Annan, by which he had been ordained.[106] After his deposition his life swiftly and tragically came to a close; he died in December 1834.

Even though the Christological position of Irving was first expressed in the ordinary course of preaching, it soon became an issue, a subject of heated debate and controversy. Irving's position can be put in his own words:

There was united in Jesus Christ, the Godhead, in the person of the son, and the manhood, in its fallen state; and that they subsisted together in one person, in such wise as that He was wholly without sin, holy and blameless in the sight of God.[107]

---

[100] A. L. Drummond, *Edward Irving and His Circle*, p. 112.
[101] H. C. Whitley, *Blinded Eagle*, p. 23.
[102] For an excellent summary of the early stages of the controversy see Irving's preface to *Christ's Holiness in Flesh*.
[103] Cited in the rest of this section as *CW*.   [104] Cited as *OD*.   [105] Cited as *CH*.
[106] It is to be questioned whether Irving was guilty of the charges brought against him. See A. L. Drummond, *Edward Irving and His Circle*, p. 219.
[107] *CW*, V.157.

For Irving this was not a side issue, nor merely an interesting speculation; it was of central importance: 'To understand how the Son of God took sinful flesh, and yet was sinless, is the alpha and omega, the beginning and the end of orthodox theology.'[108] This position was given such centrality in his thought because the saving power of Christ rested upon it; man's salvation was at stake. As with the other writers we are considering in this historical section, so it is with Irving; soteriology is dominant. Jesus assumed 'fallen human nature' and redeemed it. In one sense the atonement was made in Christ as an individual, but because He was not simply an individual but also a representative, the atonement was for all.

Irving is concerned with the kind of human nature that was assumed by the Son of God, and is insistent on its being consubstantial with ours. This point cannot be overstressed; it is a constant theme of his Christological writing. The Son of God entered into humanity as it was after the sin of Adam. 'Christ became man, and submitted Himself to the very condition of a sinner. He became sin for us who knew no sin . . . in order to give sin and Satan, death and the grave, and hell, all advantages against Him, and conquer them.'[109] He took our nature, faced our temptation, yet overcame and was victorious.

This position of Irving's gave rise to serious offence and led to the charge of heresy. Irving defended his position, and in examining his defence we shall see his adherence to orthodoxy. The main charge levelled against him was that he had relinquished his belief in the sinlessness of Christ. No charge could have been more groundless, for he was always at great pains to show that he firmly held this concept. He puts the matter clearly and unequivocally: 'What he took to work upon was sinful, sinful flesh and blood; what he wrought it into was sinless.'[110] His book *Christ's Holiness in Flesh*, in its entirety, is a defence of the sinlessness of Christ. The opening sentence sets the whole tone and theme of the book: 'If anyone shall clearly, without any apparent contradiction, assert sin to have been in Christ, either sin original or actual, either in his flesh or in his soul, he is to be assumed at once guilty of the most vital heresy.'[111] Jesus hated sin with all the hatred of God. In Him was all perfection.[112] In this book, in which he is primarily concerned to maintain the sinlessness and

[108] *OD*, p. 18. [109] *CW*, V.28. [110] *OD*, p. 66. [111] *CH*, p. 1. [112] See ibid. p. 17.

L

holiness of Christ, he still affirms the doctrine that Christ assumed 'fallen human nature', but he holds these two positions in harmony; to him they were not a discord. 'To this flesh we have applied the word "sinful" or "of sin", in order to express the state out of which God took it; the words "sinless and holy", to express the state into which God brought it, and in which he continually upheld it holy, yea most holy.'[113] Irving states that he would prefer to have shunned the word 'sinful', but had to use it if his meaning was to be clear. He is continually at pains to show, however, that the term only applies to the nature as assumed, and not to the life of Christ.[114]

Irving is concerned not simply to state his position but also to substantiate it. He constantly refers to the Bible, finding there full support for his position.[115] He also calls into court as evidence the accepted Creeds of the Church.[116] It would be accurate to say, however, that Irving shows that the Creeds are not incompatible with his position; rather than that, they support it. He believes the reason that so many reject this idea is that they confuse Nature and Person; the centre of personality in Jesus is the Second Person of the Trinity, but He assumed 'fallen human nature'. What is said, therefore, does not apply to the central personality of Jesus Christ, which was perfect and sinless, but rather applies to the nature of the humanity that He assumed. This Christological position was, he maintained, in harmony with the Scriptures and the Creeds of the Church.

To strengthen his position even more, Irving shows how various other aspects of Christian doctrine are closely related to this Christological theory.[117] Its relevance is particularly marked with reference to the work of Christ, for if 'fallen human nature' is not assumed, then 'it is not stooped into; it is not lifted up; it is not redeemed; it is not regenerated; it is not raised from the dead; it is not seated on the throne of God'.[118]

As a final way in which he can reveal the potency of his argument, Irving gives in several places a list of what he believes is lost if this theory is not accepted. It can be briefly summarized. To

---

[113] See ibid. pp. 36-7.   [114] ibid. p. 37.

[115] The most important texts cited are: Hebrews $2^{11, 14, 16-17}$, 2 Corinthians 5^{21}, Galatians 3^{13}, 4^4, Romans, 8^3, 1 Peter 2^{22}.

[116] Reference is made to the Nicene Creed, the Apostles' Creed, and the Athanasian Creed, also to the Westminster Confession.

[117] See *OD*, Part IV.   [118] Ibid. p. 114; cf. p. 96.

deny it means that Christ was not liable to all temptations by sin, it leads to a virtual denial of His full humanity, and it removes from Him His true sympathy with our sufferings and temptations. It means that His power as Mediator and Intercessor is broken, for if He did not assume our 'fallen nature', He 'never knew the fellowship of our temptations', therefore, 'how can human nature, in its fallen state, go out with confidence and affection, and without fear, to repose herself upon His intercession and Mediation'.[119] This leads to Irving's main point: to refuse to accept this position is to undermine the atonement. If Christ had assumed unfallen human nature, 'that would have been like going to seek and destroy an enemy there, where no enemy was, avoiding the citadel which he held, and making fashion of seeking him in the plain which he held not'.[120] Irving puts the position forcibly: if Christ did not assume 'fallen human nature', it means that His holiness is not a source of holiness for us, because His holiness is of a different quality from that which is required of us. He continues that, if Christ could not be holy in terms of fallen humanity, then holiness for us is impossible. 'The foundation stone, therefore, of all holiness is, that Christ came in our flesh, under the very same conditions in which we have it, and was all holy notwithstanding',[121] or, to quote the final sentence of *Christ's Holiness in Flesh* (and the capitals are Irving's), 'THE HOLINESS OF CHRIST IN OUR FLESH IS THE FORM, THE FOUNTAIN-HEAD, AND ASSURANCE TO US, OF HOLINESS IN FLESH'.[122]

In many ways Irving is a tragic figure, a man of great abilities and also of great weaknesses. He knew popularity, yet also the ignominy of being excommunicated from his mother-Church. When we examine his writings, however, and when we allow for his rather extravagant style, we find a clarity of thought, a depth of understanding, and often powerful exposition and persuasive argument. Many of his points of exposition must carry our assent.

ERSKINE OF LINLATHEN

Thomas Erskine was born in 1788 and was brought up by his maternal grandmother, Mrs Graham of Airth Castle, a strict episcopalian and a strong Jacobite. He was educated at Edinburgh University, and in 1810 was admitted as a member of the Faculty of Advocates. On the death of his brother, Thomas

---

[119] *CW*, V.226.   [120] *OD*, p. 12.   [121] *CH*, p. 73.   [122] Ibid. p. 122.

Erskine succeeded him to the estate of Linlathen. Retiring from the Bar, he devoted himself to the study of theology. His influence was quiet and unspectacular; yet, through his many personal contacts and through his writings, it was nevertheless powerful.

It is interesting to note that there is a connection between Erskine and Irving, not simply through common friends such as F. D. Maurice and Thomas Carlyle, but also because Erskine took a keen interest in the manifestations produced by Irving's preaching. At first he affirmed the genuine character of the gift of tongues, but later he changed his opinion. He died in 1870.

Erskine propounds the Christological view that is our immediate concern in two writings: *The Brazen Serpent* (1831)[123] and *The Doctrine of Election* (1837).[124]

The central point of Erskine's position is the concept of Adam and Jesus as the two heads of the human race; Adam as the head of fallen humanity, Jesus as the head of a new and redeemed humanity. The idea of solidarity is stressed; Adam and Jesus are not simply individuals, but in a deep sense representatives of mankind. He makes this parallelism between Christ and Adam consist of three main features. In the first place, both the Fall and the Restoration have been wrought through one man, Adam and Jesus respectively. In the second place, the actions of both affect the whole race. Finally, both operate through the infusion of a principle into humanity.[125] Where this last point is concerned, however, Erskine is careful to define his meaning. All men, by the very fact of birth, are incorporated into Adam and become partakers of the evil infusion, but it is only those who identify themselves with Christ through a conscious act of choice that receive His infusion of newness of life.

It was to deal with the serious situation that had arisen because of the Fall of Adam that Jesus took our 'fallen human nature' and became the Second Adam. It is again of vital importance to recognize that this Christological position is really held because of its importance for the work of Christ. Erskine expounds a representative theory of the Atonement. Christ was the Second Adam, the head of a new humanity, and 'that which the divine nature did to the human nature in Christ, was done to him in character of head and representative of the human nature; and, therefore, it is to be considered as indicating the mind of God

---

[123] Cited as *BS*.   [124] Cited as *Election*.   [125] *Election*, pp. 326-7.

to every man'.[126] Jesus Christ was our representative, and His death on the Cross and the Resurrection were the climax of His work on our behalf; 'He was indeed the head of every man, and therefore when he died, he died for every man'.[127] Jesus rose from the dead as the head of humanity, and thus declared that the barrier that kept man from fellowship with God was removed.[128]

It has already become evident in what has been said so far that to be Second Adam, to be our Representative, the Son of God had to assume our nature; this is fundamental if the representative character of the work of Jesus is to be maintained. Erskine underlines this again and again, and it is in this connection that he expresses the view that the Son of God assumed 'fallen human nature'. He turns to the Epistle to the Hebrews to find the main scriptural basis for his position. Jesus was 'truly partaker of that same flesh and blood of which the children were partakers, and on which the righteous sentence of condemnation lay, he was the real Head and not the mere substitute of the sinful race'.[129] If Christ had not truly entered into our fallen nature, 'he could not have tasted death for every man, and his resurrection could not necessarily have involved that of every other man'.[130] That He had entered into sinful humanity, humanity as it was after the Fall, is evident, and the following quotations put the position beyond any doubt:

Having become partaker of that ONE BLOOD which had sinned against God, he became in consequence excluded as a man from the presence of his Father's glory, and subject to death. . . . The Holy One of God become flesh could not stand in the pure presence of God, because the flesh was tainted.[131]

We have seen also that every suffering which he thus endured as the head contained in it an acting of holy love, and an acting of hatred against sin,—A PROTEST AGAINST SIN, the sin of that flesh which was HIS OWN, and of which he was the head.[132]

It was by this that He was able to come to grips with the power of sin and become victorious. In the person of Jesus 'it was Fallen Nature; a nature which had fallen by sin, and which, in consequence of this, lay under condemnation. He came into it as

---

[126] *BS*, pp. 36-7.   [127] Ibid. p. 42; cf. p. 77.   [128] See ibid. p. 57.
[129] *Election*, pp. 234-5.   [130] *BS*, pp. 43-4.
[131] Ibid. p. 72. The capitals in this and the following quotations are Erskine's own.
[132] Ibid. p. 97.

a new head, that he might take it out of the fall, and redeem it from sin, and lift it up to God'.[133] Again we see how strong is the soteriological setting of the theory. Jesus, by assuming this fallen nature, was able to come to grips with evil and to win the victory; 'Jesus put off the fallen flesh of the first Adam . . . and having done so, he destroyed the destroyer, and led captivity captive.'[134] Erskine attaches a very interesting footnote:

This appears to be the meaning of the word in Colossians 2[15]. The fallen flesh has been taken possession of by the power and principalities of evil: it is the armour in which they have made themselves strong; and, therefore, when Jesus overcame them, he put off that flesh, the armour in which they had entrenched themselves.[135]

Perhaps the reading of a passage taken out of context might give the impression that Erskine had jeopardized the sinlessness of Christ, but that would be a hasty and completely unwarranted conclusion. Erskine was not willing to allow the sinlessness of Christ to be abandoned, or even to be challenged or threatened. The sinlessness of His life was just as much a cardinal point in Erskine's thinking as the position that we have been illustrating. To understand how the sinlessness of Christ is maintained alongside the affirmation of His unity with 'fallen humanity', we must note carefully a distinction that is recognized by Erskine. He affirms that there is an important distinction between human nature itself and the individual personalities that partake of it. It is the medium through which their lives are lived and 'they are responsible for the use which they make of it, but they are not responsible for the condition in which they find it'.[136] To grasp the affirmation of Christ's sinlessness it is essential to understand this point. It was only by assuming condemned flesh that He could meet the condemnation, could overcome the powers of sin, death, and the devil. Despite the fact that He assumed this nature—for which He was not held responsible—He lived a perfect life, and was sinless in God's sight. He was 'one who partook of the fallen nature, and felt all our sins as if they had been his own, and yet had not personally partaken of them'.[137] It is true that He partook of the suffering and condemnation that was the due of fallen humanity, but 'not indeed on account of any flaw in his spotless holiness, but as a participator of that flesh

[133] *BS*, 37-8.   [134] Ibid. p. 132.   [135] Ibid. pp. 132-3.
[136] *Election*, p. 273.   [137] *BS*, p. 81.

which lay under sentence'.[138] Jesus assumed the same kind of nature that all fallen men possess, but in no sense could He be called a sinner, for just as He was without sin in a sinful world, 'so he was without sin in a sinful nature'.[139] This was possible because at every stage of His life His prayer was 'not my will, but thine be done'. By this continual living by the spirit rather than by the flesh, He condemned sin in the flesh.[140]

In Erskine of Linlathen the Christological theory that we are discussing is clear, and is expounded with balance, precision, and moderation. The general impression left by his writing is that he has a sound grasp of the work of Christ, and that it is for the sake of soteriology that this theory has been so strongly advocated. He does not for one instant desire to undermine either the divinity of Christ or His perfect sinlessness, but he realizes that the incarnate Son of God must be fully identified with those He came to save. The result is a finely integrated structure of thought, Christology and soteriology making a unified whole.

HERMANN FRIEDRICH KOHLBRÜGGE

Hermann Friedrich Kohlbrügge was born at Amsterdam in 1803 and was brought up as a Lutheran. He became assistant preacher to the Lutheran congregation in Amsterdam in 1827. It was not long, however, before he came to realize that there was little of the true spirit of Luther in the Dutch Lutheran Church of his day. His sermons on the radical corruption of human nature were unacceptable to his colleagues, who were of a more rationalistic outlook. As a result of this division of opinion he was deposed after only six months as assistant. He lived in retirement for several years.

He began to read and study the history and doctrine of the Reformed Church, and in 1830 sought to join it. The Reformed Church, however, fearing that its peace might be disturbed, refused to admit him. In 1833 he accepted a call to Elberfeld. Here he made a deep impression with his energetic personality and his profound and earnest sermons. The Prussian Government forbad him the pulpit; he was considered as a serious obstacle to the Government's plans for uniting the Lutheran and Reformed Churches.

[138] Ibid. pp. 279-80.   [139] *Election*, p. 368.   [140] See ibid. p. 368

Kohlbrügge lived in retirement in Utrecht for a number of years. It was during this period (1834-44) that the act of union created trouble in the Rhine region, especially among the members of the Reformed Church. In Elberfeld the Reformed Church divided, and in 1847 the dissenters called Kohlbrügge to be their pastor. He remained there until his death in 1875.

His main literary work consists of published sermons. Kohlbrügge made little impact upon the theological thought of his time, and it is only recently that his name has begun to appear in theological discussion.[141] His theology was a reaction from the *Aufklärung*; he endeavoured to reaffirm the essential principles of the Reformation. In this reaction he stood alone, at least as far as theological thought in Germany was concerned. He accepted the Reformed theology in its extreme form. He affirmed that the will was not free, accepted the doctrine of double predestination, defined justification in forensic terms, and held that justification was by grace alone. He was, however, too extreme in his thinking. He sought to make a comprehensive system and often went to extremes. Where Calvin saw difficulties and problems Kohlbrügge was dogmatic in his assertions.

Kohlbrügge writes movingly of the centrality of Jesus and of the significance of His work.[142] He has the highest estimate of Jesus; His name is indeed above every name. No one has seen God, but in Christ we see God.[143] No longer do men need to speculate over the nature and purposes of the invisible God, for God has shown Himself to us in Christ. For Kohlbrügge this revelation is seen in its fullness in redemption, a redemption wrought through the Son of God who became incarnate for us. Christ is the Mediator between God and men. Kohlbrügge affirms the full divinity of Christ, for the Son of God is the eternal, uncreated Word of God: 'The Word, in which He gave Himself utterance, was therefore nothing else than what He Himself was, it was God.'[144]

The Word became flesh. Kohlbrügge claims that it is essential to understand the true meaning of this phrase. He points out that

---

[141] There is a chapter devoted to Kohlbrügge in Karl Barth, *Die Protestantische Kirche im 19 Jahrhundert* (1952), pp. 578ff. The most important contribution to the subject is *Die Theologie Kohlbrügges*, by Theodor Stiasny (published in 1935). The present author has not been able to see all the published works of Kohlbrügge and he is greatly indebted to the work of Stiasny.
[142] See *Licht und Recht (Predigten)*, p. 52.
[143] See *Zwanzig Predigten im Jahre 1846 gehalten* (1857), p. 326.   [144] Ibid. p. 130.

the passage does not simply say that the Word became man, but that the Word became flesh. If the Son of God had simply become man, that is had assumed human nature as it was in Adam before the Fall, then our redemption would have been 'ein Komödie'. The incarnation of the Son of God meant that He stooped to the depths for us—'in such a condition as ours the Lord went about here for us'.[145] In the Incarnation we see the wonder of the condescending love of God.

Kohlbrügge tries to give adequate emphasis to both the divinity and the humanity of Christ; both aspects of His person are essential if there is to be a true redemption for mankind. Jesus Christ must be divine; a man could not save himself, still less could he save others. He must also be fully human; the divine Christ must never be allowed to over-shadow the human. Jesus was one with the rest of the human race. He shared our temptations to the full; He faced temptation in all its forms. The only way in which He was separated from the rest of mankind was that He never yielded, He never sinned.

Kohlbrügge teaches that Christ possessed 'fallen human nature'. Jesus as Son of Man shared this nature with all the human race. He accepts the doctrine of the Virgin Birth, but still maintains that the Son of God assumed human nature as it was because of the Fall. The Word became flesh for us. The clearest statement of his position is to be found in a study of the first chapter of Matthew:

We have thus in the Birth of Christ the witness how it [i.e. the Word] became flesh: born flesh of flesh . . . flesh as we are flesh . . . utterly emptied of God, removed from the sphere of God's glory; held in the very same condemnation or eternal death and curse as we are from our birth; given over to him that has the power of this death, that is the devil, as we are from the start. So He was born for us of a woman, and in this whole nature of ours, with all human affections, desires, and needs: He was made sin for us here in the likeness of a flesh of sin in our stead.[146]

Later in the same book Kohlbrügge writes that 'God has adopted a lost humanity'.[147] Jesus identified Himself with the human race, even to the point of possessing 'fallen human nature'. In

---

[145] *Die Lehre des Heils*, p. 38.
[146] *Betrachtung über das erste Kapitel des Evangeliums nach Matthäus*, p. 92.
[147] Ibid. p. 132.

only one point was He separated from the rest of mankind; He was without sin. Kohlbrügge believes that it is essential to accept this Christological standpoint if he is to uphold the redemptive work of Christ.

JOHANN CHRISTIAN KONRAD VON HOFMANN

J. C. K. von Hofmann was born in Nuremberg in 1810. He went to the University of Erlangen to study theology. Professor J. C. Krafft, who was a biblical theologian, deeply influenced his thinking, and it is from him that Hofmann's biblical theology stems. In 1835 he became Repentant in the theological faculty of Erlangen University and began to devote himself to questions that were to occupy him throughout his life—the doctrine of the inspiration of Holy Scripture, and the doctrine of prophecy and fulfilment. In 1841 he was appointed Professor. His interests were not only academic; he was an ardent supporter of missionary work, and was active in politics. He died in 1877.

Hofmann's theology, especially in his later years, showed the decisive influence of Schleiermacher. He also studied the Scriptures with care and understanding; all his theology is based on biblical exposition. The basic concept of his thought is the idea of Christianity as 'fact' rather than doctrine, the fact of the relationship between God and man mediated by Christ in which the Christian participates.

Hofmann enunciates the theory that we are investigating in 'Der Schriftbeweis'. The first edition was published 1852-6, and the second edition 1857-60.[148] In this work Hofmann is concerned to establish the authenticity of the Christian Faith. He affirms that we stand in a personal relationship with God by virtue of the Person and Work of Jesus who is our mediator. For him the centrality of Christ is the foundation of theology. He confesses the divinity of Christ,[149] but he is never guilty of neglecting His humanity; that Jesus shared our full humanity is a constant theme in his writings. He affirms also the sinlessness of Christ, and indeed discusses it at length.[150] The sinlessness of Jesus was not due to His being exempt from the temptations and trials of life: He was without sin although He was tempted in full, although He faced temptation of every sort, although He was tempted in all points

---

[148] References in this section are to this edition.
[149] See *Der Schriftbeweis*, Part 1, pp. 116-67.
[150] See ibid. Part 2, Div. 1, pp. 31-40.

as we are, although He was our brother in temptation.[151] He was fully human in the sense that He shared our nature and possessed all the qualities of humanity. Only in being without sin was He different from us.

After it [the scripture] states that Jesus was conceived and born of woman, it is taken for granted that in every respect, apart from sin, He became like those who are also conceived and born of woman.[152]

This unity of Christ with the rest of humanity was essential for His saving work to be effective: 'His work must be done within the bounds of common humanity.'[153]

When Hofmann defines this identity of nature between Christ and the rest of mankind he is quite sure that Jesus shared our 'fallen human nature'. This point is clearly made:

He will thus have so made human nature His own, that in it He belonged to humanity as it was in consequence of sin, but without being a sinner, and that He used it as a means of showing His eternal communion with God, but manifesting it within human nature as limited and conditioned by creation and sin.[154]

This Christological position is not confined to this one passage; it is to be found elsewhere in Hofmann's writings. As is his custom in other matters, he bases his belief upon biblical exegesis. He makes extensive use of the Epistle to the Hebrews, especially 2^{5-11} and 4^{14}-5^{10}. He affirms that these passages show conclusively that Jesus possessed a human nature that is like ours. He also examines the concept of the High-priesthood of Christ, which implies a real bond of unity between the One who represents and those who are represented. Certain Pauline passages are also examined with great care: Romans 8^3, Philippians 2^7, and Galatians 4^4. During this biblical discussion he makes plain his own position. When he is discussing the fact that Jesus shared our temptations and so is able to sympathize with us in ours, he declares that His struggle with temptation and evil was a real one, as could only happen 'in a human life which was subject to the limitations brought about by human sin'.[155] One final quotation will suffice to show this aspect in the Christological thinking of

---

[151] See ibid. Part 2, Div. 1, p. 37.   [152] Ibid. p. 41.
[153] Ibid. p. 54.   [154] Ibid. Part 1, p. 46.
[155] Ibid. Part 2, Div. 1, p. 74.

Hofmann. When he is discussing the important passage Romans 8³ he says:

> His son, says the apostle, came into the world with the same nature, as sons of human fathers. . . . God let His son . . . appear in the same sinful nature as ours . . . that human nature should gain the victory over sin that has ruled it since Adam.[156]

Hofmann is not concerned with Christological speculation for its own sake; he is concerned with salvation as it is wrought by the Incarnate Son of God. For him the Person and Work of Christ were inextricably woven together. He enunciates the theory that Christ possessed 'fallen human nature' because it was an essential prerequisite of His saving work. To become our Saviour, Christ had to stoop and become part of the fallen race of Adam; only in this way could He lift us to newness of life.

EDUARD BÖHL

Eduard Böhl was born in Hamburg in 1836. His father was a Lutheran, his mother a Roman Catholic. In 1854 he went to Berlin University where he studied theology; in 1856 he went to Halle, and in the summer of that year he visited Kohlbrügge in Elberfeld. This visit decided the future course of his life and thought. He came under the influence of Kohlbrügge's mind, and later he became his son-in-law.

From 1860 to 1863 he was lecturer in Old Testament in Basel. In 1865 he was appointed Professor of Reformed Dogmatics in Vienna. He held this position until 1889 when he had to retire because of ill-health. He died in Vienna in 1903, but he was buried in Elberfeld at the feet of his teacher Kohlbrügge.

In a study of the Incarnation published in 1884,[157] he affirms that God sent His Son in the likeness of sinful flesh, that the Logos entered the sphere of fallen humanity. The Son of God was the second Adam, the second representative of humanity. He entered into the sphere of sin and death; nevertheless He lived in that sphere without actually sinning, and in so doing He overthrew the power of sin and atoned for its guilt. His death was the consummation of His work of obedience which began with the Incarnation.

---

[156] *Der Schriftbeweis*, Part 2, Div. 1, pp. 83-4.
[157] *Von der Incarnation des göttlichen Wortes.*

Böhl emphasizes the truth that the Son of God assumed 'all the conditions of human nature out of voluntary love'.[158] If Jesus had not shared our nature there would have been no redemption, we should still have been waiting for a Saviour.[159] He accepts the doctrine of the Virgin Birth, but emphatically denies that it removes Christ from our humanity; the Son of God possessed our nature even to the extent of assuming 'fallen human nature'. He bases his position on the New Testament and quotes Hebrews 2[14, 17] and 4[15]. He also turns to Paul to find support for the theory; he refers to 2 Corinthians 5[21], Galatians 3[13] and Romans 8[3]. The Son of God 'was sent in the likeness of sinful flesh and as such became an object of God's anger. He came so close to us that God made no difference between Him and us.'[160] Yet it was from this situation that He became our Redeemer. He triumphed over the nature that He assumed through the power of the Holy Spirit. Böhl affirms the centrality of the Cross and Resurrection; without these there would have been no salvation. Jesus truly died and rose from the dead, but death was one of the results of the Fall. He uses this point as an argument in favour of his position that at the Incarnation the Son of God assumed 'fallen human nature'.

This teaching aroused opposition, and it was attacked by A. Kuyper, who maintained that Böhl implied that in the act of the incarnation Christ became a sinner. In 1888 Böhl wrote his defence.[161] He says that he has been incorrectly interpreted. He proceeds to reaffirm his position that Christ shared our 'fallen nature'. Jesus was 'in the likeness of sinful flesh. None of the contributory factors are missed—the order of things as they have been from Adam's fall stays unchanged'.[162] Again he appeals to the New Testament in support of his argument. He affirms that the sinlessness of Christ is not jeopardized.

In 1887 Böhl published his *Dogmatik* and in this study we also find the same fundamental Christological teaching. The human nature that the Son of God assumed was 'in substance and characteristics exactly like ours, . . . flesh that is subject to sin'.[163] He 'entered our condition thus alienated from God, or the nature which sinned . . .'.[164] Böhl accepts this Christological doctrine

---

[158] Ibid. p. 41.   [159] Ibid. p. 36.   [160] Ibid. p. 42.
[161] *Zur Abwehr. Etliche Bemerkungen gegen Prof. Dr. A. Kuyper's Einleitung zu seiner Schrift 'Die Incarnation des Wortes'.*
[162] Ibid. p. 43; cf. pp. 45-7.   [163] *Dogmatik*, p. 300.   [164] Ibid. p. 299.

because he finds it essential for the true understanding of the redemption wrought in Christ. 'Either the Son of God brings salvation to pass under conditions of life like ours . . . or else everyone has to begin all over again and fulfil independently God's claims upon us'.[165] Jesus assumed this 'fallen nature' that it might be redeemed in Him.[166] For redemption to be accomplished Jesus had to be divine as well as human. Böhl not only emphasizes the full humanity of Christ, he is also a firm advocate of His divinity.[167] The eternal Son of God assumed our humanity that He might raise 'fallen human nature', redeeming it in His own person through His perfect life, through His death upon the Cross and through the victory of His Resurrection.

HERMANN BEZZEL

Herman Bezzel was born in 1861 in Bavaria. He studied philosophy and theology at Erlangen and was an admirer of J. C. K. von Hofmann, whom as a theologian he held in the highest esteem. His main work was concerned with the Deaconess College in Neuendettelsau, of which he became Rector in 1891. In 1909 he became President of the Protestant Consistory in München and therefore head of the Bavarian *Landeskirche*. Bezzel was a convinced Lutheran and in his later years was a recognized leader of Lutheranism within Germany—in 1912 he was elected President of *Die deutschevangelischen Kirchenkonferenz*. He died in 1917.[168]

His theology was never worked out into a system, but it shows the influence of the Erlangen school with its stress on God's condescension. It was in this context that he expounded the theory that Christ possessed 'fallen human nature'. He believed that the focal point of God's dealing with men was the Incarnation. 'God is revealed in the flesh; here lies the root of our redemption and reconciliation.'[169] He emphasizes the full humanity of the incarnate Son of God and affirms that it was 'fallen human nature'. In a sermon on Philippians 2[5-11] he says that Jesus possessed not only the form of a man, 'but the form of manhood dishonoured and devaluated by sin.'[170] He came in 'the body of weakness',

---

[165] *Dogmatik*, p. 302.   [166] Ibid. pp. 307-8.   [167] See ibid. pp. 320-6.
[168] For an appreciation of Bezzel's life and work see J. Rupprecht, *Hermann Bezzel sein Leben, Wesen und Werken*. For a study of his theology, see J. Rupprecht, *Hermann Bezzel als Theologe*.
[169] H. Bezzel, *Die Herrlichkeit des apostolischen Glaubensbekenntnisses*, p. 38.
[170] Cited by J. Rupprecht, *Hermann Bezzel als Theologe*, p. 62.

He entered into 'the entire limitations of fleshly being'.[171] He came not in the form of human nature as it was originally intended by God, but 'He took the form of a servant, with which sin imprints its slaves'.[172] He was made sin for us, He accepted 'the caricature of man' that is the result of sin.[173] The Son of God was drawn deeply into the flesh: He was tempted as we are.

It is clear that Bezzel is concerned with this Christological point in a soteriological setting. The Son of God became one with us that He might become our Saviour. He entered into the post-Fall situation in order that He might redeem fallen mankind.

MODERN EXPOSITORS

During recent years the theory has not been completely ignored, and there are signs that in the future it may win more general acceptance. Several thinkers have made some argument for this theory, and others have stated it in their writings, but without giving any argument in support. This last fact is of interest; for it suggests that a theory which has been for centuries neglected, and has at least on two occasions been condemned as heretical, may now be entering upon a new phase when it will be given more general acceptance. First we will examine the position of those thinkers who have argued for the theory.

KARL BARTH

Karl Barth holds this theory, and in 1934 expressed it in an article 'Offenbarung, Kirche, Theologie';[174] his fullest exposition, however, is in his Church Dogmatics, Vol. I, Part 2. The relevant passage is to be found in the section which comes under the title 'Very God and Very Man'. In the opening paragraphs Barth gives emphatic statement to the truth that Jesus Christ is 'Very God'; he then passes on to the discussion of how the eternal Son of God was made flesh, and it is in this context that he outlines his position concerning the human nature of Christ in relation to the Fall. 'He is a man as we are, . . . equal to us in the state and condition into which our disobedience has brought us.'[175] He is one with us, yet He is 'truly God', and in this tension He is 'God's revelation to us and our reconciliation with God'.[176]

---

[171] Der erhöhte Herr, p. 4.   [172] Sünde und Gnade, pp. 9-10.
[173] Cited by J. Rupprecht, Hermann Bezzel als Theologe, p. 63.
[174] Theologische Existenz heute (München, 1934), pp. 22ff.
[175] Church Dogmatics, Vol. I, Part 2, p. 151.   [176] Ibid. p. 151.

Barth then goes on to define flesh (*sarx*) in these terms: 'Flesh is the concrete form of human nature marked by Adam's fall. . . .'[177] He does not refrain from saying that this means that Jesus has come on to our side of the gulf that sin has created, and 'it is because of this that He makes contact with us and is accessible for us'.[178] Certain biblical passages are cited to substantiate this, and the one which Barth feels summarizes the whole position is Galatians 3[13]. His comment on this is most apposite:

He was not a sinful man. But inwardly and outwardly His situation was that of a sinful man. . . . Freely He entered into solidarity and necessary association with our lost existence. Only in this way 'could' God's revelation to us, our reconciliation with Him, manifestly become an event in Him and by Him.[179]

Appeal is made not simply to certain Pauline passages,[180] but also to passages from the Epistle to the Hebrews.[181]

After this brief biblical reference Barth turns to the later doctrinal position, and again his own attitude is given unequivocally:

But there must be no weakening or obscuring of the saving truth that the nature which God assumed in Christ is identical with our nature as we see it in the light of the Fall. If it were otherwise, how could Christ be really like us? What concern would we have with Him?[182]

Again it is evident that this Christological position is set in a soteriological context; only when this is recognized is its significance and power appreciated. If Christ did not assume and possess this 'fallen human nature', then He is not a man as we are, and—what is more important—He cannot be our representative.

Barth admits that this position has been glossed over, particularly because of the desire to prevent any stain upon the character of Jesus Christ, and he quotes Luther and several Lutheran theologians to show how there is an inadequate grasp of the full humanity of Christ. Before the Reformation this same reluctance to face the issue was found. Barth then quotes from several thinkers who have in more recent times expounded the doctrine

---

[177] *Church Dogmatics*, Vol. I, Part 2, p. 151.   [178] Ibid. p. 151.
[179] Ibid. p. 152.   [180] Philippians 2[7], Romans 8[3], Galatians 3[13].
[181] 2[18], 4[15], 5[2-3].   [182] *Church Dogmatics*, Vol. I, Part 2, p. 153.

that Christ assumed 'fallen human nature'. These theologians have already been referred to in this present study.

Karl Barth is sure of the sinlessness of Christ, and this fact is emphasized in the context of Christ assuming our fallen nature:

True, the Word assumes our human existence, assumes flesh, i.e. He exists in the state and position, amid the conditions, under the curse and punishment of sinful man. He exists in the place where we are, in all the remoteness not merely of the creature from the Creator, but of the sinful creature from the Holy Creator. Otherwise His action would not be a revealing, a reconciling action. . . . Otherwise He would bring us nothing new. He would not help us. He would leave us in the remoteness. Therefore in our state and condition He does not do what underlies and produces that state and condition, or what we in that state and condition continually do. Our unholy human existence, assumed and adopted by the Word of God, is a hallowed and therefore a sinless human existence; in our unholy human existence the eternal Word draws near to us. In the hallowing of our unholy human existence He draws supremely and helpfully near to us.[183]

Within the sphere of fallen human nature Jesus Christ lived a perfect life. That which He assumed was healed; in this was our redemption. It was in the hallowing and redeeming of fallen nature that the Son of God showed Himself to be our Saviour. Jesus Christ was sinless; only as He was a lamb without blemish and spot was He able to take away the sins of the world. His perfection is to be seen in His obedience unto death. Jesus Christ had to face temptation to the full, temptation that was all the fiercer because of the fallen nature which He had assumed, but it is in the victory over temptation that His perfect sinlessness is seen.

Jesus did not run away from the state and situation of fallen man, but took it upon Himself, lived it and bore it Himself as the eternal Son of God. How could He have done so, if in His human existence He had not been exposed to real inward temptation and trial, if like other men He had not trodden an inner path, if He had not cried to God and wrestled with God in real inward need? It was in this wrestling, in which He was in solidarity with us to the uttermost, that there was done that which is not done by us, the will of God.[184]

It is generally accepted that in the central truths of the faith Karl Barth stands as a champion of orthodoxy. He affirms the

[183] Ibid. pp. 155-6.   [184] Ibid. p. 158.

M

divinity of Christ, and is sure of His sinless perfection, yet he makes a vital part of his doctrine of the Person and Work of Christ the affirmation that Christ assumed and possessed human nature as it was as a result of the Fall.

J. A. T. ROBINSON

This writer has already been quoted at length in an earlier section in this study with reference to the teaching of Paul. In his short but invaluable study, *The Body*, he expounds as Paul's position the concept that Christ assumed 'fallen human nature'. It is unnecessary to cover again the ground that has already been covered,[185] but J. A. T. Robinson's name must be included here for the sake of completeness.

T. F. TORRANCE

Dr Torrance contributed an essay entitled 'The Place of Christology in Biblical and Dogmatic Theology' to a *Festschrift* for Barth.[186] In this he states his acceptance of the theory that Christ shared our 'fallen human nature'.

The opening sentence of the essay shows that Christology is to be understood as vitally connected with the saving work of Christ, 'for in Him the Word of God has become man in the midst of man's estrangement from God, committing Himself to human understanding and creating communion between man and God'.[187] This incarnation 'in the midst of man's estrangement from God' means, so Torrance maintains, the assuming of 'fallen human nature'.

Though conceived by the Holy Spirit and born of the Virgin Mary, Jesus was yet born in the womb of a sinner, within the compass of our sinful flesh. As the Son of Adam He was born into our alienation, our God-forsakenness and darkness, grew up within our bondage and ignorance. . . . He learned obedience by the things which He suffered, for that obedience from within our alienated humanity was a struggle with our sin and temptation; . . . Throughout the whole course of His life He bent the will of man in perfect submission to the Will of God, bowing under the divine judgement against our unrighteousness, and offering a perfect obedience to the Father, that we might be redeemed and reconciled to Him.[188]

185 See especially p. 104 above.
186 *Essays in Christology for Karl Barth*, Ed. by T. H. L. Parker.
187 Ibid. p. 13.   188 Ibid. p. 18.

In this passage the author's position is clearly stated. Jesus assumed human nature as it was because of the Fall, yet within this 'fallen nature' He lived a perfect life.

The belief that Jesus shared our fallen nature is not confined to this one passage in the essay; it is expressed in several contexts:

This is the way which the Word of God made flesh takes in the midst of our sinful humanity, the way of suffering and judgement and atonement.[189]

As God and yet as Man, Jesus Christ penetrated into the midst of our humanity in order to overcome our estrangement and to reconcile us to the Father.[190]

In Jesus Christ the Word of God entered into the midst of our flesh of sin and worked out in our existence the perfect obedience of man to God.[191]

The significance of this belief that Christ shared our 'fallen human nature' is revealingly shown by the fact that T. F. Torrance makes use of it in his interpretation of the Bible and the Church. He states that we must think of the Scriptures in the light of Jesus Christ, the Word; they are 'a human expression corresponding to the Humanity of Jesus Christ'.[192] He then continues:

In the Bible, therefore . . . the Word of God comes to us in the midst of our sin and darkness at once revealing and reconciling, but it comes with strong crying and tears, pressing its way through the speech of our fallen flesh, graciously assuming it in spite of all its inadequacy and faultiness and imperfection, and giving it a holy perfection in the Word of God.[193]

T. F. Torrance is of the opinion that 'the doctrine of the Church must be formulated in the closest connection with Christology, as the corollary of it and strictly in terms of the analogy of Christ'.[194] In a discussion of 'The Atonement and the Oneness of the Church' he again states his acceptance of the theory that is the subject of the present enquiry:

We think of His mission in relation to sinful man, of His Incarnation as the incorporation of Himself into our body of the flesh of sin and the carrying of it to its crucifixion . . . of His entry into our estrangement in

---

[189] Ibid. p. 18.   [190] Ibid. p. 19.   [191] Ibid. p. 21.
[192] Ibid. p. 22.   [193] Ibid. pp. 25-6.   [194] *SJT*, VII.245.

the contradiction of sin, and of His working out, in the midst of our humanity and alienation, reconciliation with God. . . .[195]

Jesus 'penetrated into our sinful humanity . . . gathering sinful man into one Body with the Saviour, and opening up a new and living way into the Holiest'.[196] A little later in the same article Torrance states the same position, revealing clearly the soteriological significance of this Christological theory:

The Incarnation means that God the Son entered into our human alienation from God and stood in the flesh and place of man in subjection to law and judgment. He stepped into the conflict between the covenant faithfulness of God and the unfaithfulness of man and took the conflict into His own flesh as the Incarnate Son and bore it to the very end. . . . Within our flesh He was thus act of God the Judge condemning sin in the flesh, and within our flesh where man has no justification before God, He the Just in the place of the unjust stood under judgment and rendered to God the answer of complete obedience, even to the death of the Cross.[197]

The soteriological significance is again revealed when he writes:

In Birth and Baptism the sinless One incorporated Himself into our flesh of sin that through substitutionary atonement we who are sinners might be incorporated into Him as His body who was raised for our justification.[198]

The Working Committee of the World Council of Churches' Commission on Faith and Order met in Herrenalb, Germany, in July 1956. In the *Minutes* there is reported an interesting debate which is relevant at this point in our investigation. The subject under discussion was 'Our oneness in Christ and our disunity as Churches', and the point at issue was about the Church as '*simul justa et peccatrix*'. During the discussion T. F. Torrance said that the whole matter hinged on Christology.

We need to take more seriously that the Word of God assumed our *sarx*, i.e. our fallen humanity (not one immaculately conceived) and so doing hallowed it. The doctrine of the Church needs to be thought out in terms of the fact that Christ Jesus assumed our humanity and sanctified Himself. The Church is *sancta* in Christ's sanctification.

This quotation shows that Torrance was stating the Christological theory that is at present under investigation.

[195] *SJT*, VII.247.   [196] Ibid. p. 247.   [197] Ibid. pp. 251-2.   [198] Ibid. p. 252.

The reaction of at least two of those present is revealing: it shows that they did not accept the position, and reveals a fear that it might be tantamount to a denial of the sinlessness of Christ, a fear that is not justified by the position in general, and most certainly not justified in the case of Dr Torrance. 'Professor Outler pointed out that Jesus Christ was "yet without sin". Was humanity therefore fallen on purpose? Is humanity sinful in itself?' The reaction of Professor Florovsky was even more revealing, he asked: 'If the divine assumes human nature, how can this nature be anything but sinless?' These brief extracts from the *Minutes* of this meeting exemplify a discussion that has taken place more than once when the theory of Christ's assuming 'fallen human nature' has been put forward.[199]

This examination of the relevant teaching of T. F. Torrance is interesting, not simply because it clearly shows that he accepts the theory under discussion, but also because we see him using this Christological point with reference to the doctrines of the Bible and the Church. This latter point shows how firmly he has integrated this concept of the Person of Christ into his whole theological position.

NELS F. S. FERRÉ

Nels Ferré, in his book *Christ and the Christian*, shows his acceptance of the theory under discussion, though often he uses quite a distinctive terminological approach to the subject.

The full humanity of Jesus is emphatically asserted; He possessed the human nature which is shared by mankind in general. 'Only . . . if Jesus shared ordinary human nature to begin with was he genuinely part of our history';[200] it is true that in Jesus a new humanity was constituted, but Jesus 'did not begin with a transformed nature. He began where we all begin, with ordinary, actual human nature'.[201] Jesus faced the same struggle as we do, 'His victories in temptations reveal how he actually refused special status for himself'.[202] He *'was genuinely human in terms of the ordinary tensions which men must bear, both from without and from within'*.[203] Ferré maintains the paradoxical position that

---

[199] The discussion is to be found in Faith and Order Commission Paper, No. 23. *Minutes of the Working Committee, July 1956, Herrenalb, Germany, Commission on Faith and Order, World Council of Churches.*

[200] N. F. S. Ferré, *Christ and the Christian*, p. 76.   [201] Ibid. p. 77.   [202] Ibid. p. 83.

[203] Ibid. p. 89. The italics in this and the following quotations are those of the author, Ferré.

Jesus lived a sinless life, showed perfection of living, and yet possessed 'fallen human nature'. 'The raw nature of man—often explained by traditionalistic theologians as due to "the fall"— rumbled within, but these drives became the occasion for a new level of living. . . .'[204] In His earthly life Jesus was able to control and rise victorious over temptation, but temptation was not eliminated.

Ferré asserts that the Eternal Word entered 'genuinely into our humanity' and paid 'the price of our salvation from within our actual nature and situation'.[205] His humanity was identical with ours. There is no idea of a human nature specially created for Jesus. On this point Ferré is emphatic: 'If God entered man in such a manner that he did not share the full history of mankind, there was no real Incarnation.'[206] If it is asserted that Jesus, because of His Incarnation by the medium of Virgin Birth, could not sin, it is tantamount to saying that 'God . . . never assumed our full human predicament nor did He solve it from within . . .'.[207]

The soteriological aspect of the position now begins to emerge: it is only when He is our brother that He can be the first born among many brethren. Ferré affirms that

Theologically Jesus did not save us from sin unless he assumed it within himself; and sin, not finitude, is precisely our deepest problem. Jesus was 'made sin', however, not in the sense that God could ever sin, certainly not even in human form, but that the human nature of Jesus shared our whole history of alienation from God and accepted the anxiety connected with it which is the root reality of sin. *To remove Jesus from our sin categorically is to deny the Incarnation and to destroy its reality and power.*[208]

Jesus was part of the total human situation which involved 'sinful human nature' with its experience of alienation from God; it was only by becoming part of this humanity, sharing this experience, being 'made sin', that Jesus could become in reality a Redeemer. This truth is essential to a sound Christology.

The soteriological significance of this Christological position is indicated by Ferré in a chapter on 'The Atonement'. A vital

---

[204] N. F. S. Ferré, *Christ and the Christian*, pp. 91-2.
[205] Ibid., p. 96.   [206] Ibid. p. 99.   [207] Ibid. p. 10 .
[208] Ibid. pp. 113-14. This quotation also reveals Ferré's firm acceptance of the sinlessness of Christ; cf. pp. 114, 195.

part of the act of reconciliation, so he maintains, was Christ's assumption of 'fallen human nature'. It was in this way that He entered into the full human situation. God needed to 'assume in himself, *within humanity and within history*, man's sins and short-comings, and thus pay for, cancel from within, and make new and right, *from within*, what was wrong and broken'.[209] The eternal Son of God, by taking this fallen nature, 'entered into the whole heritage of human sin and with God's love and light challenged it to a fight to the finish'.[210] Jesus so identified Himself with mankind, so 'entered the deep, dark places of man's hiding from God',[211] that He could be our representative. 'God Incarnate cannot do less that identify Himself completely with sinful man and for sinful man face death.'[212] The ultimate aim of this identification was redemption. Ferré makes the doctrine of Christ's assumption of 'fallen human nature' an essential part of his estimate of Christ's Work and Person; it is not simply a Christological point, it is a soteriological truth.

C. E. B. CRANFIELD

In a volume of Christological essays dedicated to Karl Barth, C. E. B. Cranfield writes of 'The Witness of the New Testament to Christ'.[213] In this he affirms his belief that the New Testament teaches that Christ assumed 'fallen human nature'. The Son of God descended

'from the glory which He had with His Father before the world was, to the very lowest depths of human suffering and shame. This downward movement, indicated in 2 Corinthians 8⁹ by the pregnant expression 'became poor' and traced in more detail in Philippians 2⁶⁻⁸ . . . was a real and thorough-going self-identification with sinful men. The words 'became flesh' mean that without ceasing to be God, He took upon Himself not a human nature uncorrupted by man's fall, but the selfsame human nature that is ours, that is, a fallen human nature. It was with that altogether unpromising material —what Paul calls σὰρξ ἁμαρτίας (Rom 8³)—that He wrought out His perfect obedience to the Father, being 'in all points tempted like as we are, yet without sin'. 'Became flesh' and 'became poor' are not adequately interpreted unless we go as far as this.[214]

C. E. B. Cranfield then links this Christological conception with

[209] *Christ and the Christian*, p. 148.   [210] Ibid. p. 159.
[211] Ibid. p. 162.   [212] Ibid. p. 166.
[213] *Essays in Christology for Karl Barth*, Ed. by T. H. L. Parker.   [214] Ibid. p. 81.

the Cross, and the soteriological significance of the theory is clearly grasped. Why was this self-identification with sinful men? 'The New Testament gives a clear answer. It was "for your sakes . . . that ye through his poverty might become rich".'[215]

The reference to the theory under investigation is brief but unequivocal. As far as Cranfield is concerned it is necessary if the New Testament witness to Jesus is to be fully understood.

HAROLD ROBERTS

Dr Harold Roberts in his recent book, *Jesus and the Kingdom of God*, has a chapter on the Person of Christ. He makes mention of the idea of W. R. Matthews that the concept of '*libido*' must be ascribed to Jesus, and that to deny this would be tantamount to the destruction of His humanity. Commenting on this idea he asks: 'If Jesus was free from original sin, does that mean we are born with a bias which He did not share? If so, His human nature was different from ours.'[216] Dr Roberts then says that all turns on how the ambiguous term 'original sin' is defined. He turns away from the concept of 'original guilt' as 'emptying moral responsibility of an essential part of its meaning'.[217] He affirms that in some sense we are all bound up in the sin of the race, and that we possess a bias to seek our own will rather than God's, a tendency 'which has deep ramifications in the history of the race'.[218] This weakness is so strong that it makes sin highly probable, but he maintains, not inevitable. Then there comes the vital sentence. 'It would be as well to interpret original sin as a universal tendency in human nature to seek the ends of self-interest and in this tendency Jesus shared.'[219] Immediately Dr Roberts asserts the sinlessness of Christ.

It would be unfair to claim that we have here the Christological theory that we have been discussing in any developed form. Yet the implication of the sentence seems to be that the term 'original sin', when carefully defined, can be applied to Jesus; and it seems impossible to apply it to Jesus, however carefully it is defined, without placing Him within that humanity which has been affected by the sins of previous generations. Certainly Dr Roberts's thought reflects a significant change in the climate of

---

[215] *Essays in Christology for Karl Barth*, Ed. by T. H. L. Parker, p. 81.
[216] *Jesus and the Kingdom of God*, p. 78.   [217] Ibid.
[218] Ibid.   [219] Ibid. pp. 78-9.

Christological opinion to one which is more likely to find acceptable the theory that the Son of God assumed 'fallen human nature'. With the new emphasis on the reality of the humanity of Christ, this theory of His person is seen in an entirely new perspective.

LESSLIE NEWBIGIN

Bishop Newbigin's book, *Sin and Salvation*, was originally published in Tamil as a manual for the instruction of Church workers in the Church of South India. It is concerned with essentials, and states what the author believes to be the Christian Faith in its orthodox form. It is of interest to find that in this book, on several occasions, Lesslie Newbigin states the theory that Christ assumed 'fallen human nature'.

The Son of God came from the fullness of the Godhead, came into this world to be the Saviour of men. 'In so doing He has to come under the power of sin and therefore under the sentence of suffering and death which is the wages of sin.'[220] Yet, it is affirmed, He remained in perfect unity with the Father. Reference is then made to the phrases, 'in the likeness of sinful flesh', 'made flesh', 'emptied himself, taking the form of a servant, . . . being found in fashion as a man'. These mean that 'He being God, took upon Himself our manhood—that manhood which has come under the power of sin and death'.[221] There is no doubting Lesslie Newbigin's meaning as the next passage shows:

He being 'God of God, Light of Light, Very God of Very God', came down from heaven and took upon Him our sinful manhood, was born of a virgin, lived a perfect human life, died, rose again, and ascended into heaven. Taking upon Himself our sinful nature, so that He became subject to the fierce temptations of sin as we are subject, He lived a life of sinless perfection in the midst of sin. . . . Thus He met and overcame sin in our nature, from within the enemy's territory.[222]

In this quotation the whole position is put with admirable clarity and yet with commendable care.

The same position is revealed in another context in the same book. He says that man was subject to death because of sin, and adds that Jesus has put Himself completely under the same bondage. 'He has not only taken upon Himself our sin-polluted

---

[220] *Sin and Salvation*, p. 58.   [221] Ibid. p. 59.   [222] Ibid. p. 60.

nature, and lived a human life under the conditions created by sin; He has also gone with us to the last limit and died that death which is the wages of sin, died and risen again.'[223] It is by thus being identified with us that it is possible for Jesus to be our Saviour.

Here in Bishop Newbigin's book there is no exposition, no argument; the theory is simply stated as an accepted part of his theological thinking.

THE PRINCIPLES OF UNITY WHICH HOLD THESE ADVOCATES TOGETHER

Up to this point the historical material has been presented in chronological order. We must now attempt to discover whether there is any principle of unity which holds this material together. This is particularly necessary since there is little evidence for any development of interpretation in this group of advocates; the most that can be said is that the later writers tend to be more careful and precise in their statements of the theory. At first it seems difficult to see what this principle of unity can be. There are long periods when the doctrine appears to have been ignored —though it is possible to offer some explanation of that, as will be seen in Part IV. The advocates of the theory are drawn from various Christian traditions and communions. They represent a wide difference in theological outlook, some taking a theological position which is highly orthodox, and others holding views whose orthodoxy is highly questionable. Nor is it possible to show that each writer was acquainted with, and dependent on, the earlier advocates of the theory. Nevertheless, in certain cases there are such links of dependence, and these must be our first consideration.

Antoinette Bourignon was a dominant personality and she gathered around her a group of ardent disciples. One of these was Peter Poiret. He was the main editor of her works, and as such was well acquainted with her teaching. Since he himself expounds the same doctrine of Christ's assumption of 'fallen human nature', we should expect that he was, to some extent, dependent on her thinking at this point. He certainly seems to have been. We know that when he edited her works it was his custom to add Explanatory Letters. These he initialled P.P.

---

[223] *Sin and Salvation*, p. 83.

At the end of *Solid Vertue* there is 'An Accessory Letter upon Letter VI'—the one in which Antoinette Bourignon expounds her position.[224] This letter, which is initialled P.P., endorses the Christological position of Antoinette Bourignon. We can, therefore, with reasonable certainty, say that Peter Poiret was dependent on Antoinette Bourignon for this Christological point. He says in his *Divine Economy* that 'All the Truths propos'd in these Treatises are only the consequences of her Principles, or of my own disquisitions which I carry'd still deeper and deeper, encouraged by the light she gave me into all Subjects whatsoever'.[225]

The teaching of Antoinette Bourignon spread from Holland to Germany, France, Switzerland, England, and Scotland. It is with Bourignonism in Scotland that we are concerned here. The influence of Antoinette Bourignon appeared in Scotland, not during her lifetime, but between 1695 and 1715. It is not necessary to study the history of the movement in detail,[226] but certain features are significant. George Garden, who wrote *An Apology for M. Antonia Bourignon* (1699),[227] came into contact with Peter Poiret, who led him to become a devoted disciple of Antoinette Bourignon. He was responsible for the appearance of a number of her writings in English, and through his influence Bourignonism spread. In 1701 the General Assembly declared Bourignonism to be heretical. Eight points were given. Two refer to the Person of Christ: 'Her ascribing to Christ a twofold human nature, the one produced of Adam, the other born of the Virgin', and 'Her belief in the sinful corruption of Christ's human nature and in the rebellion of His natural will against the will of God'. From 1711 ministers at their ordination were called upon to renounce Bourignian teaching. The reference to Bourignonism remained until the list of questions was revised in 1889, when it was removed.

It may not be without significance that two of the adherents to the doctrine under discussion were Scots. It is true that both Irving and Erskine appeared a century later than the rise of Bourignonism in Scotland, but the possibility of their being indirectly influenced by her teaching cannot be ruled out. There

---

[224] See pp. 138-9 above.   [225] IV.xvii-xviii.

[226] For a study of Bourignonism in Scotland, see R. H. Story, *The Church of Scotland* (1890), G. D. Henderson, *Mystics of the North East* (1934) and *Religious Life in Seventeenth-century Scotland* (1937).

[227] This was published anonymously.

is certainly a similarity between the charge brought against Irving and the one against Bourignonism. This similarity has not passed unnoticed. 'The Assembly had, in effect, the same doctrine before it which 130 years after was taught and defended by Edward Irving.'[228] No further link is made between the two in this study of the Church of Scotland edited by R. H. Story. H. F. Henderson says: 'Irving's "heresies" reminded many of the old errors of Bourignonism, and on that account were deemed intolerable.'[229]

Irving refers to the teaching of Antoinette Bourignon in *The Orthodox and Catholic Doctrine of Our Lord's Human Nature*.[230] He speaks of Bourignon as 'an enthusiastic woman, who propagated certain wild and heterodox tenets . . .'.[231] He mentions that he denounced Bourignonism at his ordination, and reaffirms this position. He is amazed that 'any man in his sober sense could confound the doctrine' which he taught 'with this woman's frantic possessions and utterances of folly'.[232] He rejects her teaching, but admits his acceptance of the point that the Son of God assumed human nature as it was after the Fall. Her overall Christology is false, but it is 'much more honest than the hypothesis now current amongst our opponents, which flatly denies or avoids all the Scripture, declaring him to have taken substance of his sinful mother, and boldly asserts that he took the nature of Adam before the fall, though there had been no such nature in existence four thousand years'.[233] He praises Antoinette Bourignon for placing Jesus Christ in the stream of humanity that comes from Adam. He says that she was justly condemned 'for asserting the sinful corruption of Christ's human nature, which was not sinful, but was ever upholden holy. What he took to work upon was sinful, sinful flesh and blood: what he wrought it into was sinless.'[234] With this Antoinette Bourignon would have agreed. Irving admits that he has not seen the works of Bourignon —his only quotations are from Dr Garden's *Apology*—and has only the words of condemnation of the Assembly upon which to base his opinion. If he had read Bourignon, he would have recognized that her position was substantially the one he advocated. It is significant that he says that her ideas 'aim at

[228] *The Church of Scotland*, Edited by R. H. Story, IV.248.
[229] *The Religious Controversies of Scotland*, p. 142.   [230] Pp. 54-80.
[231] Ibid. p. 55.   [232] Ibid. p. 56.   [233] Ibid. pp. 65-6.   [234] Ibid. p. 66.

great truths, but miss the right and just expression of them'.[235]

To claim that Irving or Erskine were directly dependent on the teaching of Antoinette Bourignon at this point would be to claim more than the evidence warrants, especially considering Irving's treatment of Bourignonism. What can be said, however, is that they may have been unconsciously influenced to some extent by Bourignonism, which had at one time a certain vogue in Scotland. Certainly there is a close similarity between the point of view of Bourignon and that of Irving.

Erskine of Linlathen and Edward Irving were contemporaries. It is not easy to ascertain the precise intimacy of the connection between them. It is certain that they knew each other, but they seem to have shared other friends, rather than to have been close friends themselves. H. F. Henderson says that 'there were other living teachers who profoundly influenced Erskine, as Edward Irving . . .'.[236] Erskine was interested in the first outbreak of 'speaking with tongues' with which Irving was so greatly concerned, but later Erskine disavowed his earlier belief in its supernatural nature. In a letter to Miss Christine Erskine dated April 1827, he says that he has been reading Irving's book on the Prophecies 'and a very striking book it is'.[237] However, in a letter to Miss Rachel Erskine in November 1827, he recommends William Law's *Spirit of Prayer* and *Spirit of Love*, adding the comment: 'I really like them much better than Mr Irving's "Prophecies".'[238] One long letter from Erskine to Irving has been published.[239] It is dated 10th October 1834. The letter is addressed to 'My dear Brother', and during the course of the letter Erskine calls Irving 'my dear friend'. He was aware of the proceedings of the trial which culminated in Irving's expulsion from the Church of Scotland. In a letter to Mrs Stirling, his sister, dated May 1832, Erskine writes: 'I have just read over the short-hand report of Mr Irving's trial before the Presbytery. His defence is a very solemn appeal to the church and the world. . . .'[240] There is a letter of Erskine's to Miss Stuart, dated 13th December 1834. It reads:

You will have heard of the death of Irving. You cannot enter into my feelings on this event, as you did not know him or regard him as I did.

---

[235] Ibid. p. 79.   [236] *Erskine of Linlathen*, p. 24.
[237] *Letters of Thomas Erskine*, Ed. by William Hanna, I.109.
[238] Ibid. p. 124.   [239] Ibid. pp. 230-2.   [240] Ibid. p. 188.

He has been a remarkable man in a remarkable age. He was a man of much child-like feeling to God, and personal dependence on Him, amidst things which may well appear unintelligible and strange in this history.[241]

It is quite clear that Irving and Erskine moved in the same circles; it is also evident that Erskine took an interest in the works and career of Irving. There is no evidence to show that there is any direct influence with reference to the Christological point under discussion. Yet it seems hardly possible that they were completely unacquainted with each other's views on the subject. Erskine published his *Brazen Serpent* in 1831 and *The Doctrine of Election* in 1837. Irving's *Sermons* appeared in 1828, his *Orthodox and Catholic Doctrine of Our Lord's Human Nature* in 1830 and *Christ's Holiness in Flesh* in 1831. We have seen above that Erskine was familiar with one of Irving's books; it is quite possible that he was acquainted with others as well. Erskine was not unaware of the proceedings against Irving between 1831 and 1833, as his letter to Mrs Stirling makes clear. He must therefore have known that his own Christological views bore a marked resemblance to those of Irving. It is impossible to define exactly the connection there was between Erskine and Irving concerning this Christological doctrine, but it seems certain that Erskine was aware of Irving's teaching, and we cannot rule out the possibility of a certain amount of interdependence between them.

The theory that Christ assumed 'fallen human nature' was held by a number of Continental theologians, mainly German, during the eighteenth and nineteenth centuries. Christian Fende published his study of Ephesians in 1727. No biographical details have been discovered by the present writer, so that it is impossible for him to say to what extent he was influenced by others. His theological position is summed up by Dorner, who says that 'he denied the Trinity, the deity and satisfaction of Christ, and asserted a sinfulness of His human nature, though he at the same time allowed that it fought therewith, and overcame it'.[242] This bears a certain resemblance to the teaching of Antoinette Bourignon, who was Modalist in her doctrine of the Trinity and Socinian in her Christology, and who renounced the idea of satisfaction in her teaching on the work of Christ. There is a

---

[241] *Letters of Thomas Erskine*, I.232.
[242] *Doctrine of the Person of Christ*, Div. 2, II.376.

similarity in theological position, and Fende's book appeared within fifty years of the death of Bourignon. More than that cannot be said.

Konrad Dippel's *Vera Demonstratio Evangelica* appeared two years later than the writing of Fende. For a time he was in Holland (1711-14) and in Schleswig-Holstein (1714-19); Antoinette Bourignon had taught in both places some half-century earlier. This may suggest a possible source from which Dippel took his teaching. Konrad Dippel was also deeply influenced by Pietism, and so, though to a lesser degree, was Gottfried Menken. There seems to be no reason, however, for associating the doctrine under investigation with Pietism, for it does not feature in the teaching of the vast majority of Pietists. There is, however, reason to believe that Dippel influenced a certain Dr Collenbusch, who in turn influenced Menken. In 1848 F. W. Krug published a paper on Collenbusch.[243] Dr Samuel Collenbusch (1724-1803)[244] maintained that Jesus shared our human nature to the full, the same nature as 'every new-born son of man'. He affirmed that in Gethsemane and on the Cross this 'sinful flesh' was destroyed. It is clear that Collenbusch maintained the sinlessness of Christ. Krug, in this paper, asserts that Dippel is the source from which Collenbusch drew his teaching.[245] It is difficult to say to what extent Collenbusch drew directly from Dippel. It is possible that the influence came to some extent through Hasenkamp, who was acquainted with the writings of Dippel. Krug links Menken with Collenbusch, and suggests that Menken has systematized his teaching.[246] J. Moltmann affirms that, as a student in Duisburg, Menken came under the influence of Pietism, particularly through Collenbusch and Hasenkamp.[247] There is thus a strong case for saying that Menken drew his teaching on Christ's assumption of 'fallen human nature' from Dippel, with Collenbusch as the intermediary.[248]

There is a definite link to be traced between Kohlbrügge and Eduard Böhl. In 1856 Böhl visited Kohlbrügge in Elberfeld and the visit proved to be of the greatest significance. Böhl,

---

[243] *Die Lehre des Doctor Collenbusch, gewesen praktishchen Arztes in Barmen, nebst verwandten Richtungen in ihren falschen Principien und verderblichen Consequenzen.*
[244] See article by E. Moltmann-Wendel in *Evangelisches Kirchenlexikon*, Vol. I.
[245] See ibid. pp. 7-8.   [246] See ibid. p. 3.
[247] See *Evangelisches Kirchenlexikon*, Vol. II, Col. 1291.
[248] The present author has not been able to refer to any relevant work of Collenbusch, whose influence seems to have been more oral than written.

as we have already said, came under the influence of Kohlbrügge's thought, and later became his son-in-law. Böhl was
acquainted with some of the previous advocates of the theory.
He refers to Irving[249] and Menken,[250] but does not give either of
them his full approval. The source of his teaching on Christ's
human nature is not to be found in either of these writers, but in
Kohlbrügge, for it seems reasonably evident that it was from him
that he received the doctrine in the first place.[251] When we try to
discover whether Kohlbrügge was influenced by any of the earlier
advocates of the theory, there appears to be no direct evidence.
E. Moltmann-Wendel says that his theology was influenced by
the teaching of the Reformation, particularly Luther, and also
'die mystisch-spiritualistischen Traditionen Hollands'.[252] There
is not sufficient evidence to warrant any dogmatic assertion, but
the reference to Holland may not be without significance.
Bourignon and Dippel are connected with Holland, though
Kohlbrügge is later in date.

Hermann Bezzel is an advocate of the theory in question.
There is not sufficient evidence to show with any degree of
certainty the source from which he drew his teaching on this
point. One fact is certain, Bezzel held Hofmann in the highest
esteem.[253] As Hofmann also was an advocate of the theory that
Christ assumed 'fallen human nature', it is possible that Bezzel
was influenced by him at this point.

When we turn to the more recent advocates of the theory,
even though there is no certain dependence one upon the other,
the figure of Karl Barth appears to be central. It is not an easy
matter to decide the source from which Barth took his doctrine.
He quotes from a number of the earlier advocates of the doctrine:
Menken, Irving, J. C. K. von Hofmann, Kohlbrügge, Böhl, and
Bezzel. There is little indication which of these writers, if any,
played a determinative part in his thinking at this point. He does
say, however, 'above all, mention must be made of Gottfried
Menken',[254] and this suggests that he finds Menken the most
significant of the writers listed. We also know that Barth held

---

[249] *Von der Incarnation des göttlichen Wortes*, p. 52.   [250] Ibid. pp. 53-6.
[251] We gain some conception of Böhl's estimate of Kohlbrügge when we read the
words written after the latter's death. They are cited in Herzog, *Realencyclopädie für
protestantische Theologie und Kirche*, Band, XXIII.245-6.
[252] *Evangelisches Kirchenlexikon*, Vol. II, Col. 859.
[253] See the quotations cited by J. Rupprecht, *Hermann Bezzel als Theologe*, p. 30.
[254] *Church Dogmatics*, I. II.154.

Kohlbrügge in high regard, but this mainly seems to be for his exposition of Justification and the Grace of God. It is not possible to be dogmatic and assert that Barth is dependent upon any of the earlier advocates. One thing is certain: he was acquainted with a number of those who had expounded the theory, and to some extent, at least, his own thinking must have been stimulated by their exposition.

Certain of the more recent advocates of the theory seem to be indebted to Barth, at least in some measure. T. F. Torrance studied under Barth at Basel, and expounds the doctrine under discussion in a *Festschrift* for Karl Barth. In the article concerned he writes: 'In writing this article in honour of Karl Barth I wish to acknowledge my indebtedness throughout it to the second half-volume of his prolegomena to the *Kirkliche Dogmatik*, which I have been helping to see through the Press in an English edition at the time of writing.'[255] This is the volume in which Barth expounds the theory in question. C. E. B. Cranfield expresses his adherence to the theory in the same volume of essays for Barth, and in a footnote refers to the relevant section in the writings of Barth.[256]

Of two other writers in the present century, J. A. T. Robinson and Nels Ferré, we can say at least that they are familiar with the opinion of Barth on this matter. Robinson refers to the section in Barth and quotes from him.[257] Ferré writes: 'No matter what Barth says about Christ's assuming our fallen nature . . .'.[258]

To maintain that Barth is responsible for the increased interest in the doctrine during recent years would be to overstate the case. All that can be said is that his advocacy of the position is one of the factors which has brought it more to the fore in the present century, that certain writers admit some degree of dependence upon his thinking, that others show their awareness of his position, and that even those who do not accept this Christological position mention his acceptance of the point.[259]

When we have traced the extent to which one writer was dependent on others, has everything possible been said about what holds together these various writers? Three further points remain to be made.

The first point is of prime importance. All these advocates,

---

[255] *Essays in Christology for Karl Barth*, Ed. by T. H. L. Parker, p. 13, note 1.
[256] Ibid. p. 81, note 1.   [257] *The Body*, p. 38, note 1.
[258] *Christ and the Christian*, p. 78, note 8.
[259] See D. M. Baillie, *God was in Christ*, p. 16.

N

without exception, are of the opinion that in teaching that Christ
assumed our fallen nature they are expounding New Testament
teaching. All of them quote from the New Testament in support of
their thesis. This is true even of Antoinette Bourignon, who
claimed repeatedly that for twenty years after her 'illumination'
she never used the Bible. Yet in her advocacy of this Christological point she writes: 'And I think, Sir, you will find in Scripture
that Jesus Christ *was made Sin* itself for Men.'[260] Several of the
advocates express their point of view in the course of a biblical
study: this is so with Fende, Menken, J. A. T. Robinson, and
C. E. B. Cranfield. Hofmann was a biblical theologian, and in
Der Schriftbeweis he is concerned to expound the truth of God as
it is enshrined in Scripture. The other expositors, if not so
directly biblical in their approach to the subject, nevertheless
quote from the New Testament to substantiate their position.
There is no need to list the verses cited by the various writers;
these have been indicated when the individual writer was discussed, and many of them have been examined in the New Testament section of this present study. It is of interest to note that
several other writers, who have not been mentioned as advocates
of the theory, seem to express it when they discuss certain New
Testament passages. E. F. Scott comments on 2 Corinthians 5[21]:

Thus his physical death on the Cross had a moral value, and was
universal in its effect. By the destruction of his own flesh he destroyed
the principle of the flesh which involves the whole race in sin.[261]

Stauffer, expounding the biblical doctrine of the Incarnation,
comments on Romans 8[3]:

He took upon himself the form of sinful flesh, the burden of a life that
has been afflicted hereditarily ever since the days of Adam.[262]

Bultmann, expounding the same verse in Romans, says:

. . . having sent his own son (clad) in (our) self-same, sin-ruled flesh
and (sent him) to take sin's place, God (in condemning Christ to die)
condemned (our) sin (= Christ) in the flesh (he shared with us).[263]

Anders Nygren gives a similar interpretation to the passage:

He shared all our conditions. He was under the same powers of destruction. Out of 'the flesh' arose for Him the same temptations as for

---

[260] *Solid Vertue*, Part 2, p. 80. The italics are the author's.
[261] *MNTC*, 'Colossians', p. 48.   [262] *New Testament Theology*, p. 117.
[263] *Theology of the New Testament*, I.296.

us. . . . Christ was placed under the same conditions and under the same powers as we.[264]

C. K. Barrett's interpretation of this verse is similar:

The word 'form' or 'likeness' (ὁμόιωμα) has already been used several times in the epistle . . . and in none of these places does it mean simply 'imitation'. . . . We are probably justified therefore in our translation (the form of flesh which had passed under sin's rule), and in deducing that Christ took precisely the same fallen nature that we ourselves have, and that he remained sinless because he constantly overcame a proclivity to sin.[265]

Cullmann, commenting on Philippians 2, writes: 'In his becoming man in the flesh, and in his humbling himself unto death . . . Jesus must assume the form of fallen man in order to take the μορφὴ δούλου.'[266]

Here then is a principle of unity that holds together the exponents of the theory that Christ shared our fallen nature: they all believe that they are expounding the teaching of the New Testament, and cite the New Testament in support of their position. Their assumption is not without foundation, as we have seen earlier in our enquiry.[267] The fact that some New Testament scholars who do not specifically expound the theory in question nevertheless seem to state it when commenting upon certain passages adds weight to this position. It can thus be argued that one principle which holds the various advocates together is their interpretation of the New Testament, especially their exegesis of certain passages. It may perhaps be asked why so few have given this interpretation to the passages concerned, and why so many, who also maintain their loyalty to the New Testament, reject the theory. But this is the kind of question which arises whenever there is a sharp divergence between commentators. The problem is not unique to the present discussion.

A further point of unity which these diverse exponents of the theory possess is that they all believe that this Christological position is necessary if there is to be a true doctrine of the Incarnation. If Jesus is to be part of our humanity, if He is really to know and overcome our temptations, then He must enter into the conditions that have resulted from the Fall. There is no need

[264] *Commentary on Romans*, p. 315.
[265] *A Commentary on the Epistle to the Romans*, p. 156.
[266] *The Christology of the New Testament*, p. 178.   [267] See Part II above.

to cite the relevant passages from the writings of the advocates of the theory; these have already been given. It is a fundamental point in their argument. If the Son of God were to become one with us, then He must assume our fallen nature. If this condition was not fulfilled, then whatever Jesus might be, He would not be human in the sense that we know humanity now. He might possess a perfect humanity, but in no sense could He be said to be *homo-ousios* with us now. He would not face our problems; He would not be tempted in every point as we are; His human nature would be qualitatively different from that which we possess. This assumption might be challenged by many, but it is a point of view that is shared by all the advocates of this theory, a principle of unity that holds them together. It is interesting that certain writers who have not been claimed as advocates of the theory nevertheless seem to suggest it when they are expounding the concept of Christ's solidarity with mankind. Aulén writes:

When divine love becomes 'incarnate' and is subjected to the conditions of sin and death, the result is that it must become a suffering love. It has to live under those harsh conditions and consequences which are the results of sin. . . . But most significant is the fact that divine love in complete solidarity with men assumes the burden of all suffering, guilt, and condemnation which has been occasioned by sin. . . . It means rather that divine love in Christ enters into complete solidarity and suffers with the world toward which divine wrath is directed.[268]

A passage from J. B. Torrance gives a similar point of view:

A biblical doctrine of Christ which seeks to be true to the New Testament witness must always think of our Lord in terms of this mission to this sinful world, His identification with sinners, not only by His Incarnation and incorporation into our body of flesh and sin, but also by His life, His baptism in the waters of Jordan, His sympathy, His obedience, His suffering and baptism of blood on the Cross.[269]

Dr Eric Baker, after mentioning the passage in Harold Roberts's *Jesus and the Kingdom of God* to which we have already referred,[270] continues:

We all inherit the tendency which makes sin very probable, but it only becomes guilt when we yield to that tendency. Jesus differed from us, not in being free from that tendency, which would have meant

---

[268] *The Faith of the Christian Church*, pp. 234-5.
[269] *Essays in Christology for Karl Barth*, Ed. by T. H. L. Parker, p. 157.
[270] See pp. 176-7 above.

that He was not really Man, but in that by never yielding to it He directed His energies at every point towards doing the perfect will of God.[271]

We could take the phrase 'would have meant that He was not really Man' as a central motif in the thinking of all the advocates of the theory under discussion. If Christ did not share our fallen nature, 'He was not really Man'. Again it may perhaps be asked why so many have professed their belief in the full humanity of Jesus but have not accepted the point under discussion. No conclusive answer is possible. Whenever there is a divergence of theological position, this same problem arises to some degree.

A final principle of unity which holds together these various thinkers calls for mention. As the different advocates have been studied, attention has been called to the soteriological implications of the Christological point. This soteriological setting is to be found in all the advocates of the theory. They were all convinced that the point was essential if the redemptive work of Christ was to be effective for fallen mankind. This is not to suggest that all the writers concerned held the same theory of the Atonement. There is a wide divergence of soteriological approach. Nevertheless, all these writers found that the doctrine of Christ's assumption of fallen nature was an essential part of their understanding of the Atonement. The question of the significance of the theory for the work of Christ will be examined more fully in the final section of this present investigation.

We cannot maintain that there is a single principle of unity which holds together the material that has been presented earlier in this historical section. On the other hand, it would be wrong to suggest that we have a group of writers who are all independent of each other, simply having the one fact in common, the holding of this Christological point. There are certain definite historical links to be traced, and others are possible, though not certain. There is a most significant unity centred on the New Testament; if the teaching is found there, as these writers thought, this fact in itself unifies them. There are also two other factors which bind the advocates together: they feel that a belief in the full humanity of Jesus leads them to this conclusion; they believe that to have a satisfactory doctrine of the Atonement this point is essential.

[271] *The Faith of a Methodist*, pp. 65-6.

PART IV

The Comparative Neglect of the Theory

THE LIST OF thinkers who have held this Christological theory is not very large. On the whole it has been ignored or rejected. If it is firmly rooted in the New Testament, what is the reason for its lack of acceptance in the history of Christological thought? A question such as this is very difficult to answer, but some explanation must be attempted.

It can be pointed out that when this theory has been rejected it has been because people have feared that it might undermine belief in the sinlessness of Christ. If this fear were justified then the whole position would be untenable. Yet, as we have tried to show, all the advocates of this theory have stressed, and in no uncertain manner, Christ's sinlessness. In their thinking it was perfectly possible to hold side by side His sinlessness and His assumption of 'fallen human nature', and they do not appear to be guilty of illogically combining incompatibles. If this doctrine has been rejected for this reason, it has been rejected only because it has been misunderstood.

Another reason for this neglect might be found in concepts closely associated with that of 'original sin'. Many would agree with the verdict of Frederic Greeves when he says: 'Perhaps the most ill-chosen and unfortunate term in the whole Christian vocabulary is *"peccatum originale"*.'[1] Unquestionably it is a term which raises many unfortunate ideas, and it is obvious that we should refrain from attributing to Jesus some of the less fortunate of them. By far the most misleading conception that has been linked with 'original sin' is that of 'original guilt'. This association has been held by many of the leading Christian theologians throughout the centuries, particularly Augustine and the Reformers. It is to be questioned whether 'original guilt' can claim the support of the New Testament; certainly, throughout the years, it has had its opponents. But however this may be, there has been an obvious and understandable reluctance to attribute to Jesus 'original guilt'. The very term 'original sin' with its unfortunate, and often unwarranted associations, may have contributed to the comparative neglect of this Christological position. Yet it

[1] *The Meaning of Sin*, p. 31.

must be pointed out that most of the advocates of the theory use the term 'fallen human nature' rather than 'original sin', and some have even denied that the term 'original sin' can be applied to Jesus. It is obvious that a careful reading of these advocates would have convinced their critics that they had no desire to attribute to Jesus 'original sin' in the usual connotation of that term, and that they would emphatically have repudiated the idea that Jesus possessed 'original guilt'.

These two factors may have contributed to the neglect of the theory, but the main cause for it is to be found elsewhere. It lies in the fact that Christological thought throughout the centuries has been bedevilled by a refusal to give a true value to Christ's humanity. It is this refusal which has, of necessity, meant that the theory we are investigating has tended to be ignored. The chief cause for the lack of support given to a theory which is firmly rooted in the New Testament is thus that Christian thinking has been concerned primarily with the divinity of Christ, and has tended to neglect His humanity.

This comparative neglect can easily be seen if we trace, as briefly as possible, the movement of Christological thought in the history of the Church.

Within the pages of the New Testament the humanity of Christ is affirmed, yet even here we can detect the beginnings of the tendency to give that humanity less than its full emphasis. Jesus as He is portrayed in the Synoptic Gospels is human in the fullest degree; it was a real man who made His appearance in history, even if that man was the incarnate Son of God. In the Epistles there is the same firm grasp of the humanity of Christ. It is true that Paul's main concern is with the exalted and living Christ, but the vital point is that the victorious Christ is the one who was once incarnate and lived a truly human life, Jesus the man of Nazareth. Similarly, of the Epistle to the Hebrews it has rightly been said that 'Nowhere in the New Testament is the humanity of Christ set forth so movingly'.[2] When we turn to the Johannine writings, however, there is a tendency for the humanity of Jesus to slip into the background. This assertion needs to be stated with extreme caution if misunderstanding is to be avoided. John is emphatically anti-Docetic,[3] yet the whole picture of Jesus is

[2] H. R. Mackintosh, *The Doctrine of the Person of Christ*, p. 79.
[3] See John 1^{14}, 46^{-7}, 11$^{33, 35}$, 19^{34}; cf. 1 John 1$^{1-4}$, 2 John 7.

subtly changed and something of the grasp of the historical humanity has been lost in dogmatic considerations.[4]

In post New Testament thought the situation is different. When 'we leave the New Testament and attempt to follow the Christological controversies and speculations of the Patristic age, we are conscious of moving into a world very different from the "historical" world of the Apostolic writers, for Jesus has almost ceased to be a historical human figure and has become the "mythological" subject of metaphysical speculation.'[5]

One of the earliest Christological heresies was Docetism. This unsatisfactory teaching was firmly rejected by the Early Church. Yet despite this rejection by orthodox Christian thinkers, there was a proneness to give less than full significance to the humanity of Christ. This is seen in the emphasis on the Logos doctrine by the Apologists and Early Fathers, a doctrine which was a mixed blessing. It involved a category of thought which tended to shift attention away from the humanity of Christ. In some of the Fathers, this led to a docetic element in their thought. The most conspicuous example is that of Clement of Alexandria,[6] though the weakness was not confined to him. Origen expresses the doctrine of the *communicatio idiomatum*, but it is the humanity that is gradually deified.[7] In Athanasius there is a lack of emphasis on the humanity of Christ,[8] a fact which has been pointed out by a number of scholars.[9] Hilary has a distinctly docetic element in his Christology which springs from a preoccupation with the divinity of Christ to the detriment of His humanity. He even goes to the length of asserting that Christ's body was of heavenly origin.[10] In Hilary the weaknesses and 'ignorance' of Jesus are explained

[4] The bold realism of Mark has gone; The Baptism, Temptations, Transfiguration and Agony in the Garden are not mentioned; there is also a heightening of the miraculous. The whole picture of Jesus is subtly changed; He is confident in the Father's purpose and moves with certainty across the stage of history. He is never taken by surprise; 11[34] is the only suggestion to be found in the Gospel of His lack of knowledge. His prayers are for His disciples; He never prays for Himself.

[5] Geraint Vaughan Jones, *Christology and Myth in the New Testament*, p. 115.

[6] See *Stromata*, vi.9 (*PG*, IX.292); cf. *Paedagogus*, i.12 (*PG*, VIII.368).

[7] See *Contra Celsum*, iii.41 (*PG*, XI.972-3).

[8] See *De Incarnatione* (*PG*, XXV.95-108), viii, ix, x, xiv, xviii, xx, xlii. The same defect is found in his later writings; see *Contra Arian*, ii.8 (*PG*, XXVI.161-2), iii, 30-1 (ibid. 388-9).

[9] C. E. Raven, *Apollinarianism*, pp. 78-85; J. A. Dorner, *Doctrine of the Person of Christ*, I. ii.260. For a recent defence of Athanasius against this charge see R. V. Sellers, *Two Ancient Christologies*, pp. 41-4.

[10] *De Trinitate*, x.23 (*PL*, X.363); cf. x.16, 18 (ibid. 354-5, 355-6).

away.[11] The docetic note in Hilary is pronounced, and the inadequacy of his grasp on the full humanity of Christ is beyond question.

In Apollinarius we reach the climax of this tendency in Greek Christology to give less than due weight to the humanity of Christ. In him the denial of the fullness of the humanity is explicit. He was of the opinion that complete human nature and complete divinity could not dwell in the same person, and maintained that the Logos took the place of the human soul in Christ. Apollinarius realized that this made Christ's humanity different from ours: Christ 'is not a man but as a man, since He is not ὁμόουσιος with man in the crowning element'.[12] This position was condemned, but Apollinarius reveals a weakness that is to be found in Greek Christology as a whole. Raven says:

Apollinarius can only be condemned by those who are prepared to allow that the whole Greek school from Justin to Leontius and John of Damascus is similar . . . since the divergences between them and the heresiarch are merely verbal and superficial.[13]

Dorner makes a similar point: 'We must, however, at the same time, not forget to mention that the Church teachers of his day had not really advanced any farther.'[14]

It would be one-sided, however, to lay all the emphasis on the Alexandrian school of thought and ignore the Antiochene. The latter tended to start from the human picture of Jesus as portrayed in the Gospels. Its weakness, however, was its proneness to separate the two natures in Christ and thus split the unity of His person. There was serious controversy between the schools of Alexandria and Antioch, with the former finally emerging triumphant. Cyril defeated Nestorius, and with his victory there was a set-back for the full appreciation of the humanity of Christ. Cyril was of the opinion that in Christ after the union there was only one nature. He affirmed that the human nature was ἀνυπό-στατος.[15] Cyril tended to think of Christ as assuming, not a real manhood, but only the attributes of manhood. Dorner says that

---

[11] *De Trinitate*, ix.71 (*PL*, X.337-8), x.24 (ibid. 363-4).
[12] *Frag.* 45, H. Lietzmann, *Apollinaris von Laodicea und seine Schule*, p. 214.
[13] C. E. Raven, *Apollinarianism*, p. 297; cf. pp. 18 and 84.
[14] J. A. Dorner, *Doctrine of the Person of Christ*, I. II. 367.
[15] For a discussion of Cyril's Christology, see R. V. Sellers, *Two Ancient Christologies*, pp. 80-106.

for Cyril 'humanity is a mere attitude or predicate of God'[16] and that 'He eschewed the notion of the human nature having any personal centre, which was its sole point of unity . . . the human nature continued to subsist merely in the form of congeries of accidents, held together by the Logos as their centre'.[17] This interpretation has not gone unchallenged; R. V. Sellers, for instance, defends Cyril's use of language, and maintains that his critics do not understand the way in which he was using the terms.[18] This may well be true to some extent, but there is still a deficiency in Cyril's Christology in that he fails to give due significance to the humanity of Christ. Nestorius, who did maintain the full humanity, whatever else were his errors, was branded as a heretic; Cyril was acclaimed as orthodox. Cyril's defeat of Nestorius began the dissolution of the school of Antioch; Dioscorus and Eutyches finished the task. It is true that the teaching of Eutyches was condemned, but the school of Antioch had been crushed. At the end of this period of controversy the Creed of Chalcedon was accepted. It was a fair and balanced statement of the Person of Christ but was open to various interpretations, and more and more it tended to be interpreted in a Cyrillian sense.

Reference needs to be made to the acceptance during this controversy of a concept which has frequently been detrimental to the full appreciation of the humanity of Christ. In Cyril and Leo we see the emergence of the idea of the *communicatio idiomatum*. These two fathers did not question that there was one person with two natures which were distinct. They simply meant that 'the one person shared equally in both names and properties and experiences of both natures".[19] This interpretation is valid. Later, however, the concept assumed another meaning, that the union was so close that the natures interpenetrated each other to the point of the transference of qualities. This was the confusion of natures that Chalcedon resisted. When the doctrine was understood in this latter sense it was almost invariably to the detriment of the humanity; the divine qualities and prerogatives were thought of as being transferred to the human nature, while the divine nature was left untouched.

---

[16] J. A. Dorner, *Doctrine of the Person of Christ*, II. 1. 57.
[17] Ibid. p. 67.   [18] *Two Ancient Christologies*, pp. 95-9.
[19] J. F. Bethune-Baker, *History of Early Christian Doctrine*, p. 293.

After Chalcedon, the followers of Cyril refused to accept the decision, and the result was a further protracted period of Christological controversy. The first point at issue was whether there existed one or two natures in Christ. Monophysitism was condemned at the Council of Constantinople in 553. The Chalcedonian formula was upheld, but in the Cyrillian interpretation: Christ is one, and the two natures can be distinguished only in theory. Thus there was a further weakening of the human side of the personality of Christ. Leontius of Byzantium, the defender of orthodoxy against Monophysitism, maintained the two natures in Christ, but affirmed that the human nature was ἐνυπόστατος.

This is the point at which to refer to the two ideas of ἀνυπόστατος and ἐνυπόστατος, for both have an important bearing on the inadequate understanding of the humanity of Christ.[20] The first term expresses the idea that the human nature was impersonal. Christ was not a human person, but a divine person who had assumed human nature. Jesus was not a man, but Man. This concept has a certain value, especially soteriologically; it is dangerous, however, in that it means a weakening of the humanity and tends inevitably towards Apollinarianism. The idea of ἐνυπόστατος is more satisfactory. The humanity was not impersonal; yet it did not possess an independent personality but was only personal in the Logos. This, if carefully stated, perhaps suggests a satisfactory solution to the relationship between the two natures, but there is much wisdom in Baillie's comment that the truth which the idea contains can be stated more satisfactorily by the use of other categories. If the term is used, it needs to be defined with extreme care, otherwise it becomes simply another way of saying ἀνυπόστατος. Thus the category which was introduced by Cyril and later modified by Leontius to explain the relationship of the two natures in the one person tended to lead to an underestimation of the full humanity of Christ. This often happened when these categories were used by later theologians.

The next phase in the Christological discussion was concerned with the existence of one or two wills in Christ. At the Council of Constantinople 680-1, Monothelitism was condemned. This was a triumph for orthodoxy, but it in no way altered the position in

---

[20] For an excellent critique of these two ideas see D. M. Baillie, *God Was In Christ*, pp. 85-93.

which the stress was far more on the divine than on the human in Christ. Dorner says of the Council:

They again contrived, by means of unexpected addenda, to give to the will of the divine such predominance, that the human will was degraded from the position of a free, to that of a merely operative, power . . . constituting little more than a point of transition for the all-decisive divine will.[21]

John of Damascus, who in a sense sums up Greek orthodoxy, asserts the two natures. He makes the divine so dominant, however, that the human nature loses much of its reality.[22] 'Thus by degrees the Church's memories of the human life of Jesus faded into oblivion.'[23] It is true that the Western theologians were, on the whole, more satisfactory on this point than the Eastern, but it was in the East that Christology was most debated; the West tended to be more concerned with other problems.

During the period from the time of John of Damascus to the Reformation a significant new feature was the rise of Mariology and the mediatorial office of the saints. As a result, the humanity of Christ receded even farther into the background. Perhaps it would be more accurate to reverse the statement: it is precisely because belief in the humanity of Jesus had been weakened, with a resultant weakening of His mediatorial position, that there arose the necessity for the emergence of the Virgin Mary and the saints, who possessed a distinct humanity, and who could therefore fulfil a real mediatorial position. When, however, they had assumed this position, they tended to weaken even further the understanding of the humanity of Christ. The Christology of this period is docetic in character. Aquinas may speak for the orthodox theologians of the period. From the first moment of conception, he says, Jesus possessed the full knowledge of the Blessed;[24] even during His birth Mary experienced no pain and she remained a Virgin;[25] His prayers were uttered for didactic purposes and did not in any way reflect His devotional life.[26] The resultant picture is one of unreality.

[21] J. A. Dorner, *Doctrine of the Person of Christ*, II. 1.168.
[22] See *De fide Orthodoxa*, especially Lib. iii.17, 19 (*PG*, XLIV.1067ff), where he suggests that a deification of the human took place at the very act of the Incarnation.
[23] H. R. Mackintosh, *The Person of Jesus Christ*, p. 222.
[24] *Summa Theologica*, III.Q.ix.2 (*PL*, IV.110-11).
[25] Ibid. Q. xxviii.2 (IV.259ff), Q.xxxv.6 (IV.319-20).
[26] Ibid. Q.xxi.1 (IV.208-9).

At the Reformation the position is not completely clarified, though the theology does become more Christocentric. Calvin expresses the doctrine of '*occultatio*', in which there is emphasized the humiliation involved in the Incarnation, but he also maintains just as firmly that the divine attributes were not abandoned but were hidden as the sun is veiled behind thick clouds. In many passages Luther speaks most movingly of the humanity of Jesus; He affirms that 'The immortal God becomes something that must die, suffer, and have all the human idiomata. What would that man be, with whom God is personally united, if He were not to have true human idiomata?'[27] Despite this, there is a weakness in Luther's Christology, for he introduces as an explanation of how two natures are in one person the idea of the *communicatio idiomatum*. The defect is clearly seen in the controversy with Zwingli about the real presence of Christ in the Eucharist. Luther maintained that because of the *communicatio idiomatum* the body of Christ was ubiquitous; this was an attribute of divinity which became applicable to the human nature of Christ. Here is the *communicatio idiomatum* being used to the detriment of the full humanity of Jesus. It is thus evident that the Reformation did not completely restore the understanding of the true humanity of Christ. The years that followed saw a worsening, rather than a betterment, of the situation.

During the last hundred years there has arisen a new desire to do justice to the picture of Jesus as portrayed in the Gospels, and to emphasize His humanity as well as His divinity. This is seen in the Kenotic theory, which maintains that for the Son of God to become incarnate with a real and full humanity there must have been a laying aside, a kenosis, of some at least of the divine attributes. It is not necessary at this point to outline the various forms that Kenotic Christology has taken, or to give a critique of the theory; all that is needed is to pay tribute to the fact that this theory makes a serious attempt to do justice to the humanity of Jesus. Another school of thought that has paid attention to the full humanity of Christ is the 'Jesus of History' school. This movement can be said to have its beginnings in the writings of Ritschl, with his emphasis on Jesus as the historic founder of Christianity. The movement has many weaknesses, but its strength lies in the understanding of the humanity of Jesus.

[27] Cited by Philip S. Watson, *Let God Be God*, p. 145, note 140.

As J. S. Lawton says: 'It became the watchword of all liberal Christology—Christ's real humanity.'[28] These theologians saw that there were human limits to the knowledge of Jesus and that His moral and religious life could be understood in human categories, and by underlining these features and making much of Jesus as the teacher, they wrote movingly of the Jesus of History. This movement helped to wipe away Docetism, which had haunted Christology from the first century.

There has been a strong reaction against the 'Jesus of History' school, particularly by the neo-orthodox theologians. Their criticisms, however, are not levelled against the desire to do justice to the humanity of Jesus, and indeed this emphasis is to be found in the neo-orthodox position as well. We must agree with the criticism that this new school does not in fact pay sufficient regard to the historical Jesus, because of an excess of historical scepticism towards the New Testament record. But in their theology they accept the fullness of His humanity as much as the fullness of His divinity.

The position has thus been reached in theological thought that the humanity of Jesus is being taken seriously. We can heartily agree with D. M. Baillie's remark: 'It may safely be said that practically all schools of theological thought today take the humanity of our Lord more seriously than has ever been done before by Christian theologians.'[29] We also agree when he says that even though the Creeds of the Early Church affirmed the humanity, yet

the Church was building better than it knew, and its ecumenical decisions were wiser than its individual theologians in this matter. Or should we rather say that it did not fully realize the implications of declaring that in respect of His human nature Christ is consubstantial with ourselves? At any rate it was continually haunted by a docetism which made His human nature very different from ours and indeed largely explained it away as a matter of simulation or 'seeming' rather than reality. Theologians shrank from admitting human growth, human ignorance, human struggle and temptation, into their conception of the Incarnate Life, and treated it as simply a divine life lived in a human body (and sometimes even this was conceived as essentially different from our bodies) rather than a truly human life lived under the psychical conditions of humanity. The cruder forms of Docetism

---

[28] *Conflict in Christology*, p. 8.   [29] *God Was in Christ*, p. 11.

were fairly soon left behind, but in its more subtle forms the danger continued in varying degrees to dog the steps of theology right through until modern times.[30]

This quotation very adequately sums up the point we have been making in our brief excursion into the realms of Christological history—namely, that even though the humanity of Christ was affirmed by orthodoxy, it was given insufficient emphasis and was often ignored. This was true, with a few exceptions, until the modern period. It will readily be seen that the neglect of the humanity of Christ is a strong reason for the neglect of the doctrine with which we are concerned. When there is an inadequate grasp of the humanity of Christ, there can be little hope of the question of the relation between the human nature of Christ and the Fall being studied in such a way as to show that He assumed 'fallen human nature'.

[30] *God Was in Christ*, p. 11.

PART V

Constructive Statement

S O FAR THE discussion has been mainly concerned with a particular theory about the human nature of Christ, but frequently, both in the New Testament and Historical sections, its soteriological implications have become evident. It is thus essential to ask what is the soteriological significance of the theory that Christ assumed 'fallen human nature'. This will help to place the theory in a wider setting and draw out its general implications. This investigation is most relevant because the Person and Work of Christ are essentially related. The famous dictum of Melanchthon is profoundly true: 'To know Christ is to know His benefits.' Any theory of His Person that is not closely connected with His Work is automatically suspect. The converse is also true; any theory of the Work of Christ that is not firmly founded upon a sound estimate of His Person is to be rejected.

The main types of theory concerning the Work of Christ will be examined in turn to see in what ways our present investigation is relevant. It is only as we see this Christological discussion in the setting of these soteriological theories that a true estimate of its value will be possible.

A. THE MORAL INFLUENCE THEORY

This theory lays all the emphasis on the Cross as a revelation of the love of God, and maintains that our love is evoked as we witness this supreme revelation of God's love; 'love enkindling love'.[1]

It is not our present purpose to give an exposition and critique of the various theories of the atonement, but to see the relevance for the doctrine of the Work of Christ of the Christological position that we have been studying.

To fit the Christological position under investigation into this theory is not easy. Where there is no idea of any transaction taking place, the idea that Christ cleanses human nature in His own person cannot have a central position. Nevertheless, there would be a greater appeal to the human heart if it were seen that the love of God was such that the Son of God was willing to take our fallen nature on Himself, face the same trials and temptations

---

[1] S. Cave, *The Doctrine of the Work of Christ*, p. 133.

as we face, and yet, through the divine power that was His, live a perfect and sinless life, and through the Cross completely redeem the 'fallen human nature' which He had assumed. It must be admitted, however, that the moment this new element is introduced the moral influence theory is transformed, for in Christ's person there has taken place an act which is more than a revelation. All we can say in considering this type of soteriological theory is that the doctrine of the Person of Christ which is the subject of our present investigation is not inconsistent with it, and in fact gives it greater power and appeal.

B. THE SATISFACTION THEORY

The satisfaction theory has its classic formulation in *Cur Deus Homo?* of Anselm. He maintained that our sin had stained the honour of God, but that God could forgive if He received a satisfaction that was sufficient to 'satisfy' His wounded honour. The satisfaction must come from man, but this creates an apparently insuperable difficulty. All sin against God is infinite sin, and this means that 'there is no one, therefore, who can make this satisfaction except God Himself. . . . But no one ought to make it except man.'[2] This satisfaction Christ made. Because of His voluntary self-sacrifice on the Cross, God owed Christ a debt; yet there was nothing that Christ lacked. He, therefore, handed the recompense over to man in the form of forgiveness from the Father.

This theory has had a profound influence on a large section of Christian thought about the Work of Christ. There have been differences in detail among the advocates, but fundamentally the satisfaction theory follows the exposition of Anselm. Despite the different emphases, the basic idea is that the honour of God has been stained by human sin, and man, who stands under the wrath of God, must make recompense. Sinful man cannot do this; therefore Christ, God incarnate, makes the act of recompense on man's behalf. God is appeased, and so the atonement is a reality. The key-thought is that only man ought to make the recompense and yet only God could; therefore Jesus was the God-man.

This position, however, is considerably strengthened if the estimate of the humanity of Christ that we have been investigating is accepted. 'Only man ought', because it is the sin of man that has offended God and stained His honour, and therefore it is

---

[2] *Cur Deus Homo?* ii.6 (*PL*, CLVIII.404).

fitting, indeed it is essential, that the recompense be made by man. Thus it is of prime importance that the Son of God should assume human nature. We must go farther than this however; if man had not sinned, then the honour of God would not have been wounded, and therefore there would have been no need for man to make restitution. It is thus possible to assert that human nature as it was before sin entered in had no need to make recompense to God. It was the human nature that in Adam had rebelled and sinned which needed to face God's wrath, and from which the required retribution had to come. The Heidelberg Catechism says: 'The same human nature which has sinned should make satisfaction for sin.'[3] So we might with justice alter the saying of Anselm. Only *fallen human nature* ought; only God can. Thus, it would appear, it becomes necessary to accept the theory that Christ took our 'fallen human nature'. He remained sinless, and thus did not in any way fall from the duty of living life to perfection. On the Cross He gave up His life, and in so doing made the act of restitution on behalf of fallen humanity.

If this interpretation is sound, it means that the satisfaction theory as usually expounded falls into serious error. Those who ought to pay the retribution to the wounded honour of God are fallen men and women. If the whole satisfaction theory is not to be undermined, it is essential that this debt of honour should be paid by one who shared this fallen nature. This condition can be met only if the theory that Christ assumed 'fallen human nature' is accepted. Despite His assumption of this fallen nature, Jesus lived a perfect life, and so the sacrifice of His life on the Cross could be a satisfaction made to God and could be for the redemption of mankind.

It might be argued that by the same logic we should say that Christ was a sinner, since only sinners ought to make this satisfaction to God. This is not acceptable. If Christ were a sinner His satisfaction would not be valid and the atonement would be undermined. The assertion that Christ shared our 'fallen nature' brings Him into our post-Fall situation, but it does not jeopardize His sinlessness. In this way the atonement is valid.

[3] Lord's Day 6, Question 16.

C. THE THEORY OF PENAL SUBSTITUTION

This interpretation of the atonement is in many ways closely connected with the satisfaction theory, yet there is a significant change of emphasis. The idea of satisfaction in the Anselmic sense has gone; punishment is required by the Law of God; Christ bore this punishment in our stead. This theory was firmly held at the Reformation, though Gustav Aulén maintains that Luther was an advocate of the 'Christus Victor' theory of the atonement.[4] In recent years the theory has been subjected to frequent and serious attacks, but it would be false to suggest that it is obsolete. There are still many theologians who affirm that God must punish sin, and maintain that Christ bore our punishment in our stead, and so we are set free. Only in this way, they say, is the justice of God truly upheld, and the gravity of sin fully recognized.

This position raises many serious questions which it is not our purpose to investigate here, but it must be said that to think that Christ, who was perfect and spotless, bore the wrath of God hardly seems acceptable. For this reason it is usually argued that Christ on the Cross bore our sins, that our sins were laid upon Him, and, because He took the sins of the world upon Himself, He also came under punishment and bore the wrath of God against sin. When the position is expressed in this way the question arises: In what sense can we say that Christ bore our sins or the sins of the whole world? These and similar phrases, hallowed though they be by Christian devotion, are notoriously difficult to define. It is no easy matter to state how our sins were transferred to Christ on the Cross. Yet if we are to avoid the concept that Christ, the Perfect and the Innocent, was punished by the wrath of God, we must find the answer to the question how Christ bore our sins. The Christological theory that we have been discussing suggests a possible answer. The Son of God when He became incarnate assumed 'fallen human nature', and it was this nature that He took to the Cross and finally redeemed. When we think of the solidarity of mankind, we can see how Jesus, when He took our fallen nature and nailed it to the Cross, was bearing our sin, at least in the sense that He had entered the post-Fall situation which had been caused by sin. Though He Himself was sinless, when He

[4] *Christus Victor*, Chapter 6.

was nailed to the Cross He was at least linked with sinful mankind in that He had assumed the fallen nature which was the inheritance of all the sons of Adam. It is obvious that this exposition means a transformation of the Substitutionary theory in some of its details, but it is not our desire to defend the theory; our aim is simply to point out that the Christological position which has been the centre of our investigation can give a possible solution to some of the difficulties raised by the theory of Penal Substitution.

D. THE 'CHRISTUS VICTOR' THEORY

This theory was for a long time looked upon as of no value to modern thought on the Atonement; it was thought to be crude, primitive, out of date and hardly worthy of consideration. Gustav Aulén in his book *Christus Victor* has brought it back into modern soteriological thought. He claims that this is the classic view of the Christian Church and that it was overlooked because of the rise of the Latin and Subjective theories.[5] He speaks of it as the Dramatic theory in the sense that from first to last the Atonement is the work of God Himself. The background of the theory is the dualism between God and the Devil, but this dualism is not ultimate, since the forces of evil are created forces which have rebelled against their Creator. This theory is not merely that punishment is cancelled, but that sin itself is defeated. God in Christ comes face to face with the powers of evil; through the Cross He wins the victory; and through this victory He brings salvation to men who are imprisoned by the power of sin.

Where into this picture can we fit the Christological theory that Christ shared our 'fallen human nature'? The important point in the 'Christus Victor' doctrine of the Atonement is the clash between the power of darkness and Christ, with the resultant victory of the Son of God. In what way did this combat take place? This question takes us to the heart of the matter. In one sense the battle was external to the person of Christ. In His own nature was all the fullness of God; opposed to Him were the powers of evil, which can be seen in the scheming, calculating evil of Caiaphas, in the weakness of Pilate, in the treachery of Judas, in the failure of the rest of the disciples, in the volatile crowd who

[5] These are Aulén's designations for the two theories that we associate with the names of Anselm and Abelard.

howled for His death. In this sense the evil was external to Christ, and the victory lay in the fact that He died undefeated, His love unbroken, with His purity and holiness unstained; even in death He prayed for His persecutors, and He died for His murderers. Yet if this struggle on the Cross is to have its full power, the victory must be won not merely in an external way, it must be won in the nature of man. E. L. Mascall says: 'Only God can overcome man's ancient enemy, while the battle must none the less be fought in human nature, since its fruits are to be communicated to men.'[6] If Christ assumed our 'fallen human nature', He took upon Himself the very nature in which the powers of death and sin were deeply entrenched. Thus throughout His incarnate life there was a struggle; these powers tried to make Him a sinner like the rest of mankind, but always they were held at bay and Christ lived a perfect life. On the Cross the final victory was won when these powers that were rooted in fallen human nature were finally defeated and eradicated. In this defeat was the victory of God in Christ, and, through faith in Christ, that victory becomes a reality in men's lives.

Again it must be admitted that a new element has appeared, but it is one that fits naturally into place in the 'Christus Victor' theory. In fact it is of real value to bring in this new element. In the first place it gives a fuller and deeper exposition to the nature of the victory that was won by Christ. In the second place it overcomes one of the serious criticisms that have been levelled at the theory. It has been asked in what way the humanity of Christ is necessary to this interpretation of the Cross. Here is a definite and emphatic answer. It was by the very act of the Incarnation, the assuming of 'fallen human nature', that the battle was joined, and the final victory was itself won within human nature. The addition of this Christological position strengthens the 'Christus Victor' theory of the Cross.

E. THE REPRESENTATIVE THEORY

The Representative theory as such is, on the whole, a modern exposition of the Cross, but the idea of Christ as our representative has always played a part in theological thought. The essential point of this interpretation is that Christ as perfect man and as our representative makes a response to God on our behalf. Sometimes

---

[6] *Christ, the Christian and the Church*, p. 75.

this response is thought of in terms of perfect penitence, sometimes in sacrificial categories. Because we are sinners we are incapable of making this response ourselves. Through identification with Christ, through faith, through the Holy Spirit, through 'mystical union' (various writers lay varying emphases here), we become identified with our representative in the sight of God.

This theory has much to commend it; but, in its familiar form, it seems to possess certain weaknesses. The whole idea of a representative implies someone who has a real contact with the party who needs to be represented, who can therefore stand on his behalf before another. This theory makes Christ our representative, who stands before God on our behalf. We are united with Him and therefore His action becomes ours. Now the gulf that separates man from God is the one created by sin, and if Jesus is really to be our representative He has to come to our side of the gulf. This immediately creates a problem. To make the perfect response to God, our representative must be perfect and sinless; yet the fact still remains that if He is to stand on our behalf He must stand with us. This position can be met if our present Christological theory is accepted. He came to our side of the chasm because of the 'fallen human nature' that He had assumed, and yet, because He was sinless and never allowed this nature to gain control, He could make the perfect act as our representative. The position can be put another way. The Representative theory as it is usually expounded tends to imply that the gulf which needs to be bridged is that between man and God. This, however, is not so. If man had remained obedient, there would have been no cleavage and therefore no need for atonement. Therefore it is not sufficient to say that Christ was a man who was our representative, for this deals only with the gulf between man and God. If Christ was our representative simply as perfect man, between us and Him there would still be the deep and humanly impassable abyss, between us and Him would be the gulf created by sin. This has to be bridged before we can become united with our representative. To be an effective representative on our behalf, Christ must bridge the chasm which exists between man and God which has been created by sin; He must become identified with sinners, yet He Himself must remain sinless. This object is achieved if we accept the idea that Christ assumed 'fallen human nature'. Here is His real identification with the humanity which needs to be saved; yet because of His sinlessness He is able to be our perfect representative before God.

It would appear, therefore, that, for the Representative theory of the Cross to be fully adequate to meet the sinful human situation, there needs to be incorporated within its structure a Christological position similar to the one that is the object of our present study.

God to meet man's need sent His eternal Son, who took our nature, entered into our specific situation, and became one with needy mankind in the deepest and fullest sense. It was only through this real identification with us that He was able to be our Saviour. It is not easy to decide between the various theories of the Work of Christ; perhaps each of them presents a facet of the truth. But, as we have seen, each theory is the stronger for accepting the hypothesis that Christ shared our 'fallen human nature'. Perhaps no argument is so eloquent or so compelling as this. A Christological theory which makes a valuable contribution to each of the theories of the Cross is worthy of careful consideration. The very fact that it is not relevant only to one of the theories, but fits each of them, is in itself a powerful argument for its truth.

The full soteriological implications of the theory are not exhausted when we have seen that it makes a relevant contribution to the various theories of the Atonement. The Representative theory is, in the present writer's opinion, the most acceptable of them, and it can be shown that there it is of special value. We shall therefore make a more detailed study of its contribution to this doctrine of the Atonement.

The hypothesis under investigation affirms that the Son of God assumed human nature as it was because of the Fall. It also maintains that Jesus lived a perfect life, always triumphing over the nature which He had assumed. Finally, it asserts that this nature was cleansed upon the Cross and that Jesus rose from the dead with human nature renewed. E. L. Mascall aptly says: 'The ultimate purpose of the Incarnation is not just the re-creation of human nature in Jesus, but the re-creation of the whole human race in him.'[7] We are thus brought face to face with the question of how we are re-created in Christ. The victory was won by Him in His own person, but in what way was it made a reality for

[7] *Christ, the Christian and the Church*, p. 69.

us? It is the problem of the one and the many. How can what happened to the One, Jesus, be effective for the many, the rest of mankind.

The key to the answer may be found in the concept of 'solidarity'. The idea of 'corporate personality'[8] is vital for the correct understanding of Hebraic thought, for in the Hebrew mind there is 'fluidity of transition from the one to the many and vice versa';[9] because of the solidarity of society one person can act on behalf of the many, and what that one person does is of significance for the many. It is obvious that if this way of thinking is accepted, it is of the utmost value for the understanding of the work of redemption.

If human personality is to be correctly understood the idea of racial solidarity must be taken seriously. We are not isolated individuals, entirely separated from the rest of the human race; rather we are linked with the rest of mankind, we are bound to other people with powerful ties. This is to be understood both in terms of heredity and environment. We are linked with the human race in the sense that we draw the raw material of personality from our ancestors through the medium of heredity and we make our own contribution to the human stock through our children. We are also connected to the rest of humanity through the medium of environment. What others do vitally affects us for good or ill; what we do does not merely concern us, but has effects upon our fellow men. If the concept of the 'racial unconscious' is accepted, then we are linked with the whole human race in the depths of our psychic nature. A theory of rigid individualism can no longer be accepted; the concept of racial solidarity is essential for the correct understanding of human life. Certainly it has an important part to play in the understanding of the Christian doctrine of redemption. It means that what Christ did is effective for all men in so far as they are linked with Him. The whole point of redemption is that the results of the Fall should be reversed, that the power of sin should be broken, that 'fallen human nature' should be redeemed. Christian teaching is that this has been done in Jesus. It was a victory achieved by the One for the many.

[8] The classical exposition of this idea is to be found in H. Wheeler Robinson's article, 'The Hebrew Conception of Corporate Personality', in *Werden und Wesen des alten Testaments* (1936), pp. 49ff.
[9] H. Wheeler Robinson, *The Old Testament, Its Making and Meaning*, p. 79.

In the New Testament there are clear indications that Jesus was thought of as being a representative person; what He did was of significance for others. The term Son of Man in the Gospels has a representative significance, even if the term is interpreted as being a personal title and the corporate interpretation is rejected. The title suggests that its bearer has intimate links with the rest of mankind, especially if 'Son of Man' is connected with the idea of Adam.[10] In Pauline thought this idea of Christ as a representative figure is clearly seen. The concept of Christ as Second Adam can be adequately understood only if we think in terms of someone whose actions have a corporate significance. The figure of Jesus as High Priest in the Epistle to the Hebrews contains the same essential idea of Jesus as One who can represent the many. Clearly Jesus is not to be thought of as an isolated individual; rather He is to be seen as so closely linked with mankind that His work has significance for all.

There is, however, the other aspect of the question and this is our primary concern here. If we are to interpret the Work of Christ in terms of racial solidarity, it is not enough to realize that He is a representative figure; we must also realize that we have to be linked with Him, to become 'solid' with Him, if what He does for us is to become actual within us. This side of the matter is powerfully developed by St Paul. It is not necessary for us to make a detailed examination of this aspect of Paul's teaching, but the main points must be briefly outlined. The importance of Paul for the New Testament exposition of the theory under discussion has been indicated earlier, and if we are to understand the soteriological implications of that theory, we can turn to Paul for guidance. There are a number of Pauline phrases which are relevant here; they are closely inter-related, and are concerned with the believer's relationship with Christ. The essential key to the understanding of these ideas appears to be that of 'racial solidarity' or 'corporate personality'.

The first of these phrases is 'in Christ' ($\dot{\epsilon}\nu$ $X\rho\iota\sigma\tau\hat{\omega}$). There has been much discussion of this phrase, and a number of explanations have been given to explain the origin of Paul's conception of being 'in Christ'. Deissmann states that the source of the idea is to be found in the identification of the exalted Christ with the Spirit (2 Cor 3[17] is the all-important verse in this connection).

[10] See pp. 51-9 above.

He maintains that it is thus possible for Paul to think of Christ as an atmosphere in which we live. We are in Christ and Christ is in us.[11] This interpretation means that the individuality of the believer is affirmed; there is no mystical absorption. The personality of Christ, however, is endangered. It is also questionable whether Christ and the Spirit can be identified so closely. In this interpretation of Deissmann the phrase 'in Christ' is understood as expressing 'personal religion', a man's personal relationship with Christ. But this emphasis represents only part of the truth and perhaps not the most significant part. There is in the phrase a strong communal meaning. This aspect is emphasized by R. N. Flew, who tends to think of being 'in Christ' as inseparable from being a member of the *ecclesia*. He says that 'the roots of this phrase "in Christ" ' are to be found 'in the action of Jesus, who, as the Messiah, gathered His followers as the nucleus of the true Israel, and declared their solidarity with Himself'.[12] This corporate significance of the phrase has been underlined by many thinkers. T. W. Manson connects the phrase 'in Christ' with 'Son of Man', which he interprets in a communal sense.[13] Oepke links the phrase with the idea of the two Adams, and again its corporate significance is stressed.[14] Ernest Best has recently advocated a similar position in which the idea of corporate personality is underlined.[15] We do not wish to subscribe to all the details of exposition given by these and similar writers, but they would seem to be a useful corrective to the personal interpretation of 'in Christ' given by Deissmann. There seems to be no reason why the personal and corporate aspects of the phrase should be mutually exclusive, but the latter can hardly be denied; 'believers are "in Christ" because they are "in his corporate personality".'[16] This category is of importance for the interpretation of Paul's doctrine of redemption. His line of argument is that 'redemption is in Christ; believers are in Christ; so redemption passes over to them'.[17] Here we have 'the conception of Christ as a corporate personality, who in his own person gained the salvation of believers and of whose personality they are members'.[18] The relevance of the Christological theory that Christ assumed 'fallen human nature' seems to be clear. Jesus won the victory over this

---

[11] *Paul*, p. 140.   [12] *Jesus and His Church*, p. 153.
[13] *The Teaching of Jesus*, pp. 232-4.   [14] TWNT, II.538.
[15] *One Body in Christ*, pp. 19-30.   [16] Ibid. pp. 20-1.
[17] Ibid. p. 21.   [18] Ibid. p. 29.

nature which He had assumed; He did this as a corporate personality. In so far as we are 'in Christ' there is salvation and victory
for us. If Christ did not defeat 'fallen human nature' in His own
person, how can we win the victory over the Fall?

A second of these Pauline concepts is that of Christ as the
Second Adam. This has been discussed earlier,[19] but it needs to
be mentioned here because one of the factors involved in the
understanding of this idea is an appreciation of the concepts of
'corporate personality' and 'racial solidarity'. Adam and Christ
were not merely individuals; they were racial figures. Their
actions affected mankind. The formula 'in Christ' is linked with
the concept of Christ as the Second Adam in 1 Corinthians 15[20-2].
When we are 'in Christ' we become linked with the Second Adam
and His victory and His benefits become ours. When we are 'in
Him', the Second Adam, the results of the Fall of the first Adam
are counteracted.

Mention also needs to be made of the phrase 'with Christ'. The
idea of dying and rising with Christ has already been considered,[20]
but it is relevant here, for the concept of solidarity is a key feature
in this idea. Lohmeyer has argued that 'with' ($\sigma \dot{v} \nu$) in this
Pauline usage is unique.[21] The idea is that the believer is with
Christ in His Death and Resurrection; he has 'a part in that
event of the past'.[22] But there are also passages which speak of a
present process of dying (Rom 6[11-12], Col 3[5]). There is however no
essential contradiction. The two ideas are linked and are complementary. Our present dying to sin is dependent on the fact
that we have died with Christ. We have died with Christ, but we
need to die daily to sin. This tension cannot be escaped; it is
part of the Christian life.

In what sense are we linked with these past happenings in the
life of Christ? Some speak of the contemporaneity of Christ with
the believer. These acts were historical, but they are also eternal.[23]
This is a suggestive answer. But although it is not possible to be
dogmatic, the concept of 'corporate personality' and 'racial
solidarity' seem to give a more adequate one. This solution to the
problem is favoured by C. H. Dodd:

---

[19] See pp. 69-89 above.   [20] See pp. 89-92 above.
[21] See $\Sigma \dot{v} \nu$ $X \rho \iota \sigma \tau \tilde{\omega}$ in *Festgabe für Adolf Deissmann*, pp. 218-57.
[22] W. T. Hahn, *Das Mitsterben und Mitauferstehen mit Christus bei Paulus*, p. 88.
[23] Ibid. pp. 90-105.

Christ is the inclusive Representative of the people of God, or redeemed humanity, which constitutes in union with Him a sort of corporate personality, as natural humanity may be regarded as a corporate personality 'in Adam', its inclusive representative. That which Christ did and suffered on behalf of mankind is the experience of the people of God as concentrated in Him. Now, Christ died and rose again, and 'as One has died for all, then all have died' (2 Cor 5[14])—all, that is to say, who are incorporated in that people of God which is 'the Body of Christ'.[24]

This line of interpretation does not jeopardize the uniqueness of Christ. What happened to Jesus is the essential feature; that we are linked with Him is a dependent fact. This implies that the essential point is that the results of the Fall should have been reversed in the historical events of the life and death of Jesus. When we become part of His corporate personality the results of the Fall are reversed in us. In so far as 'fallen human nature' was cleansed in Jesus, it is able to be destroyed in us if we are 'with Christ' in His death and Resurrection.

In the present context a most significant concept is that of the Church as the Body of Christ. A number of suggestions have been made to explain the origin of this idea. It has been suggested that it is due to Stoic influence,[25] that it comes from a Gnostic source,[26] that its origin lies in the Old Testament idea of corporate personality,[27] that it springs from the speculation of the Rabbis concerning the body of Adam,[28] that it is to be explained by the Christian Eucharist,[29] that it is linked with the idea of the Church as the mystical Bride of Christ,[30] that it is dependent on the formula 'in Christ',[31] and that it is to be understood by reference to the experience of Paul on the road to Damascus.[32] It seems probable that a number of these factors have played their part in

[24] C. H. Dodd, *MNTC*, 'Romans', p. 86.
[25] W. L. Knox, *JTS*, XXXIX (1938) 243-6; *St Paul and the Church of the Gentiles*, pp. 160-2. T. W. Manson, *JTS*, XXXVII (1936); 385; G. C. Richards, *JTS*, XXXVIII (1937); 165; G. Johnston, *The Doctrine of the Church in the New Testament*, p. 87.
[26] H. Schlier, *Christus und die Kirche im Epheserbrief*, pp. 37-48; E. Käsemann, *Leib und Leib Christi*, pp. 159ff.; R. Bultmann, *Theology of the New Testament*, I.178-9.
[27] A. Schweitzer, *The Mysticism of Paul the Apostle*, pp. 116-27; A. R. Johnson, *The One and the Many in the Israelite Conception of God*.
[28] W. D. Davies, *Paul and Rabbinic Judaism*, pp. 53-7.
[29] A. E. J. Rawlinson, in *Mysterium Christi*, pp. 223ff; L. S. Thornton, *Common Life in the Body of Christ*, p. 330.
[30] C. Chavasse, *The Bride of Christ*, pp. 70-2.
[31] E. Percy, *Der Leib Christi*, pp. 18-46.
[32] E. Mersch, *The Whole Christ*, p. 104; J. A. T. Robinson, *The Body*, pp. 57-8.

P

influencing Paul's usage, though it is not an easy matter to decide which of them is its primary source. For our present discussion, however, the question of origins is not of vital importance. What is of importance is Paul's teaching about it.

It is through Baptism that a man becomes part of the Body of Christ.[33] Paul says:

For just as the body is one and has many members, and all the members of the body, though many, are one body, so it is with Christ. For by one Spirit we were all baptized into one body . . . (1 Cor 12[12–13]).

In the act of Baptism 'the person baptized is "planted" with the dead and risen Christ'.[34] This aspect of Pauline teaching is seen clearly in Romans 6[3–4]. Two of the truths which are essential to a true understanding of Baptism are that we become part of the Body of Christ, and that we are crucified with Christ, buried with Him, and rise with Him. Cullmann links these two factors together when he says: Jesus 'who sits now at God's right hand permits the person being baptized at this particular place, within his Church, to participate in what was done ἐφάπαξ on Good Friday and Easter; and this participation occurs, not by means of the transmission of understanding and faith but rather through being set at this special place, his Body.'[35] Jesus looked upon His death as a baptism.[36] It was a general baptism which He endured for all mankind. We enter into that general baptism when we are baptized and become members of His Body. In this we experience the central redemptive acts of His life. As we have already seen in the section on Paul's teaching, this concept of dying and rising with Christ is linked with the idea of Christ's assuming 'fallen human nature'.[37] If this connection is valid, and if through baptism we become members of the Body of Christ and are crucified with Him, it implies that just as He defeated 'fallen human nature' in His own person, triumphing through the Cross and Resurrection, so shall we be able to overcome this fallen nature, in so far as we are members of His body. Yet this is not something that we achieve; rather it is something that is wrought in us by Christ through the power of the Holy Spirit. 'The Christian life', as R. S. Wallace says, 'flows from the Cross because

---

[33] For a discussion on the relationship between Baptism and faith see O. Cullmann, *Baptism in the New Testament*, pp. 47-55.
[34] Ibid. p. 30.   [35] Ibid. p. 34.
[36] Mark 10[38], Luke 12[50].   [37] See pp. 89-92 above.

it has been perfected in the human nature that is crucified there.'[38] 'But', as Wallace continues, 'the Holy Spirit can bring into our life nothing but what was first worked out and perfected in the human nature of Jesus Christ.'[39]

In what sense can it be maintained that we share in the experience that Christ endured in the flesh? J. A. T. Robinson affirms that 'the Christian, because he is in the Church and united with Him in the sacraments, is part of Christ's body so literally that all that happened in and through that body in the flesh can be repeated in and through him now'.[40] Even if we should not express the point in quite these terms, the truth still remains: Christ has been victorious in His own person; as we are 'in Him' so does His victory become ours. We need to overcome 'fallen human nature'; this is possible because Jesus won this precise victory for us in His body of flesh. The essential factor, however is the victory won by Christ; our triumph is directly dependent on Him. We can only achieve what He first achieved for us. 'No matter how much we talk about corporate personality or racial solidarity we must remember that this is only part of Paul's thought, and that even within the corporate personality Christ holds a quite unique place; Christians may, as it were, stand alongside him in it ("with Christ") but he acts for them; they share in his experience and its consequences but they do not help to create the experience—that is all Christ's doing, and done for them.'[41]

We are now able to see the doctrine that Christ assumed our 'fallen human nature' in a wider context. It is not merely a Christological matter, it is related to the whole question of man's salvation. The key concepts are those of 'corporate personality' and 'racial solidarity'. Jesus is a representative person, and if we accept the idea of 'corporate personality', we can see how His actions were of significance for others. Linked with this is the complementary truth that men must become 'solid' with Christ if what He has won is to become a reality for them. Paul speaks a great deal about this under such figures as 'in Christ', 'with Christ' and the Church as the Body of Christ. It is only in this context that we can understand how Christ's defeat of the

---

[38] 'The Christian Life', in *Essays in Christology for Karl Barth*, edited by T. H. L. Parker, p. 248.
[39] Ibid. p. 248.   [40] J. A. T. Robinson, *The Body*, p. 47.
[41] E. Best, *One Body in Christ*, p. 58.

'fallen human nature' which He possessed becomes a reality for us.

One final point needs to be made. It has been argued that Christ completely overcame the fallen nature which He had assumed, and that on the Cross it was finally destroyed. If we become part of the Body of Christ, if we are 'in Christ', if we have died and risen with Him, why is it that 'fallen human nature' is still a reality in our lives? Most certainly it has not been completely defeated in us. This problem has to be faced on most interpretations of the work of Christ, but it arises in this present context in an acute form. A further reference to Pauline theology may point to the answer. Paul uses numerous compounded verbs which contain σύν. They are used to show that we are so closely linked to Christ in solidarity that what He experienced we also experience with Him. It has been pointed out that the tenses of the verbs used in this connection are significant. Frequently the past tense is used, which suggests that the Christian has already experienced what has happened to Christ. In some instances, however, a future tense is used. This double usage, both past and future tenses, suggests that Paul is describing two complementary aspects of the truth. 'The new life is given as a whole; both death and renewal are daily, continuing, present experiences, as is clear from the use of uncompounded verbs (1 Cor 15³¹, 2 Cor 4¹⁶); but not till the Parousia will that which is already given be a final and undisputed possession.'[42] As we are united with Christ, so we achieve in our lives what was achieved in His. This, however, is partial and provisional so far as we are concerned. This is because we are only imperfectly united with Him. Yet the fact still remains; the guarantee that we shall ultimately be rescued from the results of the Fall is based on the affirmation that He has cleansed and renewed 'fallen human nature' in His own person. Christ has wrought the redemption on our behalf. This is the basis of our justification and the ground of our sanctification. 'If any one is in Christ, he is a new creation; the old has passed away, behold, the new has come. All this is from God, who through Christ reconciled us to himself . . .' (2 Cor 5¹⁷⁻¹⁸).

It can thus be claimed that the doctrine that Christ assumed 'fallen human nature' makes an important contribution to

[42] A. R. George, *Communion with God*, p. 152.

Christian thought. It is a Christological doctrine which gives an insight into the way in which the Son of God became one with those whom He came to save. Its significance, however, is not confined to the sphere of Christology, for there are profound soteriological implications. Christ's victory over 'fallen human nature' means that He can be truly our Representative, and, in so far as we are 'in Christ', His victory becomes ours.

INDICES

Index of Proper Names

Index of Scripture Passages

OLD TESTAMENT

NEW TESTAMENT